Modernisation and Privatisation of Postal Systems in Europe

Springer
Berlin
Heidelberg
New York
Barcelona
Hong Kong
London
Milan
Paris
Tokyo

Roberto Ruozi · Luisa Anderloni (Eds.)

Modernisation and Privatisation of Postal Systems in Europe

New Opportunities in the Area of Financial Services

With 41 Figures and 58 Tables

Springer

Professor Roberto Ruozi
Bocconi University
Via Sarfatti, 25
20136 Milan
Italy
roberto.ruozi@uni-bocconi.it

Professor Luisa Anderloni
Genoa University
Via Vivaldi, 2
16126 Genoa
Italy
anderlon@economia.unige.it

The research has benefited by contribution of

Posteitaliane

ISBN 3-540-42777-5 Springer-Verlag Berlin Heidelberg New York

Cataloging-in-Publication Data applied for
Die Deutsche Bibliothek – CIP-Einheitsaufnahme
Ruozi, Roberto: Modernisation and privatisation of postal systems in Europe: new oppertunities in the area of financial services; with 58 tables / Roberto Ruozi; Luisa Anderloni. – Berlin; Heidelberg; New York; Barcelona; Hong Kong; London; Milan; Paris; Tokyo: Springer, 2002
ISBN 3-540-42777-5

Springer-Verlag Berlin Heidelberg New York
a member of BertelsmannSpringer Science+Business Media GmbH

http://www.springer.de

Hardcover-Design: Erich Kirchner, Heidelberg

SPIN 10734368 43/2202-5 4 3 2 1 0 – Printed on acid-free paper

Preface

After the positive experience made in 1999, with the research and consequent publication of the volume "Banking Privatisation in Europe. The Process and the Consequences on Strategies and Organisational Structures", published by Springer-Verlag, we have decided to set up a new group of researchers to study the present changes within the European postal systems and the privatisation developments.

Starting from our competencies and specific knowledge – financial markets and management of bank intermediaries – our research has basically focussed onto the posts' financial services offer and their future perspectives.

The subject is particularly interesting considering the radical changes, which are giving to the postal activity and the competition itself a new profile. And this reality paves the way to new opportunities in the market segment of financial services for retail customers and, at the same time, it brings in new threats.

Our approach is the approach of compared analysis in Europe in order to detect common trends in the development or possible specific features, as well as positioning perspectives of the different national Posts in the single market of financial services.

Our working group has benefited from the collaboration of researchers and experts with different nationality, university education and experience. Eminent representatives of postal companies, regulation and control bodies, banks and financial institutes have been interviewed and have allowed precious elements to deepen our knowledge and capacity of interpreting the present trends.

The results deriving from the comparison made are of uttermost interest and essential, in our opinion, to dispose of adequate clues to interpret the important changes the postal systems are confronted to in Europe and all over the world.

Of fundamental importance has been the participation to the conference organised by EFMA on this topic in February 2001 "Posts Offices & Financial Services". In fact, this conference has given the opportunity to discuss with qualified operators of the field as well as with representatives of international organisations about some research approaches.

The research has benefited by the contribution of the Italian National Research Council (CNR).

The volume has been printed thanks to the support of Poste Italiane S.p.A., which has shared with us the approach of a compared analysis of different systems.
Newfin – Centro Studi sull'Innovazione Finanziaria (Research Centre on Financial Innovation) of the Bocconi University-Italy has played a catalyst role of all these competencies and given the operational support to carry out the research.
Our most sincere expression of gratitude is addressed to all those that have participated to the research project and to all bodies and institutes that have contributed to the realisation of this project.

Roberto Ruozi
Luisa Anderloni

Milan, July 2001.

List of Contributions

Contents

Introduction

Roberto Ruozi and Luisa Anderloni

The postal sector is presently experiencing pressures to change its institutional framework and competitive practices as well as a strong drive towards process and product innovation with a high strategic impact. Although the patterns followed by these developments are often similar, the extent of innovation, the resolution shown by the operators in their strategic choices and the range of options available to Post Office administrators in the various countries are different.

Indeed, some of the forces that have triggered off change (deregulation and liberalisation, network companies' privatisation, technological innovation) are currently revolutionising a large number of different industries. However, their implications for the postal sector appear to be more far-reaching and complex to evaluate, possibly because, until a recent past, this segment, maybe more than many others, was immune to spurs to change and modernisation.

All this explains our interest in an in-depth study of the way the postal systems are evolving, based on a comparative analysis of the main European countries. In line with the competence of the scholars that have gathered to set up an international research team, special emphasis has been put on the prospects lying ahead of post offices in the financial sector.

The analysis of market potential in the banking and financial fields for the development and diversification strategies implemented by the postal systems, along with their main strengths and weaknesses, required however a preliminary analysis of the way the regulatory framework has changed over the years in the sector as a whole (Chapter 1).

Although the timing of further EC regulations is still unknown, the opening of postal markets to competition has partly become a fact already, owing also to an increasing demand for higher added value services that usually fall outside reserved, monopolistic areas. The postal operators are already adopting strategies that refer to a new institutional framework, where competition has a far greater role than the one envisaged by the enforced legislation. Furthermore, the rapid development of new business areas such as logistics and e-commerce has forced the European post offices to reconsider both their institutional organisation and market position.

In consideration of the experience gained to date in other public utility sectors and the signs coming from European postal systems themselves, a step-by-step pattern of institutional development has been identified. It shows how the Post Office has evolved from a public administration body to a public corporation to a formally private corporation (through the adoption of the stock company legal status) to a substantially private corporation. The last step, both in principle and in practice, can be variously shaded and take the form of privately-owned branches through franchising agreements, capital share transfers to the private sector (theoretically made to industrial partners or resulting from share exchanges with foreign operators working in the same industry or institutional investors) or Stock Exchange listing (with different levels of disengagement on the Government side, ranging from the transfer of a minority stake to the transfer of the controlling stake to total sale).

If the first three steps appear to be a fixed course, as the measures taken to complete or start it by almost all postal incumbents in 2001 seem to prove, Stock Exchange listing does not seem to be a foregone conclusion. Broadly speaking, our analysis seems to confirm the hypothesis whereby, in the postal sector too, most policy makers (governments, Post Office supervisors and managers) would still be waiting, thinking it more advisable to put off any substantial privatisation and, in particular, cautiously refrain from public announcements on the subject. In many different contexts, the reorganisation of services and the postal business is perceived as a "politically sensitive" topic. Additionally, we should bear in mind that postal organisations all too often rank amongst the largest employers in the countries we have examined. Moreover, in some countries the social function fulfilled by post offices on the territory is particularly felt, especially in the most rural, poor or economically and socially impoverished areas.

As far as privatisation prospects are concerned, implementing restructuring before substantial privatisation cannot but bring many indisputable benefits. Amongst them, a stronger guarantee that the corporation will be able to survive on the capital market, the possibility of experimenting new operating conditions from a still "privileged" position and, especially, the possibility of achieving gradual service rate differentiation in the various business segments, making sure, from the same privileged position, that the enforced regulations are really effective. Last but not least, management and staff incentive schemes may be introduced less traumatically.

Restructuring and its massive impact on human resources are usually better managed and considerably more successful when they are grafted on operativeness enhancement and supplemented by satisfactory results, not only in terms of financial performances but also in terms of service quality. Performance indicators show a positive trend. Yet, they also highlight considerably strong profitability and efficiency differentials between European countries, suggesting that, at least for some of them, the way towards recovery is still long and, may be, their pace should be stepped up.

To this end, it is unquestionably advantageous to announce well in advance that in a sufficiently long run the final goal will be privatisation, as this may encourage managers not only to improve performance but also to overcome their initial reluctance to change besides helping all stakeholders, including staff itself, perceive the benefits stemming from modernisation in the medium run.

Many an indicator has brought us to believe that the profound transformation European postal systems are undergoing - either as leads or supporting actors within the framework of alliances or partnerships that sometimes involve more protected operators in the domestic markets - will eventually have substantial privatisation as its natural outcome. At least for the most active operators wishing to play a leading role on the market.

To date, the course of privatisation has been taken by the Dutch and the German Post Offices. Their objectives, strategies and results are examined in Chapter 2. These operators have clearly been able to attain an utterly leading position at world level. Their partnerships and targeted acquisition policies have made them truly global operators, with an extremely wide geographical coverage and an equally wide and comprehensive range of business areas and market segments where their services are provided.

In a context marked by dramatic changes and new competitive trends affecting not only the postal but also the banking and the financial sectors, the future of the Post Office as financial service provider needs to be rediscussed to become the subject of deep strategic rethinking.

The analysis made in Chapter 3 shows that in highly dynamic contexts the issue is crucial: whether to be or not to be part of the supply and, if so, which range of products and services should be offered and what market targets, technologies and distribution channels should be preferred.

The results of our survey point to a variety of positions, including the decision to quit the sector taken by Northern European countries. All choices appear to have been strongly influenced both by different priorities in terms of strategy redefinition and implementation in the postal core business, together with the extent targets have been achieved in that field, and by the operating prospects of the post office branch network. In the countries where, owing to their demographic and geographical structures, the number of people addressing to the post office is low and profit margins negative, the supply of financial services based on traditional transactions and face-to-face relations may be seen either as an opportunity or, on the contrary, as an economic constraint. A positive value can therefore be assigned to the income contribution deriving from financial services, which can even play a key role in network management profitability besides generating important synergies. In many cases, the main strengths are not only the capillary presence of post offices and their closeness to customers but also their extended opening hours and their reliability, coupled with the transparency and straightforwardness of service pricing.

The most obvious target for postal financial services based on face-to-face relations is the medium-low or sometimes even the high market segment, where great attention is paid to cost reduction. The volume of resources under management may not be small, but the managerial approach privileges product standardisation and the clearness of service conditions. Their association with the postal business enables the operators to provide home services that customers see as an extension of the services provided at the counter.

The market potential in this segment may be particularly high for such new business areas as asset management, social security and basic insurance in its various forms at the stage of the mass market development. Although product simplicity and standardisation and customer attitude itself reduce the scope of consultancy, the traditional postal counter cannot always fulfil these functions. The proposed solutions vary according to the volume of assets under management and usually include areas of personal financial advice with dedicated staff at the counter or remote assistance on the phone and through call centers.

Conversely, the provision of financial services can prove unprofitable when the business generates unsatisfactory operating volumes and margins and hinders the rationalisation of the branch network, whereas the banking institutions that work on the same territory with equal market targets and spread are already meeting the demand expressed by that market segment, thus reducing its potential. This applies in particular to Northern European countries.

Midway solutions have also been identified, i.e. diversification policies that aim at differentiating counters, so that the entire range of services, including financial ones, is provided only in economically profitable areas, whereas post-office-in-shops solutions or counters within large distribution stores or mobile staff with no fixed facilities are envisaged in areas where business and profitability are low. This last option is usually feasible insofar as the opposition of the trade unions defending employment and work organisation on the territory allows, provided that there are no constraints making it mandatory for the post office to provide universal banking services, which are especially welcome in the above-mentioned areas. These considerations underlie the discussion on the role of the post office as social banking service provider in Chapter 5.

As far as pricing to increase margins and profitability is concerned, it is worth mentioning that in all European countries the main strength of the supply of financial services by the postal system is typically its lower price compared to the banking system, resulting from service standardisation and the little value added in terms of advice and customisation.

Our research has therefore focused on the answers that have already or are still being provided to the above-mentioned questions (being on the market or not, selecting products and services, market targets, technologies and distribution channels) and the structures for the intervention. The three available options we have identified have been the following: being present both at the production and the distribution stage through the organisation of the necessary processes within the postal firm; subcontracting production (delegating it to captive entities or partnership ventures) with the Post Office taking charge of product marketing and service supply; or simply taking charge of distribution on the basis of more flexible commercial agreements. As far as distribution is concerned, options range from the traditional counter, obviously redesigned according to post-in-shop or shop-in-post strategies or franchising agreements, to remote banking solutions relying on the phone or the Internet.

An evaluation of European post offices' current market positioning and mission declarations highlight the presence of three strategic groups:

- postal firms offering a broad range of financial brokerage services (Germany, France, Italy, The Netherlands, Spain);
- postal firms focusing on a limited range of basic or sometimes advanced financial products and services (UK, Austria, Belgium, Denmark and Norway);
- postal firms that are progressively forsaking the sector (Sweden and Finland).

Furthermore, other countries are still going through a transition which could evolve either in the decision to quit the sector gradually – the most likely outcome based on a number of current indicators – or in a significantly stronger position on the market thanks to sound partnership agreements (this could be the case for Ireland, Portugal and Greece).

The payment system area – where post offices have been traditionally present in Europe and significant changes are affecting processes, products and competitive trends – was therefore worth the assessment in Chapter 4.

The initial situations appeared diversified owing to the existence of cheque-based and giro-based systems (the latter having greater relevance for the Post Office) and the role the Post Office still plays with respect to the treasury services it continues to provide to the State, local authorities and public utilities owing to their public nature.

The capillarity of the postal network coupled with its home delivery service (in some countries a home cash collection and payment service is still provided) were originally the ground where the postal service grew. Over the years, however, the spreading of banks on the territory, the signing of clearing agreements between banks, the increasingly rapid modernisation of technological procedures and infrastructures in the banking compared to the postal system and, what is more, competitive dialectics between the two sectors have questioned the role of the Post Office as privileged interface for the collection of payments for the public sector and the delivery of social security and welfare benefits.

The social relevance of postal payment services has therefore gradually waned to be replaced, following the legal transformation of the entities involved, by an entrepreneurial philosophy aimed at fostering the conditions that can bring about full competitiveness for the services provided in terms of range, efficiency and prices. Thus, the supply of payment services by the postal systems has progressively widened over the years in many European countries in order to meet customers' requirements with ever increasing effectiveness. Our survey, however, has emphasised a great number of significant differences between the postal systems of the countries under examination with respect to service range and efficiency and the channels used to get in touch with customers. The shift to the Postbank as an alternative to the traditional administrative structure has obviously had positive repercussions on service range as well as on the integration and interoperativeness of the banking and postal circuits for payment services.

The advent of the Internet, the diversification of postal systems in the logistic field and their entry into e-commerce, at least in some countries, are offering new opportunities for the supply of high added value payment services with significant technical and legal innovating features (such as the e-signature, e-payment and e-paybill) in spite of their difficulty and uncertainty.

The census of the initiatives launched in this segment by the European postal systems bears witness to a swarming of initiatives. Their still early stage, however, does not allow us to take stock of the situation or venture forecasts on their lasting success.

An important aspect of the future role the Post Office will play in the banking and financial sector, which does not seem to stir particular concern in Italy whereas it is extensively debated abroad (notably in France, United Kingdom and the Northern European countries), is the supply of social banking services, i.e. payment and basic deposit services that are affordable and made available over the entire national territory to all potential customers, notably to customers that may be excluded for social and economic reasons.

Chapter 5 provides an in-depth analysis of the topic, setting it preliminarily within the wider concern for the fight against exclusion in all its expressions and the context of Social Europe and its economically-oriented missions.

The solutions being developed to fight against financial exclusion are diversified. Spain, Ireland, Italy and Greece do not seem to be particularly concerned, in spite of their banking ratios showing areas of population where that need is latent. These countries basically call upon the market to fulfil the demand, sometimes leaving the requests voiced by marginal segments unmet.

On the contrary, France, Germany and Belgium have taken a different course which relies on a voluntary bank agreement, whereby the parties commit to provide also basic banking services. This approach is being followed also by Finland and The Netherlands. Their commitment is extended to bank-post services to the extent post offices provide financial services like postal banks and sign the agreement.

A further solution is the intervention of a public entity as "mediator". This is the case for Great Britain and, under certain aspects, France. Finally, legislative coercion is envisaged, involving once again France, Portugal and Sweden. Their experience is however too recent and their data insufficient to evaluate the different European solutions.

In particular, the experience of Great Britain and France involve more directly the Post Office, based on the awareness that postal financial services fulfil a proximity need. As we have already underlined, new productive paradigms and modern life styles often make the post office branch network unprofitable, forcing rationalisation to ponder the costs and benefits of maintaining facilities to achieve merely social purposes. This may result in the provision of what the Swedish Consumer Association itself has defined a "luxury service", i.e. a service that is not consistent with economic logic and the optimisation of social services.

Moreover, the presence of the Post Office in the sometimes even high segment of banking and financial services creates a problem of image: is the image of the Post Office as lead of the social banking segment compatible with that of the leading provider of banking, asset management and securities trading, insurance and welfare services addressed to high-end demand?

Yet, in Great Britain, the project of creating a Universal Bank supported by public funding and relying on the distribution channel of the Post Office network is full on track. The strategic approach behind the project is an increased focus on efficient and automated operating modes and co-operation rather than competition with the banking system.

Our study ends with a few remarks on the opportunities that are offered to the Post Office in the Internet era (Chapter 6). New lines of strategic evaluation are suggested. The potential embedded in customer background knowledge resulting from the provision of postal services to date do not seem to have been adequately investigated yet.

The relative advantage the Post Office still enjoys compared to the other operators has been often underestimated. The Post Office can act as a "trusted information agent" in this sector. Even though, at present, it has neither the facilities nor the procedures required to do it, it can rely on a powerful brand, a customary daily contact with people and, therefore, with customers whose habits and preferences they are aware of as a result of the information they get when they provide them with payment services. While ensuring substantial more than formal compliance with privacy regulations, the Post Office could play on these strengths to develop the new services related to information and proximity that modern economy will require.

Whether the new business area suggested in our essay, still to be investigated, is closer to the Post Office core business or is more profitable than the business of more advanced financial services remains an open question our study does not answer.

Our conclusion is therefore rather an encouragement to further consideration. The dynamism of the postal system and the competitive pressure put on the banking and financial sector do not allow us to provide definite answers but only elements for a better understanding of the forces at play, the evolutionary trends and the challenges that have to be faced dynamically to formulate winning positioning strategies.

1

Changing Context for Postal Systems in Europe

Luisa Anderloni – Odile Pilley*

1.1 Transformation and Privatisation: an Inseparable Pair?

Over time, the needs met by the postal sector have evolved as a consequence of changing society and socio-economic relationships as well as technological progress. Communication is a basic need that emerges as soon as socio-economic structures go beyond basic subsistence levels. In today's world, not only has communication become an important factor of social cohesion, it has also taken on an essentially economic role.

Indeed, the postal sector is currently positioned at the centre of three economically crucial markets: the communication market, the advertising market and the transport and logistics market[1]. In some countries, the postal sector also provides financial services as part of its total offering. On this latter point, the current competitive dynamics have forced the postal systems in the various countries to adopt different strategic approaches to the financial sector in terms of what is offered and to what extent. And this, although countries with very different socio-economic realities share the same historical roots for post office provision of financial services.

Apart from regulatory issues, the boundary between postal and other services is not always clear. If we consider the type of services requested and how they are rendered, we find that the various services – derived from different production and technological processes but nevertheless aimed at satisfying similar needs – now tend to replace and compete with one another. If we consider things from the producer/supplier standpoint, we find that the various postal systems have also expanded their range of services and diversified their lines of business. The effects of market globalisation are strongly felt and postal sector boundaries are gradually expanding into new territory. What used to be simple mail delivery has now become mail delivery with specific features, package delivery, express delivery, logistics, all the way up to the integrated supply of e-commerce services[2]. Then

---

* The chapter results from a close co-operation. The opinions in this study are those of the authors and do not necessarily reflect those of the Commission.

[1] Along this line, the European Community's draft Directive submitted in May 2000 recognises the postal sector as a fundamental infrastructure for EU cohesion.

[2] As we shall explain later on, European postal firms have actually adopted different strategies in response to recent market developments. Available options have been limited

there is the impact that the so-called "integrators" have had on the European postal market. Integrators are postal companies that have set up extensive alliance and partnership structures, including airline and transport companies, for the purpose of providing package delivery, express delivery and customised products anywhere in the world[3]. Integrators have often managed to capture considerable market shares and have contributed to disrupting the inner workings of the traditional postal sector by introducing new working procedures and competitive behaviour.

This has helped to bring about a crisis in the institutional model used to define and regulate a postal sector that has traditionally been subjected to regulations for various reasons. For one thing, the postal sector is a natural monopoly that may potentially give rise to monopolistic revenue positions. The postal sector may also require state intervention to ensure the continuity of service, coverage of the entire national territory, free access and equitable treatment for all users[4].

Market-induced changes in products, innovative processes and competitive impetus from players that have adopted more aggressive development strategies (such as the deregulation that so characterises market-based economies) have made addressing the issue of how to regulate the sector inevitable. Generally speaking, this has led to varying degrees of postal sector deregulation in Europe.

Indeed, although relations between the various postal systems have traditionally been characterised by a logic of co-ordination (i.e. substantial co-operation between the various national monopolies with the aim of facilitating cross-border operations), the 1990s witnessed the emergence of international development strategies launched by the most dynamic postal companies. These latter started purchasing, entering into partnerships with, or forming alliances with local small-sized postal companies. The logic of competition was born.

This new logic of competition coincided with the need to find new ways to absorb the excess production capacity and to develop adequate levels of efficiency of traditional processes. The most dynamic postal companies also felt the need to discard their previous public service role and move towards more customer-oriented structures[5].

Both formal and substantial privatisation was seriously called into question in the wake of massive privatisation processes that shook Europe in the 80's and 90's, affecting many sectors of the economy, including a few public utilities.

As we shall explain later, when it comes to the postal sector, privatisation is a "politically delicate" matter. This explains the reluctance on the part of the government to issue any public statements or adopt official stances on the issue.

---

for small-sized postal companies and, of course, postal companies that are still in the throes of more intense and complex restructuring processes. See Figure 1.5 (§ 1.3.) for a list of the various types of products/lines of business of modern postal systems.

[3] The main integrators are Fedex, UPS, DHL and TNT.

[4] See § 1.1.2. for further details on the subject.

[5] In this case, the cause-effect relationship between adopting a more "customer-oriented" approach and the decision to privatise is not clear: both elements seem to condition each other.

The debate undoubtedly resurfaced when two giant European postal companies (the Dutch TPG in 1998 and the German DPWN in the autumn of 2000) went public. These two privatisation processes also shed light on the problem of competitive positioning on the financial market in terms of early movers and late comers.

The fact that the United States have not privatised their Postal Service, still firmly in the hands of the Federal Government, is an important testimony to the fact that there are many ways to manage the postal sector.

In order to correctly address the issue of regulating the postal sector – deciding whether to go for pure and simple deregulation of the sector and relating structures or even privatisation of postal companies – we need to bear in mind that postal companies are network utilities. By this we mean that they are public utility service providers with very specific features.

In this chapter, we shall discuss the various regulatory-based transformations (§ 1.2) and market-based transformations (§ 1.3) affecting postal systems in Europe. The aim is to provide the reader with a greater understanding of the current trends when it comes to redefining institutional models and possibly implementing substantial privatisation processes, often accompanied by major restructuring plans (§ 1.4). We shall also examine the significance of postal branch network (§ 1.5) and the conditions for profitability and efficiency (§ 1.6), which are critical factors in the dynamics of the sector.

Within the institutional and competitive context described above, we shall assess the possible role(s) of the postal sector in the area of financial services.

As mentioned in this introduction, the starting point of the analysis will be our thoughts on the role of postal companies as network utilities (§ 1.1.1). We shall go over the underlying requirements of a postal sector regulated according to economic doctrine (§ 1.1.2).

1.1.1 Postal Companies as Network Utilities

Network structures can be defined in various ways depending on whether you view things from an engineering or economic perspective. We can consider technical aspects such as physical structure and means of optimising flows by studying graphs - with the corresponding junctions, arcs, tree structures and mesh- or we can consider the economic role that networks play as an intermediary between consumers and producers/suppliers of goods and services.[6] Generally speaking, however, an efficient means of determining whether or not a given sector is truly a network structure is to check the existence of the following conditions[7]:

---

[6] Many disciplines (economy, geography, social studies, engineering) speak of the concept of network. In this study, we consider the phenomenon from an essentially economic standpoint. At any rate, understanding how other disciplines define this concept helps to interpret the phenomena described.

[7] See Curien N. (2000), pp. 15-17.

a) consumers benefit from the "*club effect*" (or network externalities);
b) productive synergies exist;
c) crossed subsidies between the type of service and customer segments are possible;
d) "border conflicts" between monopoly services and competing services are possible;
e) the sector is subject to pervasive regulation.

Actually, conditions c), d), e) are partly the result of the first two. On their own, these conditions are not enough for us to conclude that the company is a network structure.

The first condition refers to the positive external influence of consumers, manifested when each user on the market can benefit not only from his or her own consumption but also from the consumption of fellow users. Consequently, individual satisfaction increases in direct proportion to the number of users[8].

The second condition brings to light three combined effects:

- the presence of economies of scale as a consequence of considerable fixed costs;
- the presence of economies that adjust production ranges according to synergies in the supply of several services – this includes economies of joint production and economies of scope;
- network economies manage interconnection graphs as a whole instead of as separate entities, thereby optimising these graphs and generating cost savings.

Natural monopolies exist when the most efficient solution is for a single producer to realise the whole production volume[9].

At this stage, the degree of competitiveness becomes an important factor to be analysed. Indeed, it stands to reason that a company operating within a natural monopoly can be spurred to promote efficiency (i.e. applying prices in accordance with average costs), eliminating the monopoly's surplus income, with the simple threat of potential competition[10]. However, in the case of legal monopolies, supposedly intended to prevent the shortcomings of natural monopolies, we find that the absence of competition can have distorting effects. It can lead to inefficient production and generally higher costs that are either paid by the entire economy (eg. if the government decides to intervene by covering losses) or

---

[8] A good example of the direct club effect is the telephone. Although it is everywhere, the postal service is less visible since there is no preliminary condition of "interaction with users". As in other cases where there is no interaction with consumers (gas, electricity), the club effect is mainly indirect and explained in terms of expansion of the physical network and improvement of the quality of service. On network externalities see Varian H. (1996) and Shapiro C., Varian H. (1999).

[9] See Sharkey (1982). We shall go over this aspect later on when we address the issue of the regulatory requirements.

[10] See Curien N. (2000) and Baumol W.J., Panzar J.C., Will R.D. (1982) for additional information on competitive markets.

directly passed on to consumers through higher prices. Low-quality service and a lack of innovation are among the shortcomings mentioned, as illustrated both in theory and through many real experiences.

As for crossed subsidies according to type of services and users/consumers, these are derived from the presence of a network infrastructure that generates high fixed costs and therefore sharply reduced marginal costs. In such conditions, even prices policies that are based on production costs can take on different cost configurations. A typical case of a crossed subsidy is the one allocated to finance the so-called universal services. Such subsidies are aimed at ensuring that all economic players have access to service at uniform and affordable prices. This includes those consumers who generate higher costs for the company due to their geographical location on the edge of the network or due to their limited or irregular use of the services being offered.

Of course, the phenomenon of crossed subsidies can also exist for another reason, basically to compensate for price differences in various market segments caused by elasticy of demand and/or competition. In other words, policies can be implemented to have market segments that are more vulnerable to competition apply lower prices and have those that are less vulnerable apply higher prices.

This practice can give rise to conflicts if an operator moves both into a market segment where there is a legal monopoly, by virtue of reserved lines of business, and into competitive market segments. In this case, the use of network infrastructures to supply both types of market segments has been called into question. The solution of drawing a line between monopoly and competitive market is not without perverse effects. Indeed, this basically means that an attempt is being made to manage the coexistence of network operators that are more or less integrated, with reciprocal interconnections, which carry out their activities in the various links of the vertical chain of the production/delivery. And yet, these network operators are asked to work together in some lines of business and compete in others[11].

When a company finds itself in a highly regulated sector, its motivations will take on the characteristics described above. More specifically, the aims change as times and situations evolve. We shall go over this point on a theoretically level (§ 1.1.2) and shall mention the European Community's experience (§ 1.2). To conclude, when network utilities were regulated, the central issue was to correctly define the mechanisms for administrative price control. It generally happened when industries are nationalised and legal monopolies were created to further the social aim of providing universal access to basic services. Then, the need to promote efficiency and healthy competition gradually became more pressing. There is now an urgent need to decide how to best favour the interconnection of infrastructures within a context of deregulation while still preserving some of the universal service requirements. In other words, since building new infrastructures

[11] Take telecommunications in Europe, for example. European regulations require that dominant operators open up access to their own network to competitors. In other words, they are required to provide interconnection services across their own structures and standard interfaces through intelligent functions.

would be costly and socially damaging[12], how can former monopolies be transformed into network utilities that enable competing operators to have access to existing infrastructures[13]?

Postal companies are therefore network utilities that provide public services. As mentioned earlier, postal companies do have specific characteristics that influence the dynamics of the sector as well as its objectives and regulatory constraints. These characteristics can be broken down as follows:

a) postal firms have a physical network that is not technically "networked". The technological infrastructure is important for process phases that can be automated, such as mail sorting and dispatching. Unlike other networks (railways, gas pipelines, long-distance power lines, water systems, telephone/radio/fibre optic networks), postal networks are not as capillary and "invasive" on the national territory. The "network" is essentially made up of post-boxes and post offices/counters where we find the following specific features that differ from the other types of networks: management costs increase with respect to the size of the infrastructure but the occupation of "public land" (a scarce resource) and the environmental impact of postal activities is limited;
b) production/delivery processes are very labour intensive in the delivery phase[14];
c) the postal sector has traditionally described its service as being based on trust[15], which makes it difficult to delegate public functions to third parties;
d) the postal sector and postal companies in particular are often a primary source of employment, which has obvious social and political implications[16];

---

[12] Considering the impact that telecommunications networks, long-distance power lines, gas pipelines and railway networks have on the environment.

[13] According to the principle "Competition within a network cannot take place without interconnection, that is, the possibility for all network operators to gain access to the infrastructures of other network operators, and for all service providers to gain access to various infrastructures".

[14] Based on the conventional subdivision of five postal production phases: 1) collection, i.e. the delivery of items from customer - or from a location near the customer – to the first sorting point; 2) outward sorting, i.e. the initial sorting of the mail items into bundles to be delivered to the subsequent sorting office; 3) transport, i.e. the delivery of mail from the primary sorting office to the final sorting office; 4) inward sorting, i.e. the sorting of mail items for final delivery; 5) final delivery, i.e. the door-to-door delivery of mail items, studies have shed light on the fact that final delivery accounts for most of the cost of the five postal production phases. To illustrate this point, the European Commission (1992) estimates that the operational costs of managing correspondence can be broken down as follows: i) collection: 10%; ii) outward sorting: 18%; iii) transport 2%; iv) inward sorting; 5% and v) delivery: 65%. Cost functions for the various postal production phases depend on the technology used (with varying margins of efficiency improvement), on volumes and economies of scale. More specifically, for the final delivery phase (highly labour-intensive as we stated earlier), the average unit cost of postal production decreases in direct proportion to increases in customer density and volumes. See OECD (1999), pp. 29-42.

[15] Privacy of correspondence is guaranteed by the Constitution in some countries.

e) in some cases, the structure of the postal system is the only clearly visible indication of the presence of the government on the territory. This is especially true in "marginal", rural, or newly urbanised areas that face serious social problems and are generally abandoned/neglected by other private economic initiatives[17].

Moreover, if we consider the meaning of network industries as an important source of economic interconnections, we see how the efficiency of the postal system can be crucial for both economic sectors and citizens. Indeed, postal services play an important role for consumers as well as for the social and emotional life of individuals. When we speak of economic activity, we should mention the fact that some large-sized retail outlets, financial companies and publishing companies are "heavy" users of postal services. These sectors, in turn, are exposed to intense competition and are particularly reliant on the efficiency of postal services since the quality of their own services depends on the quality of the services provided by the postal system.

1.1.2 Regulations and Privatisation Processes

Although the aims and regulatory instruments of an economic sector often tend to merge, economic theory prefers to have the two categories kept separate. This makes it possible to gain a correct view of the available options when choosing which regulatory instruments are best suited to further these aims.

Moreover, these aims have not been static and rigid over time. They have evolved in tandem with socio-economic policies as well as with the characteristics of markets and technologies. Indeed, there may even be a need to counterbalance distorting effects caused by previous aims as well as mechanisms of regulation and control.

Generally speaking, we can say that the fundamental reason for regulating a sector is the presence of market failure, mainly manifested by the lack of competition resulting from natural monopoly conditions[18] as well as the presence of public good or externalities.

---

[16] Some feel that delays in privatisation of the postal system with respect to other network utilities can be attributed to unemployment concerns. See Watcher M.L., Hirsh B.T., Gillula J.W., Difficulties of Deregulation when Wage Costs are the Major Cost, in Crew M.A., Kleindorfer P.R. (2000), pp. 3-23.

[17] This need is particularly felt in the U.K. (See D.T.I. - Department of Trade and Industry (1999) and Cabinet Office - Performance and Innovation Unit (2000), Postal Service Commission (2000), in France (See Delfau G. (1999), and Larcher M.G. (1999), and in Sweden, (See Rapport Kassaservice, Batandake av betalserviceutredningen, SOU 1988: 159-1998. For further information on the subject, see Chapter 5 of this volume.

[18] The typical characteristics of natural monopolies are generally: i) economies of scale; ii) capital-intensity; iii) uninterrupted service with fluctuating demand; iv) location specificity generating location rents; v) producing necessities or essential for the community; vi) involving direct connections to customers. These characteristics have been

In the postal sector, such market failures can be explained as follows:

- natural monopolies have a cost structure that allows a company to satisfy internal market needs at a lower cost in comparison to having several companies compete with one another on that market. This naturally leads to market strength, which, if properly channelled, can benefit the entire community. Otherwise, it can generate monopolist's profit that benefits the monopolist alone;
- postal services, at least basic ones, have universal service characteristics. For this reason, it is preferable to have the postal system extend across the entire national territory in order to provide easy access to postal services at uniform affordable prices. In contrast, the free market is based on economic logic. It does not concern itself with satisfying the needs of the entire population and is naturally inclined to adopt an approach of cost-based pricing.

It is possible for the interests of the community to coincide with those of the service provider in a natural monopoly in some areas and enter in conflict in other areas. The creation of legal monopolies and the subsequent nationalisation of postal companies are instruments used to deal with such conflicts of interest. Potential abuse of dominant market positions requires the implementation of corrective measures, such as price or rate controls or other types of structural intervention.

With price controls, the aim is generally to reproduce the desirable effects of competitive dynamics when these are sacrificed to further social objectives or wider government policies for the economic system. In this sense, there are two approaches that may be used:

- Price Cap Regulation (PCR)
- Rate of Return Regulation (RRR)

PCR-based price controls are limited to setting the initial price that may be applied. Rules for later adjustments are based on objective and independent parameters such as inflation rates. In some cases, only partial adjustments are made to improve efficiency[19]. The formulas can therefore be defined differently depending on the aims and/or constraints[20]. The impact of each form of PCR-

traditionally associated with the postal system. For further details on the characteristics of network utilities, see Newbery D.M. (1999) pp. 27-30.

[19] For further information on the various forms of price cap regulation in the postal sector as well as its strong and weak points, see Crew M.A. – Kleindorfer P. R. (2000a).

[20] There are various types of PCR: *i*) "pure price cap" when different price limits are placed on the various products (different rates for first- and second-class mail, for instance); *ii*) "tariff basket" when price limits are set according to the average level of the various products weighted according to volumes (this makes it possible to restore balance to different product prices, first and second class mail in the postal sector); *iii*) "average revenue cap" or "revenue yield" which limits the total earnings of a given line of business or individual product on the basis of current or expected volumes; *iv*) "revenue cap" which

based price control can be critically examined in terms of how excess profits are distributed, how added costs are allocated, how often these costs are re-assessed and the quality of the services rendered.

RRR-based price controls are implemented only when the management of the regulated activity does not generate higher profits than the rates of return on the investment[21]. Both approaches offer advantages and disadvantages, which are shown in Table 1.1.

Table 1.1
Price Cap Regulation Versus Rate of Return Regulation

	PCR	RRR
Strong points	- Direct control over prices with immediate results for consumers - Existence of direct and strong incentives to improve efficiency, with appropriation of profits until the next price revision	- The profitability of an activity can be modulated in such a way as to reflect the lower level of risk.
Weak points	- Practical difficulty in setting the right basic price and factor x - During price revision, it is up to the regulator to properly assess and anticipate costs on the basis of production efficiency - Inflation is not always the best indicator of the "natural" cost dynamics (for instance, in the postal sector, wage factors are more important) - PCR can have an impact on operational expenses and investments.	- RRR generates incentive distortions

As far as other structural interventions are concerned, we find the creation of legal monopolies at the top of the list as the most commonly applied measure. Other measures include restructuring of industry by dismantling production

places limits on the total amount of revenues (unit prices must be reduced as a consequence of increased volumes).

[21] There are various types of RRR: *i*) "incentive return regulation", whereby higher margins are granted if specific goals such as cost reduction or improved service are reached; *ii*) "zone of reasonableness sharing", whereby higher margins wihtin a "reasonable" range are granted as compensation for cost savings, with subdivisions between consumers beyond this range; *iii*) "automatic rate adjustment", whereby there is an automatic adjustment of margins by passing through certain costs; *iv*) "focused incentives", whereby additional margins are granted if specific goals are reached, with a greater precision than in *i*); *v*) "market based yardstick", which uses benchmark comparisons of costs generated by similar activities.

processes in various ways, separating the horizontal and vertical functions of the natural monopoly and assigning them to various players. In the context of a vertically integrated natural monopoly, the main options open to policymakers are:

1. regulating the vertically-integrated (incumbent) entity as a single and indivisible entity;
2. vertically separating the components of the natural monopoly into different companies. In this case, restrictions are imposed on the line of business in order prevent reintegration from taking place and to allow other players in competitive segments to contribute their own positive effects;
3. introducing competition in competitive segments while keeping the entity vertically integrated. In this case, the entity assumes the role of public authority by regulating the terms and conditions whereby third parties gain access to components of the natural monopoly;
4. horizontally separating the natural monopoly, as a possible complement to other measures.

Governments have traditionally opted for option 1) for the postal sector, often accompanying this measure with state ownership. This has made the aims and regulatory instruments less clear and explicit.

The issue of how to structure the postal sector has resurfaced as a result of the current market context. Indeed, how does one deal with the problem of deregulating a vertically integrated sector? How can the social benefits of a natural monopoly be reconciled with those derived from competition through a work-sharing formula?

The OECD has published an efficient guide (1999) explaining the various situations and possible solutions, which we have reproduced in Figure 1.1. The OECD guide breaks down the production process according to various phases and the impact of economies of scale and economies of scope, taking into account the various factors. It argues in favour of differentiated regulation processes that place greater emphasis on reaching goals, improving performance and reducing distorting effects[22].

[22] Difficulties emerging from this approach should be considered. The subject has a high political relevance. Besides rules underlying the telecom industry can't be directly applied to the postal sector. The issues arising from the comparison of TLC and postal industries economic characteristics are dealt in Visco Comandini V. – Lettieri C. (2001).

Figure 1.1

Decision tree for choosing regulation forms of monopoly integrated structures

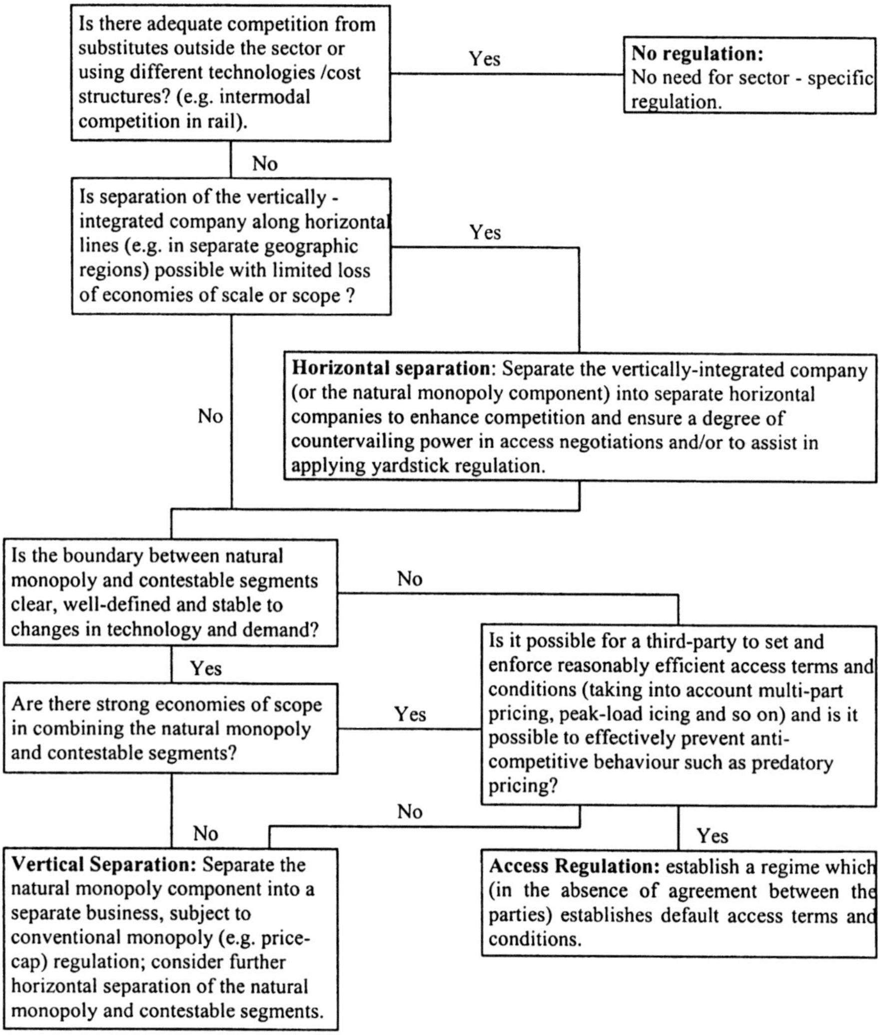

Source: OCDE (1999).

A further point concerns the organisation of the obligation to universal services (not commercial service obligation)[23]. The problem is often how to finance Universal Service Obligation (USO) having clear in mind that this is a different need than the natural monopoly regulation and also the presence of economies of scale. The following set of solutions could be possible[24]:

1. to set up a reserve area (monopoly) for the supply of some services and to use then the deriving profits to face the costs connected to the universal service delivery;
2. to create a Fund with the contribution of all operators of the sector, to indemnify the universal services performances;
3. to charge the State or public administrations. With public financing (taxation), they will have to settle the losses due to the supply of these services.

These solutions implicitly contemplate the presence of a single subject, which is in charge of all universal services and becomes the receiver of these forms of compensation. Another hypothesis consists of imposing, as general principle, that all operators of the sector will be charged, and that means that the service will be distributed on geographical base.

A further possibility would be of giving the universal service in franchising through an auction mechanism, which is then capable of considering costs and quality elements (see Figure 1.2 in the following page) at the same time.

The public nature of the subject in a sector where the correct exploitation of the natural monopolies' potentials and the possibility of offering the universal service need to be based on precise regulations, makes, in many ways, these goals more easily achievable.

Nevertheless, this fact has a contraindication, that is to say a scarce transparency in the objectives, difficulty in the measurement of results and in the balance between utilised instruments and achieved results[25]. Moreover, in general, there are margins for the alteration of competitive mechanisms with unfair discrimination of private operators.

---

[23] The principle that the geographical uniformity is desirable is not questioned in this context. What is questionable could be the fact that this could cause a distortion in the localisation choices, as the relative prices are not consequent any more with the relative costs.

[24] See N.E.R.A. (1998) and Stumpf U., "Providing Universal Service in competitive postal markets", in Crew M.A. – Kleindorfer P.R. (1997).

[25] Considering that, there are often welfare's objectives, which are not immediately measurable from the economic point of view.

Figure 1.2
Decision tree for the management of universal services obligations

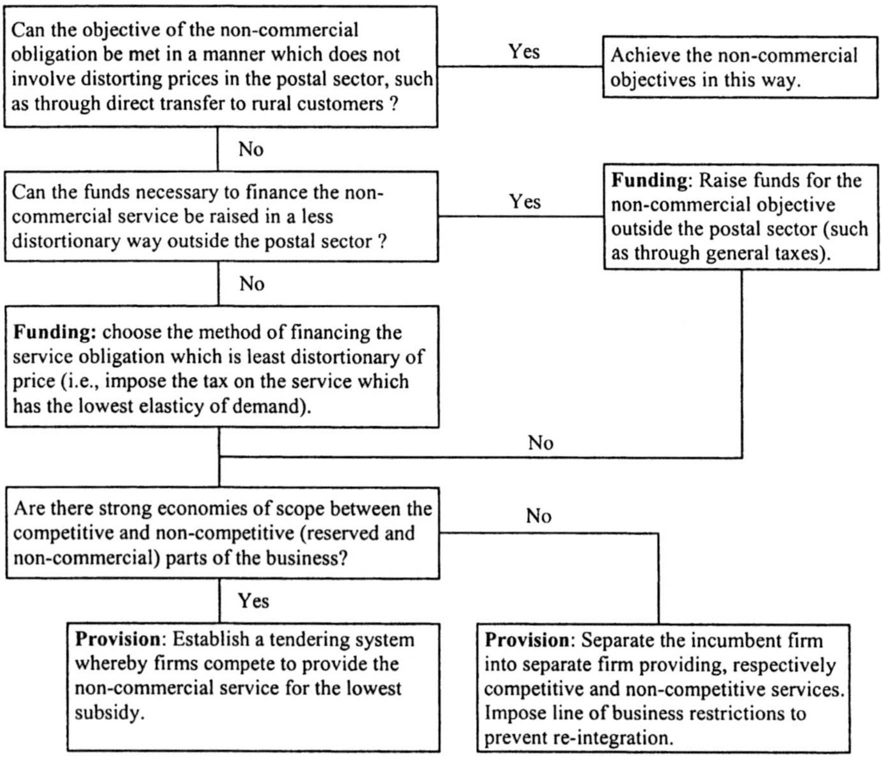

Source: OCDE (1999).

To solve these deficiencies, the setting up of a specific regulation authority could be a solution. This authority should be given specific functions, powers and competencies, it should be structurally independent so that equal treatment and transparency of attitudes are guaranteed with explicit objectives and criteria as well as obligation of making statements of the work done.

The consequent separation between the State's functions, following its way acting as regulator and controller, on one side, and as producer, which directly intervenes in economic processes on the other side, often seems to precede the following dismissal of the State from this latter function. As above mentioned, this separation is originally motivated by market failures but, as time goes by, it disappears because of the market's capacity to solve these failures or because of the risk for the public intervention to produce distortions whose negative consequences would be more serious than the advantages.

The setting up of the independent authority solves the dilemma about the State as shareholder and the State as umpire. It is even likely that this authority becomes more severe with the previously public monopolist ever, to become credible in its role of umpire.

1.1.3 Privatisation in the Postal Sector: Purposes and Trends

The purposes and trends of the privatisation process in the postal sector can be highlighted by considering, on one side, the position taken by UPU, the UN organisation in charge *"of developing social, cultural and commercial communications between all people throughout the postal service [describes in the Acts]'*. On the other side, the announcements made by postal companies and by their governments are also to be taken in consideration in this overview.

In the Beijing Resolution for a "Postal Strategy from 2000 to 2004", UPU adopts a wide formula, in particular for what concerns the juridical status of postal companies:

"The real challenge is that facing governments; they have to find the delicate balance and seek the right formula. On the other hand, they have to give postal administration the freedom to play the competition game in the context of a liberalised environment; on the other, they have to create an environment conducive to growth so that postal leaders, regulators and operators, can serve broader social interest"[26]. *Moreover: "There is no single standard system of postal reform; however, there are always some points in common: the need to obtain administrative and financial management independence, for example. There is also a need to take into account of the specific features and of all the components of each country's environment on the basis of the maturity of its markets, the level of development of the postal infrastructures and the existence of viable participants in the private sector, as well as political and governmental aspects, etc".*

In terms of strategic objectives, point 5) "postal reform and development" formulates the following statement: *"Enable, through the process of postal reform and development, postal customers to draw maximum benefit from technological, economic and regulatory changes n the postal environment".*

Earlier, during the Seoul congress in 1994, UPU called for a transformation of postal systems: they should abandon their status of departments to become economic companies with management autonomy and suitable financing forms.

So, the main objective of the above mentioned strategic plan is the possibility of offering a universal service, namely *"To ensure the provision of a universal postal service, allowing customers to send and receive goods and messages, from*

---

[26] In addition "The UPU has an anticipatory role to play as a catalyst for change: it should not be perceived as an institution responsible for protecting the status quo, but rather should be the source of changes and developments, including technological ones, which may be profitable for the Posts.

any point in the world to any other point"[27]. As a matter of fact, the communication is considered by the United Nations as a fundamental human right and the postal service is considered, in the developing countries as well a in the industrialised countries, as one of the most important means of communication for commercial, organisational and personal goals. Therefore, a special emphasis is given to the peculiarity of the postal service, that is to say their capacity of promoting economical and social development.

As far as strategies and purposes are concerned, highlighted in the postal operators' declarations, a rather varied framework is what emerges in Europe (see Table 1.2). Nevertheless, most of them seem to have a rather fence-sitting attitude.

Table 1.2
Trends and purposes in the privatisation

	Operator	Country	Purposes
Listed companies	TPG	The Netherlands	Intention to reduce the State's share holding, to 10% maximum on the medium term
	DPWN	Germany	
Private corporation	La Poste	France	Politically delicate subject: not subject to public debate
	La Poste	Belgium	Hypothesis quotation aired in 2003; afterwards it was not disavowed nor taken up again
	Consigna (The Post Office)	UK	Non explicit hypothesis[28]
	Austrian Post	Austria	To implement growth strategies to achieve "capital market capabilities" by end 2002
	Poste Italiane	Italy	To create the conditions so that the stocks can be listed (Objective 2003)
Public entity	An Post	Ireland	To enhance the wealth and economical solidity through growth. Stock option plan for employees also as motivation and incentive.

(continued)

[27] The objectives are (starting from the priority): 1) universal postal service; 2) quality of service in the international postal network; 3) economic viability of the international postal network; 4) postal markets and products; 5) postal reform and development; 6) co-operation and interaction among stakeholders.

[28] The White paper (1999) had identified 5 priorities to be achieved within the system's liberalisation and modernisation process: 1) to improve postal services for business and domestic customers through greater choice, better quality and falling real prices; 2) to maintain a universal service of postal delivery throughout the UK, and a uniform tariff; 3) to establish clear and accountable relationships between the Government, the Post Office, the Regulator and POUNC; 4) to equip the UK Post Office to meet the challenges of the changing postal market both domestically and internationally; 5) to support a viable network of post offices so as to ensure nation-wide access to a range of public and private sector services.

(continued)

	Operator	Country	Purposes
Public entity	Correos y Telegrafos	Spain	The objective is formulated in terms of "reduction of financial dependence upon the State"
	La Poste	France	Politically delicate subject: not subject to public discussion
	Hellenic Post	Greece	Hypothesis of joint privatisation and involvement of a strategic partner

1.1.4 Hypothesis along the Institutional Evolution of the Postal Systems

In principle and according to the experiences made so far in other sectors of public utilities and to the signals coming from the postal sector, the following step-by-step institutional development of the Post sector seems to be possible.

Table 1.3
Stages of evolution of institutional bases of postal operators

I	II	III	IV
		Formal privatisation*	Substantial privatisation
Public administration	Public Entity	Joint-stock company	a) Private branches management (or franchising) b) Transfer to private: - industrial partners - exchange with foreign operators - institutional investor c) Quotation

* *In a more restricted view the term "privatisation" refers only to the sell of stocks belonging to the state. In this case "formal privatisation" should be substituted with the expression "corporatisation".*

The Posts, originally set up on private initiative or by State companies, for various reasons are historically connected to the public sector, as a part of the public administration, often administrated jointly with the telecommunications sector.

This is the basic situation that is generally to be found in Europe up to beginning of the 80's.

The first step is the setting up of autonomous companies with a public model. The public nature not only of the economic subject but also of the legal form often implies the application of management rules, functioning modalities, engagement relationships, which are not to be connected to market rationale. Indeed, these rules will allow the management to benefit from some exceptions (for example:

the non-taxation of the operating income) and sometimes will impose some constraints.

The following step is the adoption of a juridical form of a private corporation. This is a privatisation process, which will lead to a new more transparent definition of the relationships between State and company following objective criteria.

On this subject, table 1.4 hereafter illustrates the present situation in Europe.

Table 1.4

Present situation of institutional set-up of postal operators in Europe

I	II	III	IV		
		Formal privatisation	Substantial privatisation		
Public administration	Public entity	Joint-stock company	a) Management of branches by private people (or franchising)	b) Transfer to private people: - industrial partners - exchange with foreign operators - institutional investors	c) Quotation
	Denmark→2001* Spain→2001* France Ireland→2001* Greece→2001* Luxembourg	Finland (1994) Sweden (1994) Italy (1998) Austria (1999) UK (2001) Portugal Belgium	*Ireland* *UK* *The Netherlands* *Germany*		The Netherlands (1994 →1998) Germany (2000)

* *Starting process to adopt the company's structure.*

In general, the postal sector seems to confirm the hypothesis that, at the beginning of 21st century, most policy makers (governments, control authorities and management of postal companies), remain in a waiting attitude - postponement of substantial privatisation operations and neutral and careful announcements seemed more convenient[29].

First of all, anticipated restructuring processes have their own advantages compared to substantial privatisation. As a matter of fact, they are able to offer better guarantees for the companies' survival on the free capital market as well as the possibility for them to experience, from a "protected" position, the market new operational conditions. In particular, they will be able to come progressively to a pricing of their services, which is correctly differentiated in the manifold segments and, in addition, from a protected position still, the possibility is given to them to verify whether the regulation is effective. And, last but not least, it is important to

---

[29] Mention has been made already on the fact that privatisation of the post office is in many cases a "politically delicate" subject.

create in a not traumatic way, the necessary mechanism to encourage management and personnel. The restructuring processes involving human resources[30] to a wide extent are more easily managed and the results are much better when they are connected to the development phases of operativity and associated to the achievement of results. And this, not only from the financial performance viewpoint, but also as for the higher quality of services and performances carried out.

To this purpose, the fact of announcing very much in advance that the final goal is privatisation, on the very long term, has undeniable advantages. As a matter of fact, this could encourage considerably the management not only in the perspective of improving the performances. Further more, this could contribute to the overcome of the initial resistances to change and to the development of the perception of the advantages among the stakeholders – personnel included – in the medium term of the modernisation of the sector.

Several elements let think that the big changes within the European postal systems, as active actors and co-actors in alliances and partnerships - which mobilise also more protected operators in domestic markets - are naturally destined to come finally to substantial privatisation. This happens at least for the most dynamic operators that are willing to take a leadership position in the market.

As a matter of fact, privatisation is functional to the availability of a large amount of necessary financial resources:

- to achieve, as time goes by and in line with the technological progress, automation and modernisation of production processes;
- to keep on protecting the traditional business areas with new and innovative products and processes;
- to allow the entry into emerging business areas, which becomes- in a global market – a new opportunity but also a threat.

Besides the financial profile, there is a further necessity to be highlighted: the need for commercial freedom to reach a competitive positioning on the market. This positioning goes more in line with substantial privatisation rather than with the subject, which is private from the juridical viewpoint but economically public. As a matter of fact, the capital is still own by the State.

Although some suitable corporate governance instruments can encourage the reproduction of market conditions also in the companies which have a private juridical structure but are a public economic subject (with suitable corporate governance instruments), there is no doubt that the market is more effective and efficient than by proxy.

Further more, the basic conditions of the State intervention or, in any case, of the public subject, can have a lesser impact onto the system of management

[30] As above highlighted, in some countries the enterprises are the ones that do the best as far as employment (manpower) is concerned in their own country.

objectives and constraints. And this can happen although, within the group's operativity, going from traditional mail activity to expresses and logistics activity, from financial and sophisticated activity to integrated services for e-commerce, the same basic conditions could even not weaken in absolute terms.

This represents a problem of balance between the objectives pursued and the instruments used to this purpose. Therefore, the needs for regulation owing to the market failure remain (§ 1.1.1 emphasises in particular the natural monopoly and the universality of service) but what is necessary are more targeted instruments which are more in line with the objectives to be achieved. Furthermore, the sector's operativity limits need to be redefined.

1.2 European Regulation

1.2.1 Foreword: the Regulation Basic Principles of the Postal Services in the European Union

As above described, the privatisation of public companies is not a real objective of the European Union, consisting of different countries with their own traditions and positions on public property and privatisation: manifold historical, economical, social and cultural factors are to be found in there. So far, the Community has adopted a neutral attitude towards public property in order to try not to sharpen the differences between countries and not to raise any debate about politically delicate matters. Moreover, in these sectors, they believe there is a major need of state's monopolies to guarantee universal services performances.

Further more, a special mention should be made on the fact that, upon relatively recent times, in Europe, the public intervention (mainly State or Municipality) in the public utilities sector was quite the rule (see Table 1.5).

Table 1.5
Economical subjects in the public utilities

	Post offices	Rails	Telecommu-nications	Electricity	Gas	Water
England	•	•	◊	⊗	◊	◊
France	•	•	•	•	•	⊗
Germany	•	•	•	◊	◊	⊗
The Netherlands	⊗	•	⊗	•	⊗	•
Italy	•	•	•	•	•	•
Spain	•	•	◊	⊗	⊗	•
Sweden	•	•	•	⊗		•

Legend: • Public property >75%; ⊗ Public property >25% and <75%; ◊ Public property <25%

Source: Parker (1998), p. 21. Data from Economist.

In the last few months the state of the industry has changed. However data shown in table 1.5 still gives a good synthesis of the starting situation.

Vice-versa, the basic principles in the Union are free competition and absence of not justified state aids that could distort the competition[31]. Nevertheless, the perspective of the Monetary Union and the engagement taken to achieve the agreed criteria in Maastricht have encouraged many Governments to choose more and more the privatisation channel in order to reduce the level of public debt. In several contexts, this is associated with the desire of developing and extending the capitals market.

There is no doubt that the change has been considerably encouraged by the community directives, in particular in the telecommunication, transport and electricity and post sectors and aiming at liberalising the markets where the public companies used to prevail.

Moreover, contrary to other economic sectors, the community policies in the postal sector have not been started in the framework of liberalisation intentions, but rather because of the need to react adequately to the development of private competition. This latter, while attacking the more profitable market's segments, was threatening the public postal administrations to be in charge of the general interest mission without suitable rules and financial mechanisms to face it.

At community level, the Nordic countries, the first experiencing liberalisation, insist on accelerating the process, while France and the Mediterranean countries are quite reluctant also because they would like to finally achieve recovery and consolidation in the markets of reference in their own countries, in a "protected" position. On the other side, United Kingdom, which is carrying out a huge process of counter automation, takes a neutral position.

---

[31] As a matter of fact, the original version of the Treaty of Rome as well as its version of the Treaty of Maastricht regulates the principle of free competition for a functioning single market but does not make any distinction between private and public companies. In general, no company is allowed to limit nor to alter the free competition through agreements (art. 85). No enterprise is allowed to abuse upon a dominant position (art. 86) nor to get any public aid (art.92). In order to avoid any competition distortion between public and private companies, a Directive has been adopted. It aims at avoiding and suppressing any state supports that could be incompatible with the single market. Some initially excluded sectors of public utilities (posts, telecommunications, water and electricity supply, transport sectors as well as the credit public bodies) have been subject to a discipline of transparency and of presumption of illegal state aid for some situations. Out of them, contributions at a loss, that is to say with cover of losses, loans at favourite conditions can be considered as some examples. See Directive 80/723/CEE, OJ L of 29 July 1980 and Directive 85//413/CEE of 24 July 1980, in OJ L229 of 28 August 1980 and Directive 93/84/CEE of 30 September 1993 in OJ L254 of 12 October 1993.

1.2.2 Setting-up of Rules, Regulations and Stages to Follow

In 1992, the Commission publishes the Green Paper on the single market for postal services[32]. This report has paved the way to a wide debate with all the involved subjects and has encouraged the setting up of a community policy for the postal sector.

In June 1993, according to the elements collected through consultation processes, the Commission sets ups the general guidelines for the development of postal service in the European market in Communication[33]. On this base, in the same year, the European Parliament adopts three resolutions on the postal sectors[34] : it invites the Commission to prepare a proposal for the development of the single market for postal services as well as a constraining definition of "universal service" and a common definition of "activities that can be reserved". On one side, this definition should be as limited as possible, on the other side it should give the suppliers full possibility to offer a universal service whose price is consistent wit the nature of the service itself.

In 1994 the Parliament, sharing the Green Paper basic approach and the Commission's way of conceiving it, adopts three resolutions[35] by fixing the development's objectives of a single market for postal services. It invites the Commission to propose to the Council the necessary measures to achieve the above mentioned objectives by 1st July 1994 (see Table 1.6).

In 1995, according to this mandate given by the Parliament, the Commission prepares a "package" of proposals comprising a Parliament and Council's draft proposal on the adoption of common rules for the development of the postal services at community level and for a better quality of services. In addition, it sets up a draft notice on the implementation of competitive rules in the postal sector[36]. The Directive (the "Postal Directive") is approved with the co-decision procedure in December 1997 and comes into force the 10th of February 1998[37].

Table 1.6

Main objectives for the development of postal services in the European Community

- *Defining at Community level a universal service that will be the minimum set of quality services which must be provided in each Member State at reasonable prices for all user and with non-discriminatory access to the universal service,*
- *ensuring the economic and financial viability of the provision of the services constituting the universal service at a reasonable price for all, by defining a sector*

---

[32] See Green paper on the development of the single market for postal services, COM(91) 476 final.

[33] See COM(93) 247 final.

[34] See OJ C 42 of 15 February 1993, p. 240; J.O. C 194 of 19 July 1993, p. 397 and OJ C 315 of 22 November 1993, p. 643.

[35] See OJ C 48 del 16 of February 1994, p. 2.

[36] See SEC (97) 2289, OJ C 322 of 2 December 1995, p. 3.

[37] See OJ L 15 of 21 January 1998, p.14.

of appropriate dimensions which may be reserved for universal service providers according to the principle of proportionality,

- *reconciling, in accordance with the objectives set out above, the rules of the Treaty and users' interests, the furtherance of the gradual, controlled liberalisation of the postal market and that of a durable guarantee of the provision of the universal service,*
- *working out quality standards for the services constituting the universal service, monitoring independently the quality of the services and publishing the results. The standards will have to be laid down at national level by the national regulatory authorities and will have to be compatible with the standards laid by the Council at Community level for intra-Community services within the universal services, on the understanding that such standards, taking account of national characteristics, must reflect a certain quality level the improvement of which should be actively sought; as regards international traffic, a similar approach should be followed in collaboration with third countries,*
- *establishing tariff principles for the universal service related to real costs and ensuring that they are applied and that any subsidies considered necessary are transparent in relation to their objective, size and scope and ensuring that they are compatible with Community law,*
- *introducing a terminal dues system based on real costs and quality, taking into account national characteristics while granting the universal services providers satisfactory protection against deflections of trade based on abuse of that systems and making provision for appropriate transitional arrangements,*
- *encouraging harmonisation of technical standards, taking users' interests into account,*
- *ensuring that fair conditions of competition outside the reserved sector exists mutually between universal service providers and between them and other operators,*
- *ensuring that the needs of users, including consumers, the interests of postal sector employees as well as the contribution of the postal sector to economic, cultural and social development in the Community are taken into account, when regulating this sector,*
- *taking account of the objectives of cohesion in the Community and in particular specific difficulties encountered by peripheral regions when measures in this area are taken.*

Source: European Parliament (1994).

1.2.3 The 1997 Postal Directive and the 1998 Commission's Communication

The Directive's main objective is to harmonise each Member State's national legislation and this by achieving three major objectives:

- to guarantee a universal service of good quality and affordable to all users, by encouraging the maximum openness of the competition sector;
- to create, at community level, a set of common obligations for all suppliers of universal service;
- to harmonise the services of the universal service, the access conditions and quality rules.

The discipline's pivot consists of three main points:

- the idea and sense of universal service;
- the instrument of reservable area and the authorisation regimes;
- the quality of services carried out.

The logic structure of the community regulation is summarised in Table 1.7.

Table 1.7
Levels of harmonisation at community level

MANDATORY HARMONISATION		OPTIONAL HARMONISATION
CORE FRAMEWORK (i.e. principles and boundaries to be applied)	**ENVIRONMENT FRAMEWORK** (i.e. only principles apply)	**TOOLS AVAILABLE** (and related principles applying)
- Universal service - Quality of service for cross-border mail - Maximum reservable area	- Tariffs geared to costs - Accounting systems - Separation regulation/operation - Quality service for domestic mail	- Authorisation & licensing - Compensation fund

Source: Toledano F. (2001).

1.2.3.1 The Universal Service

As above mentioned, the universal service's main objective is to guarantee the performance of postal services on all national territories and therefore on the entire territory of the Community by respecting the three following principles[38]:

[38] It should not be forgotten that this is a general concept which applies to several sectors. Finally, see the official document from the European Commission, Communication COM (2000) 580 def. "The general interest services in Europe". In short, these are unavoidable services for the normal consumption and production activities.

- equal treatment and equal conditions for everybody;
- continuity, namely unceasing supply of the service;
- functionality and adaptability to technological progress;
- transparency in pricing, management and financing.

On this base, the Directive sets up the minimum features of universal service that must be guaranteed in all Member States and the performances that are to be included in the universal service. As for the geographical extent, the Directive states that the universal postal services concern domestic services as well as cross-border services (see Table 1.8).

Table 1.8
The postal universal service in the Commission's 97/67 Directive

Minimum features of the universal postal service	Minimum performances to be included in the universal postal service
Availability each working day and for not less that five days a week – unless there are geographical circumstances the national regulation authority considers as exceptional conditions – of at least: – a collecting service of mail sent; – a home delivery service or at the address of any legal or natural person or, as exception given at the discretion of the domestic authority, a delivery at the requested places.	– collecting, sorting, transport and distribution of postal mailings up to 2 kg; – collecting, sorting , transport and distribution of parcels up to 10 kg[39]; – services for registered mailings and for mailings with declared value.

In other terms, the universal services address the needs for offering a performance capable of respecting the essential needs and of guaranteeing a equal treatment to all users, avoiding any form of discrimination.

As far as the geographical cover of it, the Directive states that the universal postal services concern domestic as well as cross-border services.

As for the tariffs for the universal services, the following criteria are applied:

- prices must be affordable and must be able to guarantee the supply of affordable services to all users;
- prices must be connected to costs but each national regulation can opt for the application of a single tariff on the whole national territory[40];

[39] The national regulation Authority is given the right to raise the weight limits for parcels to the upper limit of 20 kg.

- tariffs must be transparent and non-discriminatory.

Similar principles have been elaborated for cross-border universal service supplies, in particular for what concerns the terminal costs[41].

From the pricing principles according to the costs derives the setting up of criteria for a bookkeeping separation (distinction between reserved services and not reserved services) and bookkeeping systems of costs with analytic charging of direct and indirect costs[42].

1.2.3.2 Reserved Services and Authorisation Regimes

To be able to offer universal services, the 67/97 Directive proposes a reservable area that each Member State can assign to the postal operator in charge of the universal service. In this area, there is a monopoly regime.

In other terms, the reserved services represent a "monopoly" which is to be carved out from the universal service. The area is limited to collecting, sorting, transportation and distribution of internal mails, through express or not express delivery, identified on the base of two vectors, namely price and weight (see Figure 1.3 in the following page).

The first of these two vectors fixes the limit at a price which is lower that five times as much of the public tariffs applied to a mail of primary level of the quicker normalised category, no matters where it is to be found. The upper limit is 350 grams.

Exceptionally, that means in the cases when that could be useful to keep the universal service, also the cross-border post and the direct advertisement by correspondence[43] can continue to be reserved in the limits of price and weight that are prefixed by correspondence.

For services that are not reserved and lie outside the application field of universal services, national regulations are allowed to introduce any general authorisations and other individual licences procedures in order to protect the essential needs and the universal service[44].

---

40 The application of a single tariff does not exclude the universal service supplier's or suppliers' right to conclude individual agreements for prices (art. 12) of the Postal Directive.

41 See art. 13 of the Postal Directive.

42 As specified in art. 14 of the Postal Directive.

43 Art. 2, point 8 of the Directive states: "communication addressed to a significant number of people, which consists only in advertisement or marketing material, which contains the same message but different name, address and number of identification of addresses, plus the further modifications which do not change at all the message nature to be sent and delivered to the address the sender has written to the sending itself or on its envelope".

44 Consistently with the community principles for the regulation of activity sectors – general or individual sectors – they must be transparent, non-discriminatory, balanced and based on objective criteria.

If the obligations connected to the delivery of the universal service are charged with a unfair financial imposition for the supplier of this service, the national regulation any set up a compensation fund[45] in order to guarantee the performance of the above mentioned universal service. In addition, it can decide that the concession of authorisations will be subject to the obligation to give financial contribution to this fund[46].

Figure 1.3
Present monopoly area (reserve) and hypothesis of reduction

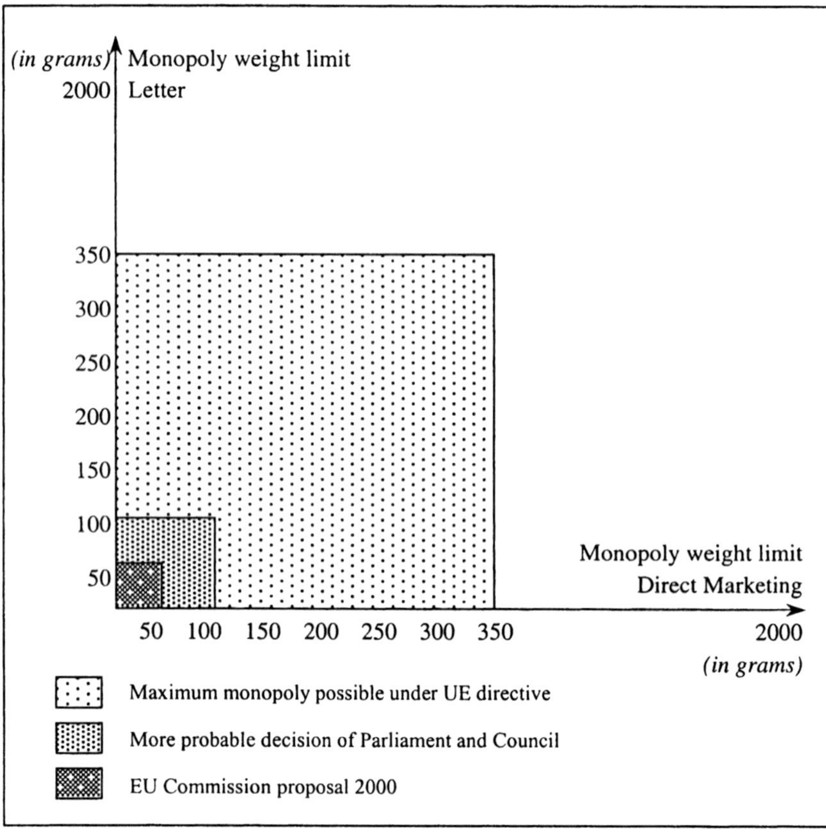

[45] Art. 9 of the Postal Directive states that it has to be administrated by independent beneficiary (or beneficiaries).
[46] Proposed by the doctrine, mentioned in § 1.1.2.

1.2.3.3 The Promotion of Quality of Postal Services

For what concerns the quality of postal services, the Directive is willing to promote the improvement of quality and the efficiency recovery in the users' interest and of companies in general.

In principle, the factors that contribute mostly to the definition of the quality as regards the postal services are:

- speed
- reliability;
- security;
- easy access.

As far as "domestic" postal services are concerned, the community regulation simply sets up the basic criteria for the evaluation of quality and gives to the national authority the task to fix the level of these criteria. Moreover, it adds that the quality standard should concern, in particular, the times necessary for delivery, regularity and reliability of the service[47] to be guaranteed. Vice-versa, for cross-border services, the objective is much more simply defined, in function of the average duration for the standard products to be sent[48]. Therefore, the initial standards to be taken have been defined as benchmark, which should be achieved for all flows within the intra-community traffic and for each bilateral flux between two Member States[49].

Table 1.9
Quality objectives for intra-community cross – border post

AVERAGE DURATION	OBJECTIVE
D + 3	85% of mailings
D + 5	97% of mailings

In line with the community principles for the consumers' welfare in the different economical sectors, the community regulation on abusive provisions in the contracts between consumers is extended to the postal activity. In addition to

[47] The rule is enhanced by the provision that external bodies comparing to the universal service suppliers, annually or more often, assess the quality of performances.

[48] In technical terms "of the sendings belonging to the regulated quicker category". The duration is calculated from the entry to the destination of delivery, according to the D + n formula (D represents the date of deposit and n represents the number of working days between that date and the date of delivery to the addressee and according to particular conventions in the ** note in the enclosed document of the Postal Directive.

[49] The national objectives must, of course, be coherent with the cross-border objectives.

this, the adoption of special procedures for claim management becomes unavoidable[50].

1.2.4 Proposing a Further Liberalisation

In the year 2000 the Commission has elaborated a proposal for a new Directive for the postal sector, to amend 97/67 EC in order to further expand the competition margin in the postal sector[51]. This initiative is a reaction to the market developments (improved efficiency and performance, growing integration of new business areas from express mail to parcels, to transport and logistics, geographical expansion with cross-border acquisitions). But it is also a commitment to what had already been foreseen with the first liberalisation in 1997[52], as well as a reaction to political pressures[53]. In brief, this liberalisation would involve:

- the opening of a further 20% of the USP turnover starting from the year 2003[54];
- a subsequent liberalisation of the postal market starting from 2007 (with a level to be decided on the basis of the current market situation);
- some accompanying measures (special services, access, redress procedures, cross-subsidies).

The benefits of the further expansion of the market are of course to be found in the promotion of a market that is more efficient, innovative and careful to the quality of services. It should be able to exploit the potential offered by new

[50] These procedures need to be transparent, simple and of limited charge. For what concerns claims, special mention is made of losses, thefts and damages or non-observance of the rules of quality of the service. See Art. 19 of the Postal Directive.

[51] See COM (2000) 319 final.

[52] See art. 7(3) Directive 97/67/EC: "*As a further step towards the completion of the internal market of postal services, the European Parliament and the Council shall decide by the 1st January 2000 and without prejudice to the competence of the Commission, on the further gradual and controlled liberalisation of the postal market, in particular with a view to the liberalisation of cross-border and direct mail, as well as on a further review of the price and weight limits, with effect from 1st January 2003, taking into account the developments, in particular economic, social and technological developments, that have occurred by that date, and also taking into account the financial equilibrium of the universal service provider(s), with a view to further pursuing the goals of this Directive*".

[53] See Conclusion of the Presidency, Lisbon European Council, 23rd and 24th March 2000, within the framework of the economic reforms for a complete and fully operational market it is deemed necessary "*to speed up liberalisation in areas such as gas, electricity, postal services and transport. ...it aims at achieving a fully operational internal market in these areas*".

[54] This opening is expected to be divided as follows: 16% through the delimitation of the reservable area to 50gr/a multiple of 2.5 the basic price; 3% from the opening of outgoing cross-border mail and 1% removal of price limits on express mail.

technologies and find targeted solutions for consumers and companies whose needs have become more complex with respect to the past. Such "step-by-step" liberalisation is regarded as compatible with the aim of offering a universal service, by granting both a suitable number of branches and making them accessible with consistent prices. Finally it should keep into account the social constraints to keep sustainable levels of employment in the sector.

The criticisms made to the proposal and the resistance to change, are essentially based on the following points[55]:

- the sustainability of the supply of postal services and of uniform prices in rural areas;
- the relationship between special reserved services and areas open to competition;
- the impact of liberalisation on employment levels;
- the impact of liberalisation on keeping a condition of economic balance for Universal Services Providers;
- realism in setting the timetable for opening the market.

There is no doubt that the market needs to know with sufficient advance the regulation framework being drawn up in order to reduce uncertainties and plan investments. However the degree of consensus in the various countries and different political areas leads to the conclusion that it will take quite a long time to reach the necessary compromises.

1.3 What Transformation and Which Causes?

The analysis carried out so far underlined the regulation process as one of the factors explaining the on-going developments in the postal sector. This might be a flaw in the illustration of certain topics, whose understanding requires the analytical consideration of some elements of the institutional framework. On the other hand, a primary role in defining the developments in the sector and the widening of its borders is played by market factors and competition, alongside the institutional elements.

It is possible to find converging aspects in all European countries on some development lines in the sector:

- technological progress and new technological application;
- globalisation of economies and internationalisation of the markets;
- concentration of economic sectors;
- restructuring of production processes on the basis of organisational flexibility criteria and generalised use of outsourcing for corporate functions;

---

[55] See Toledano F. (2001) and European Parliament (2000).

- demand for efficiency from the customers;
- dissemination among companies of new commercial policies aimed at setting up a personalised relationship with the customer alongside mass communication;
- more frequent use of one-stop shopping.

The direct consequences of the developments in the regulation framework and of the institutional constraints mentioned above also include:

- deregulation and liberalisation of markets;
- more stringent budget constraints in countries belonging to the Monetary Union;
- political aim of the Governments to safeguard their political credibility as administrators by introducing efficiency measures[56].

These are all general trends, which characterise in a pervasive way all economies and affect all sectors to a different extent. This means that they should be taken for granted and assimilated by any sector that is going through a vital development phase. It is not an overstatement to say that in the postal sector the shock wave is particularly strong. In this case, the impact could be really dramatic considering that the sector in the past has always been safeguarded from competition. In addition, it was administrated in such a way that the criteria of suitability of production processes and of products/services with respect to the potential of new technologies and the new types of demand, generally speaking were not sufficiently taken into consideration. Furthermore, as it will be underlined by the following analysis, the above mentioned trends have clearly been identified by operators as stronghold to be duly stressed and used in order to penetrate traditional market segments of postal activity and to open up new ways of entering adjacent operation areas.

The sector of the supply of postal services in advanced countries can be regarded as mature and thus subject to revitalisation through radical changes in the operating concepts and growth drivers.

The competitive threat in particular has different forms and origins. The most dynamic operators have integrated their own business areas both vertically and horizontally. They have diversified their supply by trying to take greater advantage of their segments and expanding the range of customised solutions.

As for technology, it is relevant in the area of process automation (for example in sorting), transport, but also storage of goods, computerisation of back office activities and for the development of track & tracing techniques and related products. From this point of view it should be mentioned that in many cases in the past decades postal companies had neglected the need for computerisation and

[56] See Campbell R.M., Regulatory and Governance Changes in Liberalised, Commercialised Postal Environments: a comparative assessment, in Crew M.A. – Kleindorfer P.R. (2001b).

automation of their branches. This was due to the fact that their strategic vision was aimed at satisfying customers who were not particularly sophisticated and sensitive to the efficiency profiles of processes and/or because the resources made available by the economic subject were scarce.

Furthermore, there is high potential in Internet applications both for related activities, which the New Economy generates on traditional or less traditional demand for postal services (package delivery for e-commerce), and for the exploitation of new business areas. Within this group we find hybrid mail products, the supply of Internet connections, E-mail addresses, web pages, up to E-commerce platforms, electronic signature and data transmission with suitable safety and protection solutions.

As a consequence of the globalisation and internationalisation of economies the adoption of world-wide borders for commerce and economic activities is extended also to small and medium-sized enterprises which manage within a global framework their own corporate processes of procurement, production and sale of goods and services. This in turn leads to an increase in demand for services of communication, transport and payment; more in general there is a call for assistance on a global scale and service suppliers must be able to compete on this level. The latter is a critical factor for success. In view of the competition coming from other forms of communication (telephone, fax, Internet) mentioned above as a threat, the ability to operate choosing a global approach and using the most advanced technological solutions in order to enrich the range of products on offer becomes the real competitive edge.

An example of how partnership relations and alliances can be a way of responding to globalisation is illustrated in Figure 1.4, where the target is only the domestic market with reference to the four main postal operators in Europe (Deutsche Post, TPG, La Poste and The Post Office - now Consigna). Indeed, in order to map the phenomenon throughout the whole of Europe an extremely wide-ranging approach is necessary.

The concentration of economic sectors is partly a consequence and partly a concurrent cause of economic globalisation. The growth in size of operators, often through processes of external growth in order to reach objectives faster, is a response to the need to exploit economies of scale, strengthen skills in a wider ranging area, acquiring market power and finding better ways of diversifying risk.

On the other hand, if you exclude the postal sector in the narrow sense of the word, traditionally subject to a monopoly, the other segments of parcel and express mail delivery, transport and logistic functions on a European level have been extremely fragmented up until recent years. In addition, their operations activities are often limited to regional areas. This means that there are pressures and opportunities for profitable structural recomposing through concentration processes which should allow supply structures to reach a size suitable for the characteristics of the demand.

Figure 1.4
Global competition in a global market

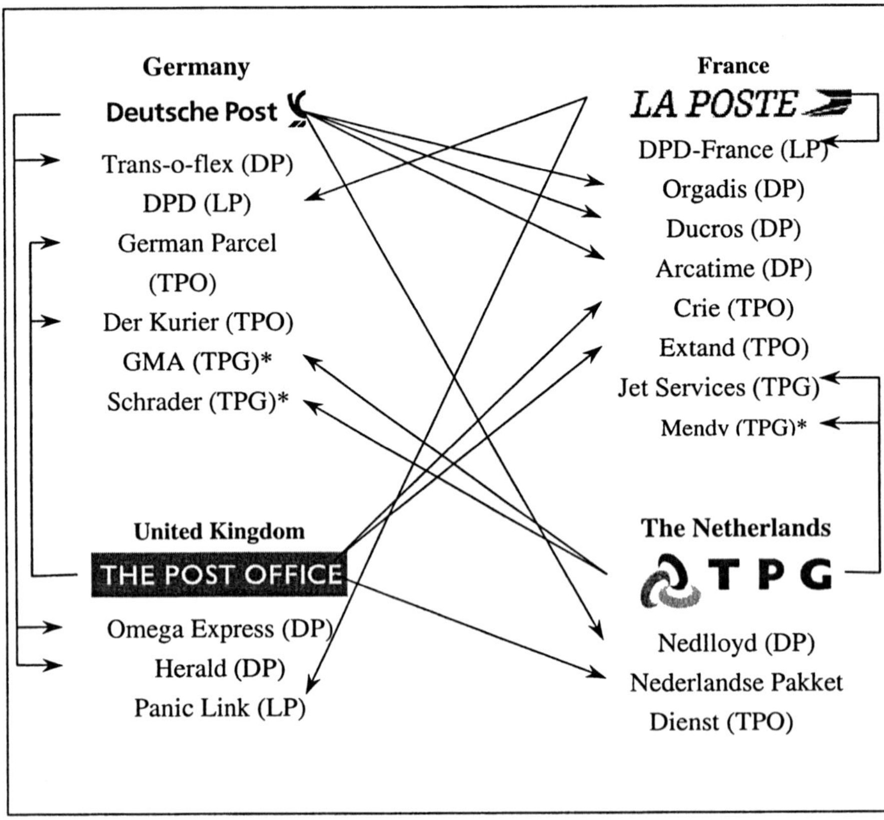

Legend: DP = Deutsche Post; LP = La Poste;
TPO = The Post Office; TPG = TNT Post Group.
Source: Toledano F. (2001).

The restructuring of production processes on the basis of criteria of organisational flexibility has lead a growing number of companies, even those belonging to different economic, manufacturing or commercial sectors of the old and of the new economy, to assess the option of outsourcing some of their corporate functions. An immediate impact on the "traditional" postal sector is caused by the production of hybrid mail and by the development of integrated logistic services. In the latter area particular relevance should be attributed to those areas for productivity and efficiency gains that can be obtained by resorting to specialised operators. The latter adopt ad hoc organisational models and operational instruments, being strongly oriented towards the optimisation of processes which thus become the core business of the activity, supported by targeted localisation choices and by advanced reference technologies. The relevant elements to be considered also include the growth in professional skills of the human resources and their motivation because the staff has to operate in highly specialised structures, rather than in auxiliary services with respect to the main production processes.

As for the demand for efficiency by the customers, this is a result of the degree of competitiveness, which is generally higher in global markets. Not only that: as already underlined, this is also the result of the trend of postal services for communication and transport to jeopardise with their quality level, the very quality of the performance by third parties[57].

Last but not least, the adoption of direct marketing techniques aimed at conquering new markets or increasing customer loyalty is undoubtedly a trend that generates demand for delivery services and expectations in terms of performance quality[58].

The trends mentioned above have forced the Post to reorganise the production processes for traditional activities and to adjust the supply in order to take advantage of the potential of new technological applications and to respond to market demands as well as to the challenges presented by competitors. It is also necessary to make strategic positioning choices in the definition of the sectors.

The two main elements in defining the strategic positioning are, on the one hand, the range of products on offer and the market segments by lines of product/requirements covered and, on the other, the geographical coverage of the supply.

With reference to the first element, the following strategic business areas have recently emerged:

- mail
- express delivery
- logistics
- financial services
- support services to e-application and integrated e-business services.

As for the second element, the geographical dimensions that can be used as possible strategic reference take on the following configuration:

- domestic coverage
- regional operations

---

[57] A very clear example of this are sales by correspondence, subscription press but also the large number of other instances where the customer or supply relationship is based on the interaction of communication / postal delivery.

[58] The experience in the US seems to indicate that the reduction in the correspondence volumes generated by competition from replacement products is more than compensated by the growth of direct advertising by mail, with or without address.

- pan-European operations
- global operations

The companies can choose the way of positioning themselves along these two axes either through internal growth processes or through more accelerated and aggressive external growth processes. There is a wide range of possible solutions, from commercial alliances to equity-type alliances and those based on the creation of joint ventures, to more complex process of M&A. In general, a constraint/opportunity in terms of strategic positioning choices is generally represented by the need /opportunity to improve the degree of use of the network and to create scope economies with a combination of products that can be extremely heterogeneous.

The competitive threat comes from various fronts: from global operators as well as niche operators and in particular from replacement products provided by integrators (global operators and regional couriers), alternative products such as E-mail and Internet solutions, from specialised delivery agencies on a local and regional basis.

Generally speaking the competitive variables are represented by:

- price;
- quality, in terms of speed and reliability of performance;
- image and service customisation;
- territorial coverage;
- easy access;
- product innovation and ability to respond timely to new needs and to rapidly offer new solutions in order to take full advantage of the potential offered by new available technologies.

In actual fact, however, these variables have different specific characteristics and weights depending on the market segment. Furthermore, due to their different history, their exposure to competition varies (see Table 1.10).

Table 1.10

Estimation of parts of turnover per segment and type of operator

	Monopolist	**Private companies**	**Total**
Letters	45.7	2.2	47.9
Packages	6.5	10.9	17.4
Express mailings	4.3	30.4	37.7
Total	56.5	43.5	100.0

Source: European Commission (1992), p. 262.

For what concerns the different business areas, the growth perspectives and the competitive variables are differentiated and different in each European country.

In short, three considerations can be made on this purpose.

Within the mail activity, the main challenges are the improvement of productivity and flexibility of costs in the network. The demand volumes are exposed to the erosion of substitutes – based on different technological supports – and of services that have a different price but offer better conditions in terms of speed and reliability (typically the express services). Besides the activity of express forwarding, in this area, it is very important to improve the quality of service, by expanding the network's productive capacity (density and efficiency) and its geographical cover. And that means investments in vehicles of different type and also, as it happens in the more advanced experiences, in planes, hubs, warehousing and infrastructures). The interfaces with the clients whose operativity is suitable to meet the needs of the several segments considerably contribute to the success of it.

It is in direct mail that the analysts see a growing demand. This demand is less exposed to the competition of electronic replacement because it is complementary to the E-commerce, particularly in its B2C formula. In the value chain, this sophisticated activity meets several specialised operators among which also the postal operators for the accomplishment of their central task consisting of the "distribution of direct mail articles". Moreover, in a rationale for diversification of the activity they can successfully integrate functions that are in many ways related and create therefore direct mail enterprises, which work as specialists in the sector[59]. The most dynamic postal operators have started to be strongly present in this type of activity[60], which has interesting development potentials in Europe and can represent one of the revitalisation way of the traditional sector. This one, in turn, has reached its maturity[61].

For what concerns the sector of logistics, it is now basically considered in its modern framework of effective highly automated and integrated services. In this perspective, it is relatively recent and comprises several formulas such as the contract logistics (from order management to warehousing to order processing, from shipping, to transport & delivery) to the most specific forms concerning warehousing, shipping and transport & delivery. The Post Offices have entered this sector for several reasons. First of all, this is an expanding market (growth is expected to grow by 15% in the next two years in the USA and by 10% in Europe) – contrary to the overstocked market. Further more, there is the strategy of taking advantage of synergies with the postal segment of forwarding parcels and express mails. With the latter, in particular, there are common factors and overlapping in the relationships to the clients, common technological structures (management systems of transport and track and trace) as well as common warehousing and

---

[59] To identify the value chain in the direct mail sector, see Arthur Andersen (1998), p. 5.

[60] Reference is made basically to TPG and to DPWN.

[61] For an analysis of the growth drivers of the direct marketing activity in Europe and about the perspectives for the postal sector, see in details Arthur Andersen (1998).

sorting infrastructures. In 1996, it has been the Dutch Office that has identified first this opportunity and diversified the portfolio of activities with the acquisition of TNT Ltd. Now these companies are regrouped under the brand TNT logistic, whereas DPWN has entered the sector in 1999 with the acquisition of Danzas, followed by other shopping operations on the domestic markets[62]. In 1998, also the French Post joined, with 50% sharing, Publi-Trans, integrator of logistics services. During 1999 it brought this share to 100% and started in this way a considerable competitive run. At present, among the "big" commercial post operators, only the British Post Office (now Consigna Ltd) did not realise any significant acquisitions in the sector, although this is mentioned in the strategies. The British logistics market, this is also to be mentioned, is one of the most consolidated and effective markets in Europe where the big logistics empires have just started their activity. Therefore, the entry into the sector seems possible only through strong M & A processes. In the other countries, the entry into the logistics is quite easier because of the strong fragmentation of operators and because the operational margins are little, in particular if the processes are not optimised with suitable models and the support of the operational research techniques and considerable investments.

Finally, for what concerns the financial services, this is historically a field of operativity given to the Posts (often, in the past, it was not often seen as a business area but an obligation of universal services), in particular for what concerns the post-giro systems and deposit collection. In spite of not substantial differentiation of the structures of offer[63], these have represented a kind of saturation of productive capacity and of relationship to the clients of postal counters (see § 1.4). Nevertheless, considering the joint deep structural transformations and competitive relationships in the bank and financial sector, several operators revised their intervention with also external strategies which could also be extreme, that means also of complete exit from the business area or, with a integral a very competitive presence[64].

The above mentioned structural dynamics and competitive attitudes brought to a new definition of the limits of the postal activity. The fact of using vectors such as weight and volume on one side, and speed and reliability of deliveries on the other side, allows it to identify the following business areas. These are fields of intervention for highly specialised operators often belonging to "poly-functional" structures with the presence of postal operators (see Figure 1.5).

---

[62] The two postal empires seem, however, to be differentiating their strategies: the first toward contract logistics, the second one towards to-end-solutions.

[63] As we will see later, this is often a more recent strategy aiming at improving and consolidating the brand's image.

[64] See in much more details Chapters 3 and 4.

Figure 1.5
The borders of the modern "postal" activity

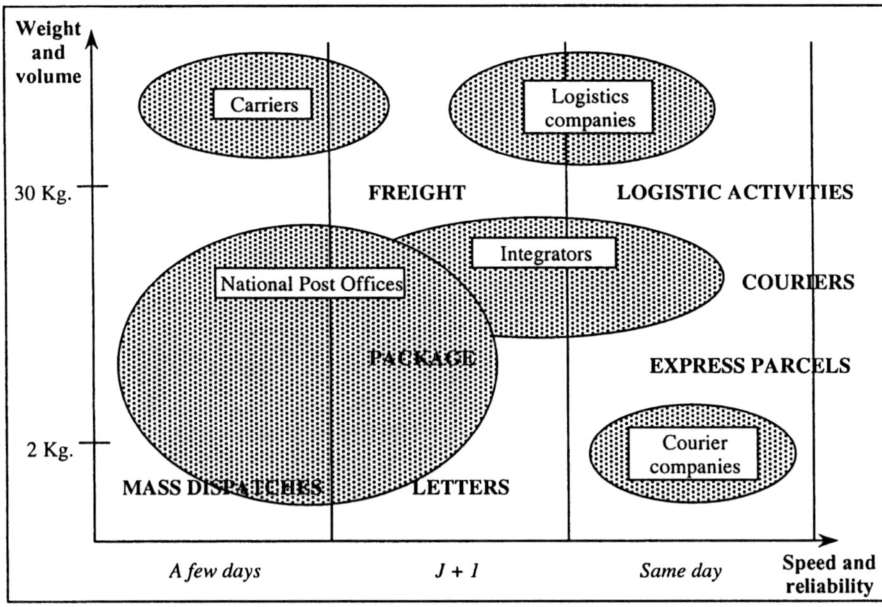

Source: Our adaptation from Commissariat Général du Plan.

To conclude, crossing of the two vectors of development, i.e geographical cover and market segments, we see that in Europe there are very differentiated strategies (see Figure 1.6 in the following page).

Nevertheless, since the market calls for global services and the competition becomes more and more sharper, the Posts are currently taking positions of domestic niche and will be probably obliged to act as protagonist in market segment that are open to the competition.

All this has already and will always have a significant impact on the organisational structures which gives relatively poorly articulated solutions for production lines must evolve toward divisional structures to come to group structures with sectorial holding. After growth and conquer of market segments with acquisitions and alliances, this development calls for rationalisation and integration of the several acquired companies. It also calls for the setting up of a brand structure, which is able to encourage the investments in marketing. These are necessary to conquer significant market share in a context with high development potentials, but with very strong competition. In fact, they all need to operate according to globalisation rationales and with operational volume sable to take benefit from the economies of scale.

Figure 1.6
Geographical cover with market segments

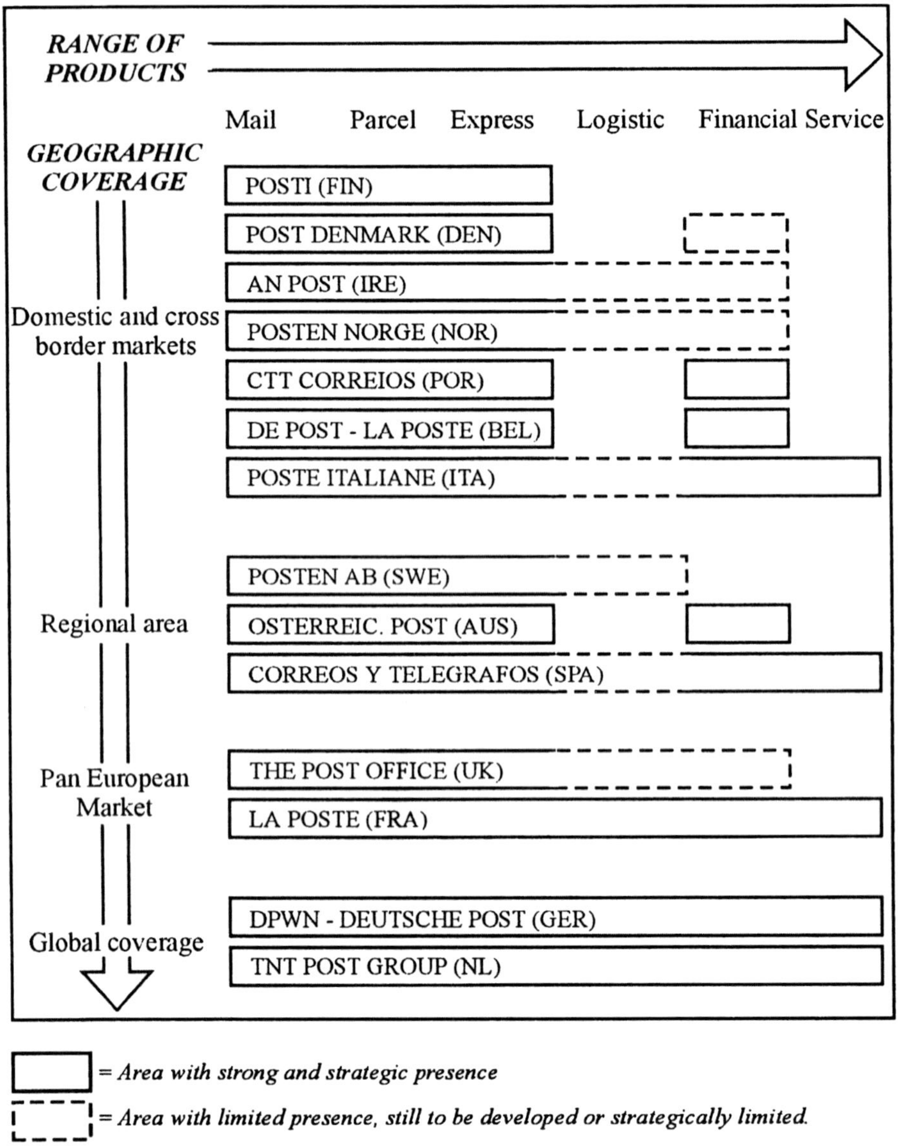

1.4 The Branch Network

Traditionally, the post office branch network is one of the qualifying features of the company's network nature, which has been previously discussed. These physical structures distributed across the entire national territory, along with door to door postal delivery and the retrieval of mail posted into the appropriate boxes, have fulfilled the function of proximity services. Traditionally, in almost all countries post office branches perform front office activities for postal services in the strict sense (letters and parcels) and for payment by post services (gyro payments), as well as some back office functions.

The advent of information technologies and the spread of the Internet have unhinged the rationale for this organisation in as much as the network of branches is no longer a prerequisite for delivery of these services. Therefore, at least in principle, the branch network, which, in the traditional organisation of the business, constituted a strength and a barrier to entry for other operators, may turn into a handicap. The high management costs (staff and fixed capital investments in real estate or resources absorbed in rentals) and, recently, also the investments required for their refurbishment and for the computerisation of the workplaces have inevitably led to a questioning of their function and of ways to achieve optimisation of these functions.

The answer to this question is not easy and, most importantly, it cannot be a single solution as the profitability of branches varies widely according to their location, that is to say according to the type of customers served and the operating volumes achieved. The branch network's situation in the early 80's reflected the management rationale, which had stratified over time, of postal companies more or less throughout Europe inspired by the public administration model and the provision of universal services. In fact, in some countries, the provision of a broad network of branches has formed a, sometimes official, part of the obligation to provide a universal service.

A mapping survey carried out in 1998 demonstrated the widespread acceptance, by legal obligation or by custom and practice, as well as by political and trade union pressure, of the concept of the branch network as an obligation to provide a universal service (see Table 1.11).

Table 1.11
Obligations incumbent upon the organisation of post office branches

Country	A	B	C	D	Exceptions and other notes
Austria	X			X	Absence of specific standards relating to number and location of branches.
Belgium	X				At least one post office per municipality and maximum distance of 5 Km between branches.
Denmark	X				Joint responsibility of the Ministry and the Danish Post.
Finland	==				
France	==				The Ministry has ultimate authority as regards the reduction of the number of post offices with a moratorium since 1993, but La Poste does not measure the profitability of individual branches.
Germany	X		X		The PUDLV draft establishes the maximum distance between branches in the newly urbanised areas.
Greece	==				
Ireland	X			X	Attempts to close unprofitable branches in rural areas in the early '90s failed due to political opposition.
Italy	X				Difficulties in closing branches in rural areas due to political opposition.
Luxembourg	==				Rural branches are considered to be operating at a loss, but no data is available.
The Netherlands	X		X		In general guide lines of the postal system.
Portugal	X			X	As a general rule CCT is free to close branches, but the possibilities are limited by political considerations.
Spain	X			X	As a general rule, Correos is free to close branches, but the possibilities are limited by political considerations.
Sweden	X	X			In accordance with the Postal Services Act of 1994.
United Kingdom	X		X		The Government is committed to maintaining a network of post office branches across the whole country.

Legend: A: **Part of the USO** C: **Defined in other written form**
B: **Defined by law** D: **"Custom and Practice"**
X : part of the UPO == : not specified in the USO

Source: NERA (1998), p. 30.

However, within the traditions of the different countries there exist various institutional organisational solutions. Alongside the owned branches, there are solutions such as agency agreements or franchising (that is to say granting of an operating licence to independent parties) or by joint management initiatives. These can be combined with other commercial activities (sale of stationery or office supplies, sale of magazines and newspapers, service stations, grocery stores) in order to exploit management synergies. Such flexibility also relates to the opening hours and the range of services offered.

In some more recent experiences, alliances for the management of branches have been established with some of the large retail chains in order to put the function on a more commercial footing.

The problem of low profitability, or, more often, of operating at a loss, which affects branches located in rural or poor urban areas, is crucial in some countries, where often the local post office represents the only form of state presence and also the only surviving economic and social activity. This issue is particularly critical in the UK, Ireland and France, but is also felt in Sweden and Norway where, as the right to vote is exercised in the post offices, the idea of their closure has been viewed as a threat to democracy.

The problem of re-conversion of post offices operating at low levels of profit is therefore undoubtedly a very complex one.

The European experience is quite varied with the countries in the Mediterranean Basin tending towards the more traditional solutions and the Nordic countries having tried for a longer time to set up the previously-mentioned more flexible approaches.

In The Netherlands, the branch network is managed by a dedicated company (Postkantoren B.V.), which is a joint venture owned in equal shares by Postbank N.V., of the ING Group and PTT Post. This network provides services for the Postbank banking business, for the PTT Post postal business and for other third parties by means of commercial agreements. With more than 2,500 branches, of which a part are franchises and some have adopted a formula of shops in post under the Bruna brand, Postkantoren manages one of the most extensive commercial networks in the country[65]. This is the result of a post office branch policy, which has been underway since the early 90's and took a farsighted approach to the problem of the decline in the traditional proximity services. These services have been eroded by the advent of computers and remote operations and focused on partnerships and more flexible commercial solutions in order to cope with the over-capacity in the system and to exploit the potential for cross-selling.

[65] The structure of the Dutch post office branch network is currently in a dynamic state of evolution with a progressive reduction of owned properties and a reorganisation of those managed with more flexible commercial formulas.

Table 1.12

Types of post office branches in The Netherlands

	1997	1998	1999
Owned branches	694	635	553
Branches operated under franchise	162	188	219
Branches operated as sub-agency	1,435	1,449	1,475
Bruna Bookshop service points	332	305	292
	2,623	2,577	2,539

Source: Postkantoren Balance Sheet.

In 1997, a second modernisation programme was launched in the aim of dealing with the physical layout of the branches and to improve commercial agreements (with KPN Telecom and public agencies, the national lottery, and the ticketing provider for transport services). Further purpose was the training of staff in order to foster commercial attitudes and to raise professional motivation. A particular focus was laid on the need to achieve a more rational use of resources with proposals for self-service equipment for routine transactions and direct contact with staff for special assistance and consulting[66]. The network has been reorganised commercially into three different types:

- "Mega Post Office" with continuous opening hours from morning to evening. These branches are located in commercial centres and business areas. The separation of front and back office functions has the aim of improving the commercial focus of the front office;
- "City Post Office" with continuous opening hours from morning to evening. These branches are located in small town centres or within suburban shopping centres, to serve a clientele of private individuals and SMEs;
- "Service" points for private clients, located in high frequency areas. These are designed along the lines of a shop and offer products for packaging and support services.

The situation regarding the distribution of branches in the country appears satisfactory and in the recently passed Law governing the postal services there is no explicit mention of any obligation in terms of the distribution of the branch network.

Also in a country such as Belgium, where there is no tradition of franchising for post office branches - but where their management is entirely in the hands of the post office organisation -, since the second half of the '90s a programme has been launched for the modernisation of the network by the establishment of an operating unit. This unit' s name is "Point de Vente", and it has been charged with the mission of converting the network to a commercial approach and making it profitable, in as far as this is compatible with the Post Office's commitments towards the State[67].

---

[66] In this country too every attempt at rationalisation is met with resistence due to the fear of weakening the strength of the unions and incurring job losses. Such initiatives are therefore agreed with the Unions because there is a great sensitivity to the threat of strikes and political action.

[67] The axes along which the modernisation was arranged are: i) lay out, with improvements in terms of user-friendly space for the public and separate rooms for personalised service (there were 65 offices at the end of 1997, rising to 462 by the end of 1999) and by the creation of organised queuing lines; ii) information for clients and marketing communications; iii) training of staff (commercial, managerial and behavioural training as well as technical training); iv) call center; v) telesales units; vi) computerisation of workplaces and network linkup of the IT infrastructure.

Along with the closure of some branches, as part of the initiatives for the rationalisation of the network, improvements have been made to the service with late evening opening times one day a week and on Saturdays in some branches.

In 1999, the "Point de Vente" units' mission was focused on the promotion of sales of both La Poste products, as well as those of its partners and other third parties. This purpose was to be achieved by means of the branch network, thus combining the three objectives of satisfying the customers needs, creating an adequate profit margin from the business and providing a quality delivery of public service. A new affiliate, Post-shop, in partnership with GIB Group, enters into this scenario, for the sale of stationery and office products.

As for the legal obligations for the distribution of branches, the preamble to the management contract stipulated between the State and La Poste for the period 1997-2001, envisages that: "*L'Etat veille à ce que La Poste fournisse un service public de qualité, notamment en ce qui concerne la densité du réseau et les performances en matière de distribution. Un adaptation des taches de service public à l'évolution des besoins de sociétés et du contexte européen s'impose. Le dynamisme de La Poste à l'égard des nouvelles technologies est encouragé*". In art. 4, concerning the relationship with customers, a judgement indicating that the need for proximity to the customers is generally met, is formulated with regard to the density of the branch network. The principle is stated that the Post Office should have the freedom to adapt the network according to the needs of the customers. However, all the projects for modifying the network which alter the density of branches to any significant degree[68], must be submitted to the State as part of a concerted procedure. Furthermore there remains an obligation to keep at least one branch open for each municipality. In general, there is also a provision for obligatory opening hours of at least a few hours per week beyond the working hours of the clientele. The undertaking is also considered to organise the branches in such a way as to avoid queues involving waiting times in excess of an average of four minutes.

In France traditionally great attention is given to the arrangements for the post office branch network . Already in the contract for the plan for the 1995-97 period, between the four points defining the mission and the tendency of the post one reads: "*Les missions en matière de contribution a l'aménagement du territoire*", with an involvement of the Poste in public initiatives for the support of rural and socially disadvantaged areas such as the city suburbs[69]. On the same subject, as

[68] This refers to the closure of post office branches which are more than five kilometres away from the nearest branch.

[69] In fact art.4 stipulates: "*La Poste, conformément à la loi du 2 juillet 1990 et à son cahier de charge, contribue à l'aménagement du territoire. Elle propose sur l'ensemble du territoire [omissis] un service public de qualité qui répond aux besoins de toutes le catégories d'usagers, ménages ou entreprises, en particulier en zone rurale et dans les banlieues*". Further it explains that: "*Pour optimiser l'efficacité de son réseau, la présence de La Poste sera analysée au niveau le plus pertinent avec les collectivités locale concernées. L'offre de service pourra intervenir dans le cadre de formules adaptées aux caractéristique locales: i) association avec les collectivités locales, les entreprises*

regards investment policy, only at the end of a list of other priorities does one encounter a generic commitment to *"rénover et maintenir l'ensemble des infrastructure existantes (réseau de bureaux et bien immobilier, parc de véhicules, parc informatique)".*

In the new contract for the period 1998-2001 the problem of the post office network is a leitmotiv which is recurrent in more than one of the six points in the mission and strategic trends. In fact, it is demonstrated explicitly with a reference both in point 3 "*Des service de proximité pour tous et de qualité*"[70], and in point 4 "*Le réseau des points de contact et la participation à l'aménagement du territoire*"[71]. Then point 5 "*La politique des ressources humaines et l'amélioration des relations sociales*" envisages both specific training programmes and career management models and incentive systems for staff working in "sensitive" urban areas. As a reward for this social commitment on the part of the branch network, La Poste benefits from a favourable tax treatment[72].

Sweden, which, like Finland, liberalised the postal market some time ago, has also envisaged that, as part of the Universal Postal Service, amongst the other requirements "*the density of the points of contact and of access points shall take account of the needs of users*"[73]. This obligation is met either by means of the traditional post offices (in competition with the bank offices), by the "*post office in shops*" and by the "*rural postmen*". In order to keep those branches going which are not profitable and which have no commercial justification for their operations, Posten Ab receives an annual subsidy from the State of 23.8 million Euros (200 million Swedish crowns). According to the Swedish authority controlling the postal system, this subsidy is less than the actual cost and therefore cannot give rise to crossover subsidies to help other areas of the Swedish postal

---

publiques et les administrations de l'Etat (point multiservices, points publics), ii) recherche de partneriats avec d'autres services publics ou parapublics ainsi qu'avec des acteurs économiques locaux, en particulier les commerçants des zones rurales, pouvant offrir des prestations postales pour le compte de La Poste".

[70] In particular, there is mention of the need to improve the quality of the client welcome, to promote the use of new technologies and Internet access as much in cities as in rural areas, and to take an active role in facilitating the changeover to the Euro, especially with those segments of the population who will experience the greatest difficulty. In order to meet this need ad hoc training courses are planned for staff who are in direct contact with clients.

[71] In this it is stated that La Poste, which is present across the entire country, must adjust its network of points of contact to meet the needs of the population, taking particular account of demographic, social and economic developments and of any projects for the promotion of the territory, and seeking a financial equilibrium. The special nature of the specific needs of rural, urban and the so-called "sensitive" areas (with more acute social problems) is highlighted as is the need to develop appropriate criteria to assess their relative needs. Emphasis is once again given to the development of partnerships with other public entities in order to achieve a joint effort which could benefit from synergies.

[72] In accordance with art. 21 of Loi 2 Juin 1990, referred to in the programme contract.

[73] In accordance with the Postal Service Ordinance (1993:1709) issued by the National Post and Telecom Agency in Section 8.

operations[74]. The reduction in the number of post office branches constitutes a response to changes in the customers' buying patterns, which are now tending towards more convenient solutions[75]. The replacement of traditional branches with post office in shops, with longer opening times and a wider range of services, seems to meet the customers' needs. The PTS report judges the level of distribution of the service across the country to be acceptable[76].

In Great Britain the problem of the modernisation of the Post Office has been dealt within a White Paper which has exposed the sector's problems[77]. Among the reform programme's five objectives we draw attention to: *"Objective 5 – To support a viable network of post offices so as to ensure nation-wide access to a range of public and private sector services".*

The observation which gives rise to the proposition is that the postal network – which with 19,000 branches is the most extensive in Europe – has historically represented an important component which was appreciated by the country's social and commercial infrastructures. In the current competitive context, in order to provide an economic justification for this system and to generate the necessary resources to ensure its viability, as a point of access to postal services in the strict sense (Royal Mail and Parcelforce Worldwide) and as a channel by which the government delivers services such as the payment of pensions and other social benefits and, through certain selected offices, issues documents such as driving licences and passports, the aim of reinforcing this poly-functionality becomes an important priority. Historically, the activities carried out on a contractual basis for the government and its agencies have contributed significantly to the networks' turnover, accounting for over half. However, technological advances open doors to other alternatives for the delivery of these services and therefore place the nature of the above-mentioned role of the post office branch in doubt.

Both commercial and social aspects are taken into account in considering the criteria for future development and flexible solutions are recommended in order to

---

[74] See National Post & Telecom Agency (2000).

[75] The development of the type and number of branches is summarised as follows:

Table 1.13

Types of post office branches in Sweden

	1990	1993	1999
Traditional post office	1,934	1,494	922
Post office in shop and other offices service point	120	398	853
Total number of fixed service point	2,054	1,892	1,775

Source: National Post & Telecom Agency 2000.

[76] The offering was completed by the 2,700 rural postmen (who serve approx.700,000 families and 5,000 businesses) who offer what in effect amounts to branch services door to door.

[77] See DTI - Department of Trade and Industry (1999). The objectives have already been referred to in this Chapter under note 28.

reconcile the coverage of rural areas with the economic constraints[78]. In the face of this need the Government has the responsibility for defining the initial parameters such as minimum criteria for accessibility to branch services (i.e. the percentage of the population living within a given distance). The POUNC commission has been assigned a consultative function with regard to the matter of branch networks and their control, to ensure that the development of the network takes place without neglecting the less populated and socially deprived areas. Similarly, there is an obligation of transparency imposed on the Post Office regarding policy in matters of branch location[79].

Moreover, it is remembered that from 1986 the Post Office was reorganised into 3 business units: Royal Mail Letters, Royal Mail Parcel and Post Office Counters. In 1987 a company structure was given to these divisions and so "Post Office Counters Limited" became an associated company under the total control of the postal group. In implementing the reform project set out in the White Paper, in October 1999 the Post Office Group restructured its business areas into units which generate business for the network (described as "market-facing units") or which provide services to customers for the market-facing units (and, thus, described as service-delivery units). The Post Office Network obviously fits into this second category.

In Great Britain, the branch network which offers postal services, has traditionally been based on a network of owned properties (called *branch* or *Crown Offices*), operated by Post Office employees and on branches managed by sub–postmasters who generally run another retail activity alongside the postal business[80]. A minority of them (one thousand, approximately) are run in the form of a franchise (with brands such as Spar, Alldays, Forbuoys, Star News and

[78] *"It is the aim of the Government and the Post Office to maintain access to counters' services in, for example rural communities. POCL goes to great lengths to maintain post offices in these circumstances, setting them up in village halls, petrol stations, pubs and even domestic premises, when no other solution can be found*".

[79] This is through the statement in the yearly accounts report on the development of the branch network in rural and deprived urban areas.

[80] In urban areas typically cigarettes, sweets, newspapers, magazines and stationery; in rural areas the village shop. In the London area and other major cities most of the sub-post offices are managed by families of Asian origin.

Table 1.14

Types of branches in Great Britain

	1993	1994	1995	1996	1997	1998	1999
Owned branches (Crown or branches)	917	800	699	653	606	601	600
Privately managed agencies*	19,041	18,922	18,908	18,761	18,645	18,407	18,175
Total	19,958	19,722	19,607	19,414	19,251	19,008	18,775

* *That employ approx. 4,000 people in addition to the owners.*

Source: Post Office Annual Report.

Dillons)[81]. The management of postal services by sub-postmasters who run other retail businesses, constitutes a point of attraction for the customers and increases the retailer's sales of products, as well as the remuneration. This latter is set as partly fixed and partly variable, according to varying proportions which are established in the contracts[82]. However, estimates indicate that for the Post Office about 4,000 submasters (that is to say a little over 20% of the total) operate at a loss, generating less revenue than their costs, with an overall loss in the order of £35-40 million for the Post Office Group.

The main problem for the Post Office has been the delay in the network renewal and automation programmes during the period of the Thatcher government. At that time, in riding the long wave of traditional efficiency enjoyed by the country's postal system, there was a lack of farsightedness which prevented the structures from being adapted to suit the new technologies and working methods.

The Horizon programme was first launched in 1996. This was called for initially in response to a need to deal with the problem of benefit fraud and secondarily, due to the need to increase the efficiency of payment services within the postal circuit. The project, which had a time span of eight years, involved the organisations responsible for welfare and pensions. The technological solution first adopted was the magnetic card, with eventual developments towards more automated systems. However, the project suffered various delays and rethinks and so was eventually subjected to a complete review. In the meantime the benefits agencies' reached a decision to extend the entire payments system to a direct payment into bank accounts within the period 2003-2005 and therefore magnetic card option was dropped while in the meantime a benefits book with a bar code system is used. Project Horizon has therefore assumed a degree of post office branch automation and has a budget of about £1 billion, of which approximately half is government funded. By 1999 about 1,500 branches were due to be automated and the remainder at the rate of 300 a week in order to reach completion by the summer of 2001.

The automation of the branches represents the starting point for a commercial new launch of the network. In addition to postal services in the strict sense, the two following business areas have been identified, which are actually traditional ones but which are being re-launched as part of a policy decision: payment services connected with the banking system and public services.

---

[81] The ratio is that only approx. 3% of branches carry out 20% of all transactions and are located in the areas where there is the greatest demand (high streets or city centres) and the remaining 97% are managed privately. The trend however, is towards a reduction in the points of contact with customers and the directly managed share (which has reduced from 4.6% in 1993). However it must be remembered that in 1988 a programme to convert from owned branches (branch or Crown offices) to privately run sub-post offices had been launched which affected approximately 900 branches. The target is to retain an owned network which should cover approx. 15 % of the volume of transactions.

[82] See CABINET OFFICE – Performance and Innovation Unit (2000), pp.29-30.

With regard to the former, the White Paper points out that "*The post office net has an unrivalled reach into both rural areas and urban deprived areas. Thus some 60% of rural parishes have a post office whereas less than 10% have a bank or building society*". The development strategy in this regard was identified in the White Paper as being by means of partnership agreements with the banking system, whereas the subsequent evolution of the difficulty of social banking also gave rise to the idea of a Universal Postal Bank [83]. On the second front, there is an explicit political call to make it possible to retain the branch network even in non-profitable areas in concert with other public bodies which use this channel for the delivery of their own services. So, the need is also made for a widespread territorial presence also in areas where there is a low volume of transactions their own[84]. In other words the problem is presented as how to balance the needs of economic equilibrium with the requirements of a social nature[85]. Trust is placed in automation to enhance the poly-functionality of the branches with commercial agreements with third parties, in the development of the franchising and agency options[86]. However, but for extreme cases, the solution can only come from the contribution of the local communities, which have the immediate responsibility for their area[87].

---

[83] See Chapter 5, in this volume.

[84] In fact, point 19 of the White Paper, concerning objective 5 - To support a viable network of post offices so as to ensure nation-wide access to a range of public and private sector services -, the following warning is given: "*The Government has repeatedly made clear its wish to see a thriving nation wide network of post offices. There may be a difficult transition as demand for traditional services declines whilst new services and new ways of working may still be at an early stage of development. The Government stands ready to play its part in easing this transition with an eye in particular to supporting those post offices of special value to the local community. The Benefits Agency will continue to use the counters' network on the same basis as it does now until 2003, when the new arrangements for paying benefits by ACT will be introduced over a two year period. A number of other Governments and agencies also use the counters' network for the delivery of these services .....*"

[85] In fact the text continues thus "*There is an understandable wish on the part of these Departments and Agencies to find the most cost-effective means of delivering their services to their customers and giving their customers a range of choices for accessing their services. But this needs to be balanced against the importance of avoiding too sudden a change in POCL' [Post Office Counters Limited] financial circumstances, with the damage that this would cause*".

[86] In point 4 of the Objective referred to in the White Paper one reads "*It is primarily this sharing of overheads between combined business that makes the franchised and agency network an economically efficient means of delivering Government and other services, compared with stand alone, directly operated post offices*".

[87] In fact in point 20 one reads "*The future of The Post Office counters' network lies above all in its continued attractiveness to clients and customers as a channel for accessing products and services and to sub-postmasters as a business proposition. If, for whatever reason, the customers stay away from an individual post office, neither the Government, nor the Regulator, nor indeed Post Office management will in the end be able to prevent its closure. If local communities value the presence of a post office outlet, as so many clearly*

It should also be borne in mind how in Great Britain, within the general reflections on the future of the postal system and its network of branches, the need to equip the system with a financial regime which is more appropriate to the commercial context has been brought to light. In fact, it should not be forgotten that "*The Post Office has a good track record of profitability and has been a net contributors to public finances over a long period*", while, the modernisation of the structure itself requires large margins of self-financing[88]. Further more, a greater freedom of recourse to loans in order to fund its growth, especially through acquisitions and joint ventures.

In the German case, the reunification of the country had drawn attention to the problem of the extreme fragmentation and inefficiency of some parts of the network, especially in the new Länder and in the areas with a low population density.

As part of the wave of restructuring programmes of sectors of the economy which led to the approval of many laws by accelerated processes, the reform of the postal system also received political consensus from the various sides and it was possible to implement it with great determination and expeditiously. If in 1994 there was a total of approximately 26,000 branches, by the end of 1999, the restructuring had reduced the number to 13,984, while the law stipulated that up until 2003, the number of branches was not to be less than 12,000. Out of these, at least 5,000 were to be managed by employed staff[89]. In this context the Dutch model was followed. That means a ratio fixed between the number of branches and the total population, regardless of its density. The network, on its side, was completed with more flexible solutions (agencies operating under franchise which offered longer opening times and mobile services with the use of pre-paid cards

---

do, their best guarantee of retaining it lies in making full use of the facilities on both sides of the business".

[88] To this end the financial regime has been reviewed so that the Government, on the basis of the Strategic Plan, sets a profit target for the postal businesses as a whole, but leaves a considerable share to the Post Office for self-financing (50% of net profits for the year '99-00 and 40% for subsequent years) for financing on capital account.

[89] Decree July 1999. The development of branches is shown in the table below.

Table 1.15

Types of post office branches in Germany

	1995	1996	1997	1998
Directly managed branches				
Deutsche Post	13,983	11,981	10,000	7,788
Postplus	= =	19	80	118
Mc Paper	= =	= =	14	40
Franchises				
Agencies	2,998	4,604	5,236	6,483
Shop-in-shop	= =	= =	1	53
Mobile services (number of employees)	15,000	16,700	17,000	17,000

for postal services and also offering payment services on post office accounts). In parallel to the above, in 1998, a four year programme for the modernisation and re-styling of the owned branches was launched which aimed at a more functional layout of space and equipment.

In Italy, instead, the branch management model reflects the experience of the Mediterranean countries: the owned network, which is very widespread has remained substantially unchanged since the '50s. With the corporate restructuring plan the new organisational model has been approved, based on the "divisionalisation" of services and on giving responsibility to the management for results, which will include the "Divisione Rete Territoriale"(National Network Division)[90] and a major post office layout review and re-styling project has been launched[91].

The "Rete 2000" (Network 2000) project is aimed at improving the quality and efficiency of post offices, with a new layout for those which have the heaviest usage and a re-styling for those with lower volumes of work. The new layout envisages a more functional and user-friendly design giving priority to the reduction of queues and waiting times. The main aspects being tackled are the simplification and automation of procedures by means of computerisation and the linking up of the network of branches. In addition, optimisation of the national coverage, redesign and upgrading of the premises, increase of the staff available to serve the public, change and extension of opening hours and an active management of the queues by means of the "single line" are also important to this purpose. The new post office design for those areas with heaviest use, provides separate consulting as for customers, self-service points, multi-media signs, innovative security systems and special access for the disabled. This is in line with the solutions devised in the more advanced countries.

The post office computerisation process and network link-up was completed in the early part of 2000, providing every office with at least one workstation and thus closing a serious gap in comparison with the banking system and, in general, with the standards of other European countries.

In Italy, there has not been any consideration given to the potential offered by shop in post or post in shop solutions or by privately managed franchise agencies. This is due to the fact that in this country there is no existing tradition of "private" management of branches by means of agency or franchise systems. There is not either any particular political sensitivity to the problem of impoverishment of rural areas and city suburbs consequent to the closure of public infrastructures and commercial outlets.

The analysis of the post office branch network structure and the management problems in the main European contexts has highlighted the extent of the areas of

---

[90] This is alongside the Divisione Corrispondenza (Letters Division), the Divisione Espresso-Logistica Pacchi (Parcels Express-Logistics Division), the Divisione BancoPosta (PostBank Division) and the Divisione Filatelia (Philately Division).

[91] The size of the budget is 11 billion lire in 1999 and 220 billion lire in 2000 (between 5-6 million € in 1999 and approx. 114 million € in 2000).

difficulty with regard to the economics of the business. At the same time, it has pointed out the branches' capability to meet the needs of customers, with themes that are recurrent and in many respects shared in common, as well as the variety of manifold solutions. These latter are put into practice with varying stages of experience and, therefore, with varying degrees of rooting into the social contexts and the buying patterns.

Therefore, the quantitative data relating to the absolute size of the branch networks (Figure 1.7), or to the size of the average area of utilisation served by each branch (Figure 1.8), assume a different meaning depending upon the specific characteristics of each country.

Figure 1.7
The size of the branch networks in the European countries

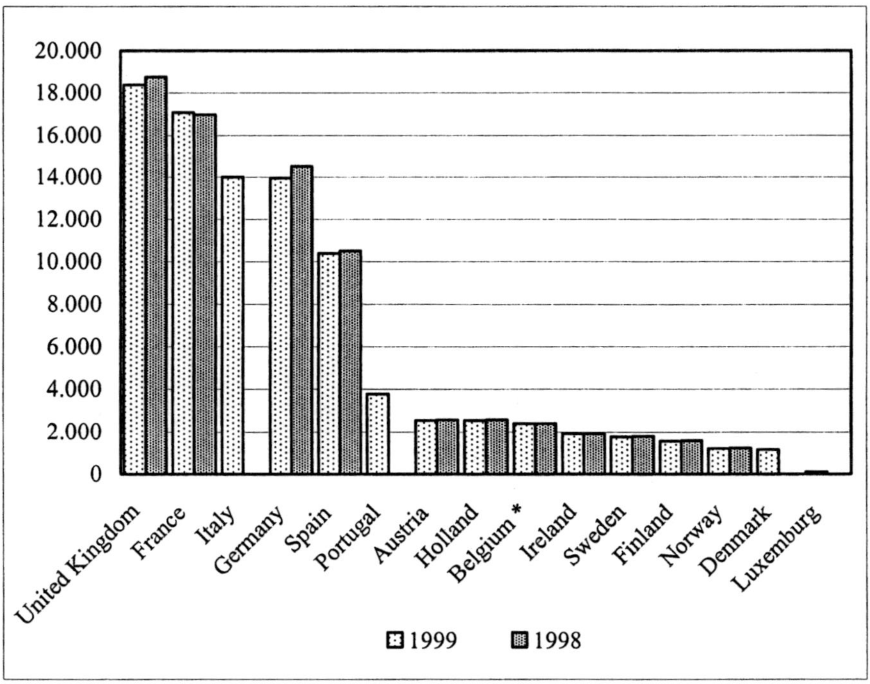

** Belgium: estimated data*
Source: processed on the basis of UPU data and company financial reports.

Figure 1.8
The post office branch network: average n° inhabitants per branch

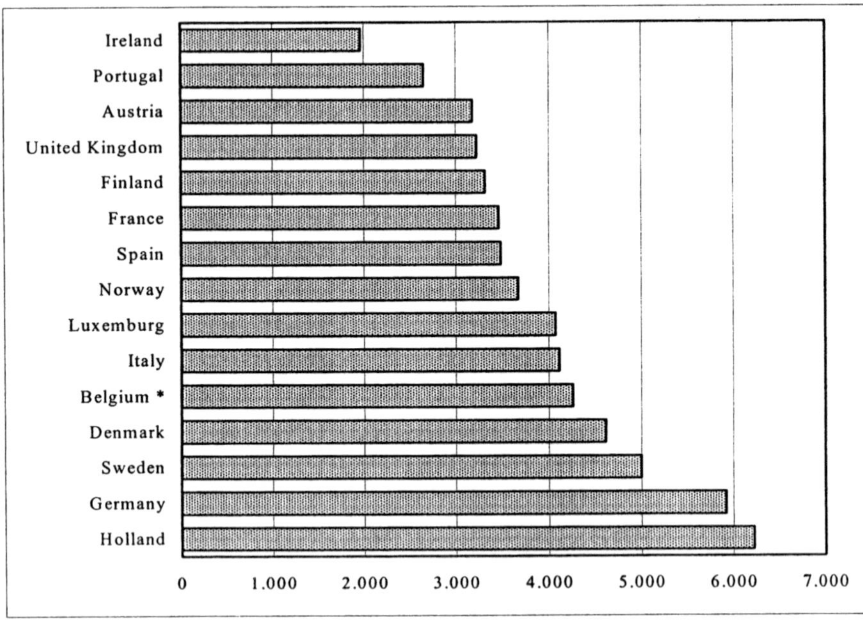

* *Belgium: estimated data*
Source: processed on the basis of UPU data and company financial reports.

1.5 Profitability and efficiency

The institutional set-up of postal companies in Europe, their strategic positioning in respect to geographic coverage of the market and of the areas of business has been analysed. Some solutions have been adopted to improve the efficiency, productivity and profitability of the branch network so as to transform even marginal locations from an encumbrance into a competitive advantage. And all this provides useful clues to the differences encountered in the various systems in terms of profitability and efficiency.

As regards the profitability, the analysis of the financial accounts and in particular of the two ratios of ROE and ROA, calculated on a result presented as EBIT net of extraordinary items, brings to light a wide range of differences in performance levels. However, the situations are in a state of constant evolution, also as a consequence of processes of external growth achieved by means of acquisitions and restructuring efforts, which in some cases are still underway. Such causes combine to bring about a discontinuity in results even from one year to the next.

The judgement following a comparative study is inevitably only valid as a rough approximation. It cannot be accurate as the accounting practices are not perfectly comparable and the reference to specific data emphasises some aspects, which relate to the economic context. Even the efforts made to consider a longer track record than two years would be nullified owing to different reasons. These could be the absence of data for those companies which have only achieved legal and financial autonomy in the last two years or the poor significance of such indicators if applied to subjects which had not yet adopted a privatised type of legal structure.

The companies which have already followed the path of, even substantial, privatisation and of the quotation of their shares, are those which register the best performance. TPG and Deutsche Post are at the top of the ROE ranking along with the postal companies of the Nordic countries and France, which boasts a consolidated record of high performance (see Figure 1.9).

The British Post Office is ranked in a not very brilliant position. It is currently feeling the financial burden of the process of computerisation and especially of automation of the branch network which was launched late, as mentioned earlier, and with hiccups and changes, which did not come without a cost.

If one considers the ROA parameter, the range of performance variability is less wide. Nevertheless, it becomes more difficult to identify homogeneous groups of operators. And this confirms the existence of discontinuity in the indicators given the effect of significant external growth processes, which do not always reflect their economic potential in the very short term (see Figure 1.10). TPG, the first to complete its globalisation processes and achieve world-wide coverage and - by now consolidated - entry into a broad spectrum of different areas of business[92], dominates the ranking. DPWN, for its part, which with a total asset of 77,118 million € in 1999 (as against TPG's 6,222 million €) is in pole position in terms of size of the group[93], is still in the stage of putting its assets and its relative performance in order.

---

[92] It is interesting to note that for TPG in 1998 and in 1999 the domestic turnover represented a share of 43% and 39%. respectively. In the same period DPWN's share was noticeably higher (97.9% and 78.4% respectively), notwithstanding the group's speedy international growth being clearly evident. For France and the UK the domestic markets still remain decidedly more important (with respective values of 94% and 91% and of 98.7% and 95.9%).

[93] Followed by France with 43,600 million € and the UK with 10,769 million €.

Figure 1.9
*Financial performances: profitability coefficients measured with ROE**

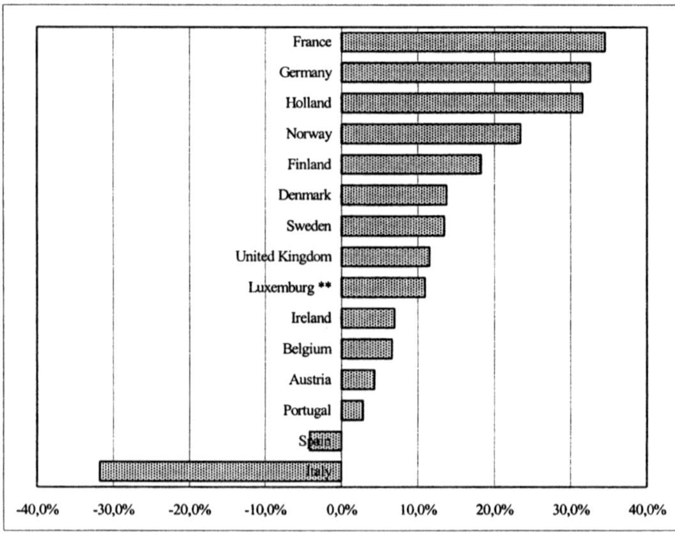

Figure 1.10
Financial performances: profitability coefficients measured with ROA *

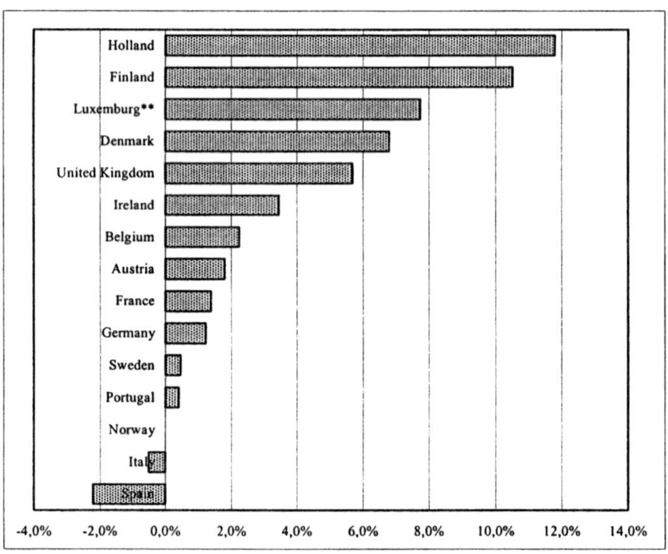

* EBIT after extraordinary items; ** The comparison with the Luxembourg reality is not homogenous as the postal and telecommunications activities are run by the same business.
Source: analysis on the basis of financial reports 1999.

As for the conditions of profitability, a comparison at international level can be easily carried out only for what concerns the mail activity and according to the evaluation criteria based on average time necessary to deliver mail. Also in this case, the indicator for expressing an evaluation of efficiency is only approximately valid as it analyses only one of the several and manifold factors connected with the postal activity. For example, special emphasis has been laid on the fact that one of the efficiency prerequisites requested by the market is the time – hopefully limited – the users have to spend at the counter or the frequency of deliveries, besides the reliability and other requirements connected with the quality of service.

However, the average delivery time is an objective criteria for comparison and represents an engagement sanctioned at community and national level in the postal law or in the programme contracts as guarantee of control.

In general, a clear improving trend is to be seen as far as home services (see Figure 1.11) as well as cross-border operativity (see Figure 1.12 and Table 1.16 in the following pages) are concerned.

As for domestic operativity, the best countries, namely the Nordic countries, Germany, United Kingdom and France, immediately followed by Austria and The Netherlands, used to deliver, already in 1998, more than 80% in average of sending by the third working day. Therefore, in their cases, there is no major difference in quality, also because progresses depending also upon the investments in the infrastructure are more difficult.

The countries with the lowest performances, namely Portugal, Belgium, Ireland, Italy and Spain, have registered significant progresses year after year. In these cases, the gap to be filled used to be deeper and, therefore, several very strong initiatives (automation and opening of new sorting centres, processes re-engineering with identification and removal of inefficiency niche) became necessary. The still existing differences are only partially justified by the different distribution of population on the territory and by the quality or road infrastructures along the country.

Figure 1.11
J+ 3 average standard (domestic mailing delivery)

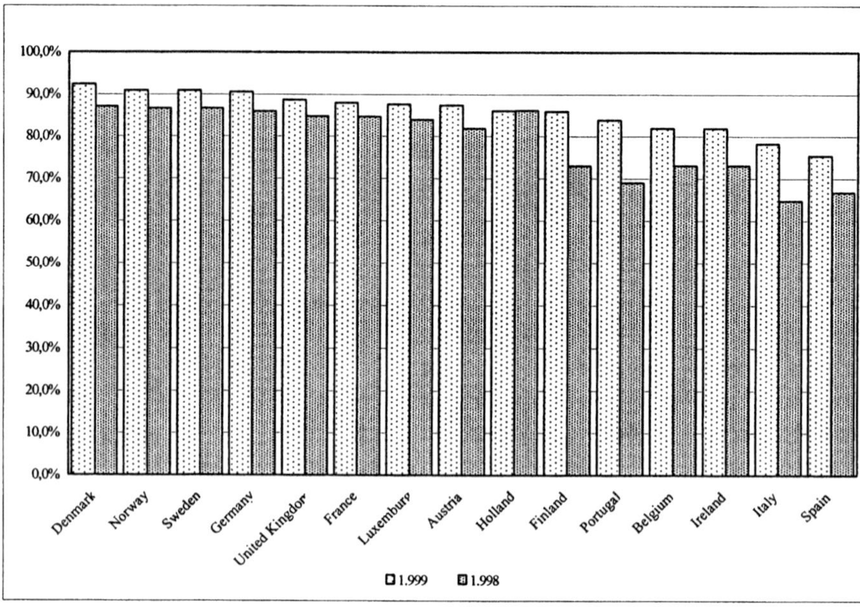

Source: IPC.

As for the international operativity, assuming a longer lapse of time, a clear improving trend is to be registered. Within the European Union, from the comparison of the 5 demographically biggest countries emerges the much bigger efficiency of Germany, France and Great Britain. Disparity in quality of service throughout Europe continue to decrease. The improved performance for the year 2000 is the result of the commitment of all Member Posts to adopt more efficient processes and to improve the quality of the services. Some postal operators have contributed significantly to the overall improvement in 2000, especially Poste Italiane, Correos Y Telegrafos of Spain, Norway Post, Iceland Post and Finland Post.

Figure 1.12
Average delivery days

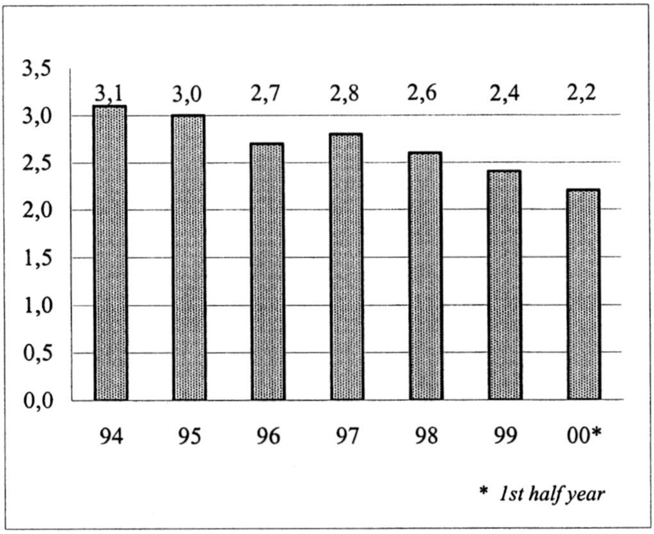

Source: IPC.

Table 1.16
Percentage on time within J + 3 standard (Years 1998,1999,2000)

			DESTINATION				
			FRANCE	**GERMANY**	**ITALY**	**UNITED KINGDOM**	**SPAIN**
ORIGIN	**FRA**	00		96,7	88,1	95,1	88.8
		99		95,8	75,5	95,8	89,3
		98		95,3	45,8	93,3	78,6
	GER	00	94,3		91,6	94,3	86,4
		99	93,3		76,2	95,3	84,1
		98	92,4		49,6	92,1	67,1
	ITA	00	89,6	92,6		92,0	84,7
		99	83,1	86,1		85,7	74,2
		98	69,3	74,6		65,7	55,2
	UK	00	89,7	94,6	88,5		85,2
		99	92,2	94,2	75,4		86,0
		98	91,4	90,4	47,3		70,1
	SPA	00	88,6	91,3	78,7	90,6	
		99	86,1	85,9	66,3	88,3	
		98	82,6	82,7	36,8	79,8	

Source: IPC.

Further more, what is also to be highlighted is the different intensity in use of the service itself; the variability range of number of average sending per year per inhabitant (and, therefore, the average number of daily mailings) (See Figure 1.13).

Figure 1.13
Average daily pieces per capita in 1998 and 1999

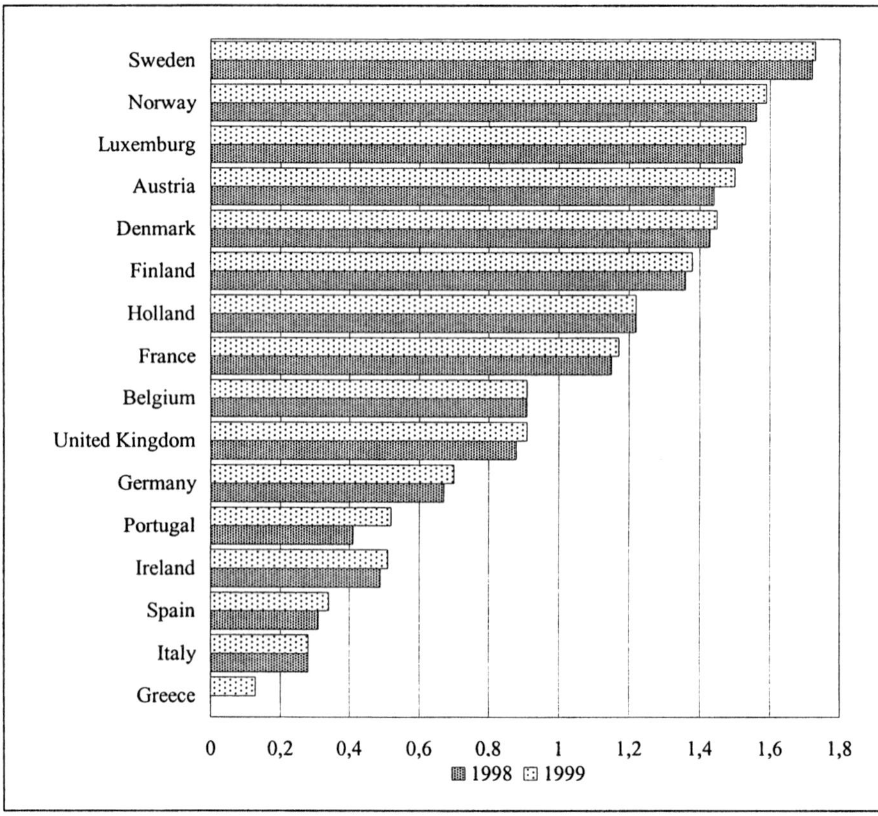

Source: Processing on UPU data and business balance sheet.

There is no doubt that this reflects at the same time different lifestyles and habits. Nevertheless, a simple reading of the available data show a significant link between service efficiency and level of use. The Scandinavian countries, The Netherlands and France are the countries that use the most the Post's communication channel. They are followed by Belgium, United Kingdom and Germany, where the average delivery time is considerably worse that benchmark.

Further more, considering the type of network of the activity and, as already highlighted, the presence of strong economies of scale, it is legitimate to think of a possible link between efficiency of the service and per capita operational volumes. Upon this link a virtuous or vicious cycle is anchored, following the way the service is perceived: efficient or, on the contrary, inefficient.

1.6 Conclusions

The postal markets are going to - or are already experiencing - a new stimulating competitive run. The time when that is going to happen is still uncertain but the inexorability and, at the same, the rapid development of new extremely advanced markets, with strong added value (such as logistics and e-commerce) have encouraged the European postal enterprises to reconsider the institutional models as well as their positioning on the market.

A thorough comparison has shown that the modernisation of institutional forms has achieved different stages of development[94], with the Dutch TNT-Post Group and the German DPWN in more advanced positions, and Spain, France, Ireland, Denmark and Luxembourg operating with public bodies' bureaucratic models, that are in the rear.

The other operators are to be found in intermediate positions with different stages of evolution. In several contexts, the institutional evolution is a politically delicate subject because of the postal system's traditional, sometimes social role and of its network of branches.

This positioning corresponds to the adoption of more advanced strategies of global operativeness only in the cases of TPG and DPWN respectively.

As a matter of fact, in the consideration of the two vectors - range of services or areas of business, on one side, and geographical cover on the other side – some strategic groups have been identified[95].

The strategic positioning and the performances are to be explained by manifold factors:

- size
- level of diversification
- stage of development
- quality of services.

For what concerns the measurement of performances, the quality which is evaluated in terms of average time necessary to the delivery of ordinary mail in the domestic markets and for cross-border sendings, a general improvement is to be seen. However several differences remain to be solved. To this purpose, the rears are busy trying to develop automation and reorganising projects. Although it

[94] See above mentioned Table 1.4.

[95] See above mentioned Figure 1.6.

is not statistically demonstrated in this particular context, the efficiency of the postal system has an impact on consumption models, that is to say the average sendings per inhabitant and therefore on operational volumes. These volumes, at least from a logical viewpoint, have an impact on the possibility to carry on the process with better-cost effectiveness and therefore they have an impact on the effectiveness with which these processes can be set up and started. So, it is important to get out of a vicious circle, by setting up a strong strategic orientation and conditions of dynamic development for modernisation against stagnation. A better effectiveness is possible also by reorganising the work. This is a politically delicate subject and, in several contexts, it has shown different possibilities of being managed. The choice of international alliances seems to be the most successful one also in the perspective of giving power to innovations in the processes as both the new technological contexts and markets ask for a quick modernisation of the processes.

Taking into consideration also the results in terms of profit, the situation of postal enterprises in the different countries is considerably differentiated. Most operators have not yet achieved the necessary level of profitability for going to the public through public offers. However, as for the evaluation of economical performances is concerned, a great deal of caution remains necessary for the interpretation of the resulting data. As a matter of fact, it can not be forgotten that this is not merely a question of bookkeeping methods, which makes the comparison of data not an easy task, but also of manifold operational modalities with the wide range of functions that are carried out by the postal network with public objectives. The access and presence into some captive market segments of operativity, justifies, besides the strictly postal business itself, the introduction of rules aiming at avoiding undeserved subsidies and competitive differences. Further more, this intervention generates financial flows and brings an income, which is not easy to be evaluated but that can have an impact on the indicators that we are trying to analyse. Moreover, the reference to precise data of the most recent years emphasises the relevance of possible phenomena connected to the economic situation and short time trends. Considering the juridical autonomy, besides the economic and administrative autonomy very recently acquired, it is not possible to extend the analysis through a longer and very significant laps of time.

For what concerns the perspectives connected to the profit of the postal activity, besides the price effects generated by the presence of competition, another question remains open, that is to say whether the traditional postal product (mail delivery) has achieved the maturity of its development cycle and whether the substitutes (fax, telephone, hybrid forms of mailing, e-mail and, in general, Internet) will make the traditional postal activity outdated. The analysis of the situation of the last two years shows that in all European countries the average number of pro-capita sendings is slightly growing or, at least, remains constant. The strategic reactions that are apparently prevailing are to be identified in the search for a non domestic but also cross-border or even foreign positioning, through alliances and, in particular, through the development of emerging markets (direct marketing, personalised advertisement and services with considerable added value for supporting the e-commerce).

However, strategic vision and availability to support the considerable risks connected to the uncertainties of the new economy development remain necessary factors to enter this context in a durable and successful way. Both conditions are much more likely to be present if the original problems connected to the institutional set-up have been solved and profitability as well as efficient management are present conditions. These conditions are necessary to generate, respectively, considerable financial resources, technological reputation and market strength. These factors are essential to a successful positioning. Moreover, the potential of this positioning must be recognised on the demand and the client's side, as well as on the partner side, with which important alliances can be set up.

The TNT Post Group and DPWN cases, as well as the cases of the British Post Office and the French La Poste clearly show this reality. The latter examples, in spite of their delay comparing to the best examples mentioned, are based on a long tradition of efficiency and profitability in their own countries and become at the same time reliable and favourite partners.

In this global framework of the postal markets in the new millennium, a question remains open: what role will the traditional postal branches play in the new economy of virtual relationships? In the most advanced contexts, these "windows" are loosing most of their traditional features, with new choices of externationalisation of the management which is assigned to third parties. The latter are also in charge of commercial functions and succeed in realising synergies and encouraging new development trends of the network's functions.

The choice of associating the supply of bank services to the postal activity has been imposed by the non recent evolution of postal systems in many countries and it has been therefore brought forward on the wave of tradition devoid of a modern strategic vision. Therefore, the critical revision of this choice is a significant challenge for the post enterprises' success in the new institutional context and market framework.

1.7 References

ARRIGO U. – BECCARELLO M. (eds.) (1999): I Servizi Postali. La convergenza europea nel settore pubblico, Ciriec/Franco Angeli, Milano.

ARTHUR ANDERSEN (1998): Study on the Impact of Liberalisation of Direct Mail, in http://wuropa.eu.int/ISPO/infosoc/telecompolicy/post/en/European1.htm

CABINET OFFICE – PERFORMANCE AND INNOVATION UNIT (2000): Counter Revolution. Modernising the Post Office Network, http://www.opengov.gov.uk

CREW M.A. – KLEINDORFER P.R. (eds.) (2001a): Current Directions in Postal Reforms, Kluwer Academic Publishers, Dordrecht.

CREW M.A. – KLEINDORFER P.R. (eds.) (2001b): Future Directions in Postal Reforms, Kluwer Academic Publishers, Dordrecht.

CREW M.A. – KLEINDORFER P.R. (eds.) (1999): Emerging Competition in Postal and Delivery Service, Kluwer Academic Publishers, Dordrecht.

CREW M.A. – KLEINDORFER P.R. (eds.) (1997): Managing Change in the Postal and Delivery Industries, Kluwer Academic Publishers, Dordrecht.

CURIEN N. (2000): Economie des Réseaux, La Découverte, Paris.

COMMISSARIAT GENERAL DU PLAN (2000): Services Publics en Réseau: Perspectives de Concurrence et Nouvelles Régulations, La Documentation Française, Paris.

DELFAU G. (1999): La Poste un Service Public en Danger. Constat et Proposition, L'Harmattan, Paris.

D.T.I. – DEPARTMENT OF TRADE AND INDUSTRY (1999): Post Office Reform: A world class service for the 21st century, White Paper, July.

EUROPEAN PARLIAMENT (2000): Rapport sur la proposition de directive du Parlament européen et du Conseil modifiant la Directive 97/67/CE en ce qui concerne la poursuite de l'ouverture à la concurrence des services postaux de la Communauté, Final A5-0361/2000

EUROPEAN COMMISSION (1992): Green Paper on the Development of the Single Market for Postal Service, COM (91) 476.

GEDDES R.(1998): The economic Effects of Postal Reorganization, The Journal of Regulatory Economics, n° 13, pp. 139-156

LARCHER M. G.(*rapporteur*) (1999): Sauver La Poste: est-il encore temps pour décider ? , Rapport d'information n° 463, Sénat.

LARCHER M. G.(*rapporteur*) (1997): Sauver La Poste: devoir politique, impératif économique. Rapport d'information n° 42, Sénat.

IPC – International Post Corporation (2000): Improving the Quality of International Mail, in http://www.ipc.be

IREPP-INSTITUT DE RECHERCHES ET PROSPECTIVE POSTALES (1998): La Poste dans tous ses Etats, Cahier n° 22.

MMD (1999): Modelling and Quantifying Scenarios for Liberalisation, London, February.

NATIONAL POST & TELECOM AGENCY (2000): The Liberalised Swedish Postal Market and the Situation Seven Years after the Abolition of the Monopoly, July.

N.E.R.A. (1998): Costing and Financing of Universal Services in the Postal Sector in the European Union, Brussels-Luxembourg.

NEWBERY D.M.(1999): Privatisation, Restructuring and Regulation of Network Utilities, The Mit Press, Cambridge-Massachussetts

POSTAL SERVICE COMMISSION (2000): Preserving Access to Post Offices in Rural Area. A discussion paper, December, in http://www.psc.gov.uk

OECD (1999): Promoting Competition in Postal Services, Directorate for financial, fiscal and enterprise affairs – Committee on competition law and policy, September.

PARKER D. (ed.) (1998): Privatisation in the European Union. Theory and Policy Perspectives, Routledge, London.

PILLEY O. – ANDERLONI L. (1999): European Post Offices in Financial Services. Competitors or Strategic Partners, Lafferty Publications, Dublin.

PRICEWATERHOUSECOOPERS (1998): Study on the Impact of Liberalisation of Community Cross-border Mail, in http://europa.eu.int/comm/internal_market/

en/postal/evolvframe/studies/index.htm
PRICEWATERHOUSE (1997): Employment Trends in the European Postal Sector, in http://europa.eu.int/comm/internal_market/en/postal/evolvframe/studies/index .htm
RODRIGUES S. (1999): Services Publics et Services d'Intérét Economique Général dans la Communauté Européenne. Eléments de Droit Comparé et Analyse du Droit Communautaire, Université Paris I – Panthéon Sorbonne (*mimeo*).
SHAPIRO C., VARIAN H.R. (1999): Information rules. A strategic guide to the network economy, Harvard Business School Press, Boston.
TOLEDANO F. (2001): A Necessary Evolution in Postal Regulation, Contribution to the Conference "Postal Offices & Financial Services", February 12-13, EFMA, Paris.
UPU-UNIVERSAL POSTAL UNION (1999): Beijing Postal Strategy, Resolution C 103/1999 in http://www.upu.int
UPU-UNIVERSAL POSTAL UNION (1999): Statistics in http://www.upu.int
VARIAN H.R. (1999): Intermediate Microeconomics. A Modern Approach, W.W. Norton & Company, New York.
VISCO COMANDINI V. (1995): La Privatizzazione delle Poste Italiane fra Vincoli Istituzionali e Ricerca dell'Efficienza, in "Rivista di politica economica", n° XII.
VISCO COMANDINI V. (1994): Monopolio Pubblico e Concorrenza nei Servizi Postali. Elementi per un'analisi economica, Franco Angeli, Milano.
VISCO COMANDINI V., LETTIERI C. (2001): Comparing Postal and Telecommunication Networks: Similarities and Differences, in "Journal of Network Industries", n° 2.
WATERSON M. (1992): Privatisation and the British Post Office, in "International Review of Applied Economics", n° 1692.
WORLD BANK (1996): Redirecting The Mail: Postal Sector Reform, The World Bank.

2

The Experience of Floatation: the Cases of TNT – Post Group and Deutsche Post AG

Francesca Arnaboldi – Ekkehardt Bauer*

2.1 Introduction

In the last ten years the European Postal sector has been undergoing significant changes owing to liberalisation and globalisation processes, as well as the new technologies.

TNT Post Groep, the Dutch post office, was the first postal incumbent who went public through an IPO. On June 1998, KPN's (the telecom company) ordinary shares were split into two new shares: on one side, telecom company share at an opening price at Euronext (Amsterdam) of € 33.58, on the other side, a second postal incumbent, with an opening price of € 22.46, for every one held.

The stocks of the Deutsche Post World Net AG were first traded on all German stock exchanges on November 20th 2000. It started with a price of € 21.40, +1,9% relative to the issue price of € 21.00[1], valuing the company at € 23.4bn and in the middle of the € 18 to € 23 indicative price range[2]. The offer on the flotation of the Deutsche Post World Net AG included the sale of 278.20 million to 319,93 million[3] shares, that were in the possession of the Kreditanstalt für Wiederaufbau, i.e. 25% to 29% of the capital with participation in earnings going back to January 1st 2000. The offering was reported to have been eight times over-subscribed.

Both companies are leaders in Europe in the postal sector and have got a strong financial position, high levels of efficiency and increasing earnings. The chapter deals with the reorganisation process leading to each company's IPO.

---

* The chapter results from a close co-operation. However, §§ 2.1, 2.2 and 2.4 are more specially attributable to F. Arnaboldi and § 2.3 to E. Bauer.

[1] All rates from the Frankfurt stock exchange.

[2] See Elliott R., Flower S. (2001).

[3] If the Greenshoe-Option is fully exercised.

2.2 The TNT – Post Groep Case

2.2.1 Introduction

2.2.1.1 Privatisation in the Netherlands

The Netherlands' economy is heavily dependent on international trade, especially with its European Union partners such as Germany, Belgium, the UK and France. Both levels of exports and imports (about 60 per cent of GDP) clearly show its openness and its sensitivity to foreign political and economic developments. Because of its mercantile tradition and of the small size of its home market, the Netherlands have developed a strongly internationalised and concentrated economy with foreign and Dutch – controlled.

The privatisation process has not been very substantial, simply because state-ownership has traditionally been limited. Apart from some minority state shares in the steel industry going back to the post-war reconstruction programme after the Second World War and the chemicals/mining industry which can be traced to the days of coal mining as well as participations in ailing firms, public enterprise in the Netherlands has largely been restricted to the traditional public utilities (post and telecommunication, energy, railways, airlines, airports), some development agencies and banks.

As a rule, government interference in daily operational issues and in long term planning of public undertakings has been low. The main exception was the PTT (and to a certain extent NS Dutch Rail) where the government took an active part in the decision-making process on tariff setting, wages, labour conditions and investments. The privatisation programme had no explicit ideological motivation. Denationalisation was simply considered a pragmatic instrument to economise on the state budget and to strengthen the market sector. Officially, the goals were the reduction of state bureaucracy and the improvement of efficiency within government, the reduction of public expenditure and the budget deficit as well as the stimulation of entrepreneurship and market responsiveness to economic revitalisation. The Dutch government showed a clear preference for reorganising the public sector by retaining the core competencies of policy making and by privatising in a gradual way. Privatisation met with little political opposition and legal – constitutional problems were minor. At first, the privatisation programme, in general terms, was opposed by the civil service unions. They saw privatisation as an excuse for restructuring civil service considered as inefficient and ineffective by the State and feared occupational as well as income and pension rights losses. The public sector unions became more moderate and co-operative when they saw that particular labour conditions such as job security, wages and social securities were safeguarded. Privatisation only implied a possible transfer of members from public sector to private sector unions.

The Dutch way of privatisation is characterised by a two stages approach, emphasising an incremental adjustment of the public enterprises to the new market conditions and avoiding the radical option of selling immediately a majority of the state assets. As a first step, state enterprises are restructured and brought under private law, without touching upon ownership and market conditions. In the next step, the independent state – owned company is given some space to become a market – driven corporation, before its shareholdings are sold off. Employment levels are protected as much as possible, in order to overcome any resistance to any changes within the personnel. The transitional period (*Verzelfstandiging* , in Dutch, or corporatisation) contributes to the company value offering by gradually building up the tension and allowing the players to get used to the modes of doing business in an economy, which is open to competitive market forces.

From the legislative point of view, by the early 90's, Dutch competition policy does not prohibit any anti-competitive practices but tries to limit abuse of economic dominance and collusion in the marketplace. Legislation on the ex-ante scrutiny and control of mergers and acquisition were absent. The only existing regulation required mergers candidates to inform their employees' council and/or the relevant trade unions. Competition legislation in the Netherlands has been based on a case-by-case judicial review and the enforcement by law of privately conducted cartel-agreements. From 1992 onwards a series of anti-trust measures were effectively implemented as a consequence of the adoption of EU Regulation. Like in many other smaller countries, since the adoption of the new competition, the State has adopted a lenient position about competition Act.

A full postal market liberalisation in the EU was expected in 2003. Nevertheless, there is still no consensus among Member States on the schedule for full liberalisation to take place. A European Commission proposal to reduce the maximum weight for reserved letters from the existing level of 350g. to 50g. in 2003 was changed during bill's first reading. The revised bill now proposes a reduction to 150g. starting in 2005. This cuts the estimated share of the European postal market from 20% to 5%, which would be opened to competition and adds a two years delay. Also worthy of note is a failure to endorse the proposed date (2007) for full market liberalisation[4]. The delay is due to the fact that there are still major differences in efficiency, quality and customer orientation levels among the EU public postal operators. For TPG, a remarkably positive scenario would be a slight reduction in the weight limit and an opening up of the direct mail, which would allow it to protect its domestic markets while entering other Member States' direct mail market. The reduction in the weight threshold to 50g. in standard mail will probably have a minimal impact on the major operators in Europe, as 70 - 80% of European volumes are below this weight. The Dutch regulator had already lowered the weight threshold in standard mail to 100g. in

---

[4] Speech by Commissioner F. Bolkestein, Strasbourg, December 13rd 2000.

June 2000. Although it is premature to analyse the long term effect of this, there has been little impact to TPG so far.

TPG and the postal sector's performance are evaluated in a positive way with an interesting strategic development. The strategic focus will shift on e–business services and on more rapid growth of mail, express and logistics divisions dismissing non-core businesses progressively[5].

2.2.1.2 Outline of Section 2.2

TNT Post Group's historical background is provided in § 2.2.1.1 with a brief introduction on privatisation in the Netherlands and the situation of the European postal legislation. TPG's profile is introduced in § 2.2.2.1, with the analysis of historical data. Since the postal operator is a separate entity from Postbank which operates the postal financial services, § 2.2.2.2 is dedicated to the financial services area. The terms of the agreement allowed both companies to focus onto their core-businesses with a better orientation of their investments.

The experience of floatation is reviewed in § 2.2.3. The steps of the privatisation process of KPN are briefly taken into account to explain better the situation of TPG in 1998. Starting from the placement's goal, the role of the public sector is shown through the analysis of corporate governance rules and the changes they are facing. Finally, the evaluation of the floatation is provided through a comparison with the German experience of Deutsche Post AG privatisation.

2.2.2 TNT Post Groep

2.2.2.1 The Group and the State of the Industry

TPG is a global company providing mail, express and logistics services under the Royal PTT Post and TNT brands. With its 130.000 employees TPG provides services in more than 200 countries. TPG is the world's first postal incumbent to be publicly quoted. TPG is carefully and safely moving into other areas than traditional mail represents. Its mission is to achieve a recognised world leadership position through excellent customer service and through a strong market position in Europe[6]. In October 2000, TPG announced a JV with Royal Mail, called "The Preference Service", aimed to be UK's leading "infomediary", in the supply of data to direct mail companies. TPG's corporate strategy is to build a leadership on high brand – awareness, impeccable reputation, above – average profitability and

---

[5] Sella Asset Management Studies, "Il Sole 24 Ore", November 25th 2000.
[6] TNT Post Group, Annual Report 2000.

growth. TPG is listed and traded on four stock exchanges. The main market for trading in Ordinary Shares is the Amsterdam Stock Exchange, the others are London Stock Exchange, Frankfurter Börse and New York Stock Exchange. At December 31st, 2000 the issued share capital was 218 million and consisted of one Special Share – the Golden Share – and 479.166.412 Ordinary Shares. The State of the Netherlands is the holder of the Golden Share.

TPG annually pays interim and final dividends. TPG remains committed to pay a stable dividend of NLG 0.80 (0.363 €) per Ordinary Share of NLG 1 in the years to come. The Management Board of TPG is willing to pursue a dividend policy with a pay – out in a range of 30% to 35% of its profits reflecting its expected growth levels and investment strategy[7]. Payout in 2000 was 31% and it was 41% in 1999[8].

Figure 2.1
Shareholders

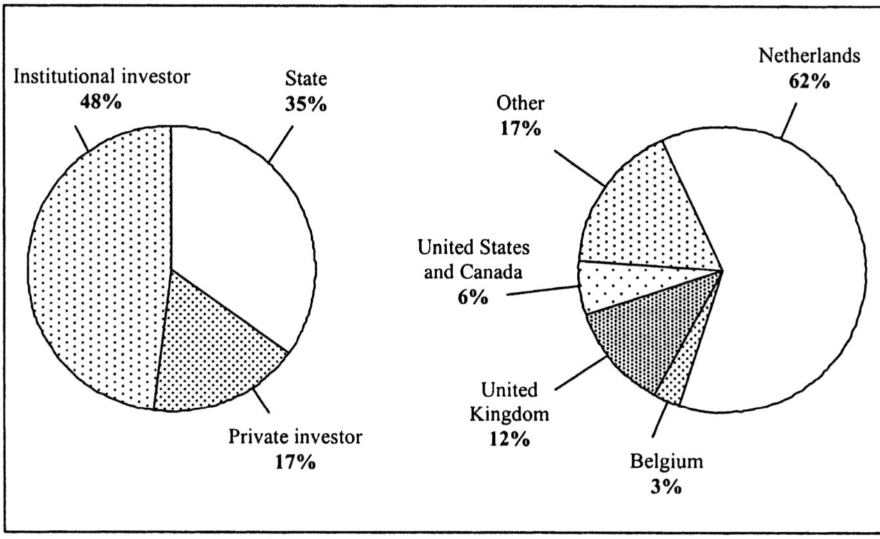

Source: Depot Bank Research.

In year 2000 the revenue growth was over 16% and the net income growth was around 25%. The Mail division performed solidly, managing to improve its margin to 20.8%. For the first time revenues of the Express division surpassed

[7] TNT Post Group, Annual Report 2000.
[8] http://www.tntpost-group.com:about TPG/frequent question, April 9th, 2001.

those of Mail contributing 4,145 million (41,3%) of TPG's total revenue. Express operating margins improved to 5.1% over the full year and 6% in the second half of year 2000. E – commerce development, especially in the business-to- business sector, is fuelling demand for express services. Logistics division has significantly strengthened its position in the targeted markets and industry sectors through a series of acquisitions, which increased revenue growth by 43.2% and operating income by 46.5%[4].

What had previously been considered a low growth utility seems to be going to be transformed by technology, private capital and dynamic management. With the IPO of UPS in November 1999 and the IPO of Deutsche Post one year later, investors were being forced to come to terms with major "new" entrants into what had been considered as a mature sector of quoted transport and logistics companies. Post, express and logistics companies possess strong network, characteristics which support concentration of business towards market leaders. Customer expectations regarding service levels and global scope have risen sharply over the past decade, which also support economies of scale. A signal of the attractiveness of the sector is the fact that postal and logistics companies generate more operating cash flow than 94% of other major quoted businesses.[9]

The key industry trends the leading global integrators FedEx, UPS, TNT and Deutsche Post face are globalisation, deregulation, outsourcing and e-business.

Globalisation is the key driver for the ongoing consolidation in the logistics industry. While partnerships and alliance are possible, direct acquisitions are also likely, given the shortage of attractive bid targets and new commercial freedom for postal operators. First mover advantages are evident given a diminishing number of attractive independent targets. However, on a global basis the sector is still quite fragmented. Emerging well-funded postal operators have the potential to become global leaders offering sole-sourcing of sophisticated delivery services even if mergers or takeovers between national incumbents could remain a "step too far" over the next two years. In the European telecommunication industry where deregulation is far advanced, there has not been a single merger between incumbents in the traditional business[10].

Deregulation is an important trend in Europe for TPG and for Deutsche Post, especially for their Mail division. Germany decided not to liberalise its market before 2007. The total available (non-monopolised) mail market is expected to increase to around € 14bn with the liberalisation. In this scenario TPG's target revenue of € 450 - € 650 mn would imply a market share of only 4 – 5%. However, a more gradual liberalisation process is expected in Germany, in line with the rest of Europe overall. That would reduce the available market to € 5bn and imply a market share of 9 – 13%[11].

---

[9] Hawkins D., Murphy S. (2000).

[10] Sanderse M., Ripper A., Steegers P. (2001).

[11] See Sanderse M., Ripper A., Steegers P. (2001).

Industries and companies that globalise need to restructure and streamline their supply chains. As a growing number of companies simultaneously refocus on their core business, by outsourcing, the third trend global integrators are confronted to, is experiencing remarkable growth.

Finally, e-commerce give an opportunity to delivery companies to leverage off their current role and move into higher margins service provisions. Physical delivery offers direct face-to-face customer contact on a regular basis, the only point in an Internet-based supply chain where this is possible. Control of this physical customer relationship is therefore a key strategic strength and should allow for service expansion as Internet business models mature.

2.2.2.2 The Financial Services

The original postal financial services arm, Postbank, is now an integral part of the international financial services group ING. Postbank, the direct financial services subsidiary of ING, and TPG have formed a 50:50 joint venture, which owns the postal services networks, Postkantoren[12]. Web based messaging and bill payment systems offer electronic (and in some cases paperless) alternatives to physical mail delivery. Post offices can establish a profitable position in this market as trusted intermediaries between banks, businesses and individuals. Post offices would be taking control of aggregating, processing and administrating bills and statements from multiple billers over the web. However without implementation of Electronic Bill Present and Payment systems, post offices risk total disintermediation in the corporate billing market. There is a genuine window of opportunity for them to establish themselves as they are still perceived as trusted intermediaries and can offer billers electronic as well as physical solutions. However this advantage could erode quickly as ISP or software and outsourcing providers such as Checkfree, Bottomline Technologies and bill aggregators such Paytrust and Cyberbills move in aggressively.

Postbank, 100 per cent State owned, was originally formed in 1968 from the merger of Postcheque-en-Girodienst (1918) and Rijkspostspaarbank (State Postal Savings Bank, founded in 1881)[13]. Both banks were using post offices for their cash transactions and had similar type products. The merger seemed to be the natural step to exploit synergies even if many problems remained unsolved[14].

---

[12] http://about.ing.com/en/index.html, June, 9th 2001.

[13] This paragraph describes a short profile of Postbank and of the process which has led to the constitution of ING Group. See Chapter 3 for further information.

[14] A statutory regulation effectively barred Postbank from selling securities and insurance products preventing the organisation from penetrating the high - net - worth market. To resist competitive pressure Postbank developed the home banking concept through Girotel in 1986. However it remained ill equipped for the business market and lacked critical skills in the intermediation of securities, in insurance (with the exception of travel insurance) and in credit.

In 1986 Postbank was incorporated to allow for greater management flexibility and in 1989 it merged with NMB, to form NMB-Postbank Group. Postbank had its limitations as a commercial bank. For instance, it was not allowed to act as a stockbroker, neither did it have access to the wholesale market. Therefore it sought to approach a commercial bank. The NMB Bank was looking for reinforcement of its own position in the personal market, at which it was relatively under-represented, in view of its being the third largest bank in the Netherlands[15]. As the Postbank and NMB Bank complemented each other, they decided on a merger[16].

By a change in Dutch financial services regulation prompted by the adoption of the Single Market and allowed for a much closer co-operation between banks and insurance companies, a new bancassurance group was set up in 1991 through the merger between NMB – Postbank and the insurance company Nationale-Nederlanden. The entity was renamed Internationale Nederlanden Groep (ING) in 1994. Nationale-Nederlanden was established on 3rd April 1963, a result of the merger between the National Life Insurance Bank and the Netherlands Insurance Company est. 1845. The merger company has experienced a period of expansion through acquisitions. Nationale-Nederlanden developed into the largest insurance company in the Netherlands. As a result of extensive acquisitions in the United States, Canada and Australia, the company generates over half of its revenues from international business[17]. ING Group expanded through the acquisition of investment. In 1995, Barings bank, the American insurer Equitable of Iowa Companies in 1997, the Belgian Bank Brussels Lambert in January 1998, the German BHF-Bank in 1999 and the American insurer ReliaStar in 2000[18].

It is to be regretted that TPG and Postbank had not positioned themselves as first movers in electronic commerce where they are uniquely placed to combine the electronic payment and document transmission aspects with the logistics of international delivery.

Postbank is one of the most efficient retail banking operations in Europe[19]. Postbank's unique distribution strategy, with a low reliance on standard bank branches, has been identified as key to its efficiency. Via the giro account Postbank offers a wide range of services in the field of fund transfers, current accounts, savings, mortgages, debit cards, consumer credit, investments, life and non – life assurance. Postbank is the clear leader in travel policies and direct

---

[15] http://about.ing.com/en/index.html, June 2nd 2001.

[16] As a result or that, the group obtained full banking status and became the fourth largest bank in the Netherlands with 40% of market share in deposits accounts, 47% in electronic fund transfers and respectable share of the savings (16%) and loans (12%). See Chapter 3 for further information.

[17] At the time of the merger the interest of the Dutch State in NMB Postbank Group was 49%, which was reduced to 8.2% upon the merger. Following later sales the State interest in ING Group has diluted to less than 1%.

[18] http://about.ing.com/en/index.html, June 2nd 2001.

[19] Pilley O., Anderloni L. (1999).

banking. Funds transfer capability, large databases and continuously improved database management, customer orientation, absolute dedication to convenience through integrated delivery, brand management, mass communication and systematic gains in economies of scale are essential to Postbank's successful strategy.

2.2.3 The Floatation of the TNT Post Groep

2.2.3.1 The Process of Constitution of a joint – stock Corporation in the Postal Sector

The Dutch telecommunication regime, based on the 1989 Postal Act (and on the secondary legislation, collective labour agreement and agreement with the Unions about the transition period), relied upon a core PTT monopoly of infrastructure provision and the supply of the basic telephone, telex and data services. The 1989 legislation revised the close link between KPN/PTT Telecom and the government by hiving off the company from the state apparatus and separating the carrier's operational and administrative activities. KPN, renamed PTT Nederland N.V., was given corporate autonomy and became a joint-stock company, ceasing to be a state enterprise on 1st January 1989.

The goal of the process was to achieve government's policy of privatisation, since it strongly believed that the market could do better than the State in ruling the company. Besides a State – owned company has less freedom in implementing its merger and acquisition policy (see e.g. Telefonica – KPN failed merger, the case of the agreement between KLM and Alitalia).

Employees changed overnight their status of "civil servants" by receiving two letters, one from the government, which fired them and the second from PTT Nederland N.V., which hired them. A transitional law transferred everyone to the joint-stock company giving the option not to accept the new condition of work within three years. After that period employees could not go back to the civil servant status any more[20]. The employees generally accepted the new work condition since they were better rewarded, and job satisfaction improved.

This process of "corporatisation" was followed by privatisation through an international public offer (IPO). In June 1994, the State sold the first tranche of 30% of its shares, reaching almost seven billions guilders, and the combined postal/telecommunications company was listed on the Amsterdam Stock Exchange as Koninklijke PTT Nederland (KPN). In 1996 after selling the second tranche of 25% the State no longer had a controlling interest in KPN. The sell generated six billions guilders.

---

[20] Interview with Mr. C. de Weerd, Nepostel, April 4th 2001, The Hague.

The company was listed in NYSE in October 1995, in London Stock Exchange in June 1996 and Frankfurter Börse in July 1996.

As of 20 November 2000, KPN has a total of 1,203,654,498 ordinary shares outstanding with a nominal value of € 0.24 each.

Accordingly to the present legislation, the government will retain at least a third of KPN shares until 2004. Government influence in KPN's corporate evolution is ensured through a golden share construction implying that for "critical" issues, like the sale of a new tranche, mergers and acquisitions, large investments and substantial tariff increases, KPN needs political approval[21].

In June 2000, the government informed the Parliament that it considered the State's withdrawal from KPN as desirable, considering the new circumstances in the telecommunications market. The exact timing of this withdrawal is however still uncertain and depends on the market conditions. The discussion would concern both holding of the percentage of ordinary shares as well as the special share. The State would hold the special share, until the number of ordinary shares would be substantially diminished, although a percentage wasn't explicitly defined.

In relation to the new equity issued on 20th November 2000, a lockup period of 180 days had been agreed. In this period no shares would be sold by the State to avoid an excessive dilution of their value.

Table 2.1
KPN Shareholders

	Number	**%**
Owned by the State of the Netherlands*	417,547,253	34.7
Marketable shares (free float)	786,107,245	65.3
Total	1,203,654,498	100

**Excluding the special State-owned share.*
Source: KPN, Annual Report, 2000.

[21] http://www.kpn.com/br1/aboutkpn/aboutkpn April 2nd 2001.

Figure 2.2
KPN Shareholders

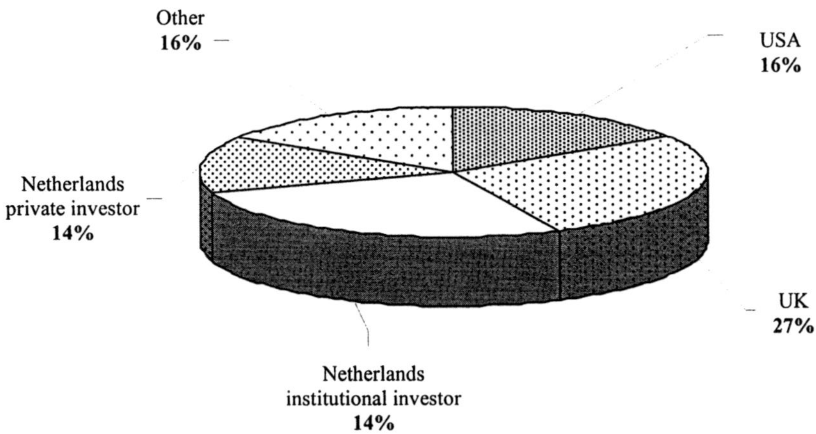

Source: KPN, Annual Report, 2000

In 1989, at the time of the formal privatisation, both the postal and the telecommunication activities were under the supervision of the Dutch Minister of Transport, Public Works and Watermanagement and it was decided for historical reasons not to separate the postal and telecommunications businesses. However, in the nine following years, these businesses have in fact become separated each with different focus. The differences have become apparent in particular in management methods, in internationalising strategies (for telecom branch, acquiring companies country by country; for post branch, acquiring a global network through a single merger) and scale of investments with PTT Post being more labour – intensive and PTT Telecom being capital – intensive.

On 2nd October 1996 KPN and TNT, a world-wide operating transport and logistics group, announced that KPN was going to make a public bid for TNT. The two companies had enjoyed a close commercial relationship since 1992, when TNT Express Europe, TNT Skypak and TNT Mailfast combined with the mail services businesses of KPN and the post offices of Canada, France, Germany and Sweden to form GD Express Worldwide (GDEW)[22]. GD Express Worldwide originally was a joint venture created to oppose the move into Europe of the large operators. TNT owned 50% of GDEW.

---

[22] http://www.tntpost-group.com: about TPG/history, May 28th 2001.

The friendly take-over between KPN and TNT was completed in December 1996[23]. TNT had already been listed and had a different company culture, more market-oriented and innovative, compared with KPN's. Moreover, the market had already known it as TNT has been listed on the Sydney stock exchange since 1961. This contributed to accelerating changes in corporate culture in the postal incumbent. At that time, the news that a traditional postal incumbent took over a dynamic world integrator was unexpected. TNT was created in 1946 and built a strong brand reputation of fast delivery services all over the world growing through take-overs and interests acquired in other companies[24]. Its weakness was in its high level of debts – a problem for all integrators, which doesn't exist for post offices, since their cash flow situation was excellent: as a matter of fact, their customers pay in advance. After integrating the Express activity in the traditional mail business, the structure of balance sheet is changing for post offices since now they are counterparts in contracts with delayed payments.

In 1997, KPN began the process of integrating the postal branches (PTT Post, GD Express Worldwide and TNT). The structure of the group consisted of Royal PTT Nederland, the holding company, and two separate legal entities fully owned by the parent, PTT Post B.V., which was the result of the above mentioned integrating process, owner of the mail, express and logistics activities, and PTT Telecom B.V., the new telecom company after the demerger[25]. PTT Post had total operating revenues amounting to 15,267 millions of guilders and total assets to 12,292 millions of guilders in 1997 compared to 15,780 and 30,046 millions guilders respectively of KPN[26].

In June the same year, the Management Board announced the approval of a resolution authorising the demerger of all mail, express and logistics operations. On Friday 26 June 1998 the Shareholders' AGM approved this demerger and PTT Post was denominated as TNT Post Groep (TPG). The legal aspects were formalised on Sunday 28 June 1998 and TPG was listed as a separate stock on the exchanges in Amsterdam, New York, London and Frankfurt the following Monday[27]. More background information on the takeover is given in § 3.3.

After the demerger, PTT Telecom B.V. changed its name into KPN N.V. and the structure of the company was re-shaped to face the new situation. In the last two years, the mobile and fixed line businesses have split into two, each with different focus and investment needs. Therefore, as of June 5, 2000 KPN's ordinary shares with a nominal value of NLG 1.00 have been split to a ratio of two new shares for every one held. At the same time, the nominal value of the share has been redenominated from guilders to €. This means that every share of

---

[23] TPG–TNT Post history, http://www.tntpost-group.com/english/profile/history/content.html, April 3rd 2001.

[24] http://www.tntpost-group.com: about TPG/history, June 2nd 2001.

[25] Interview with Mr. C. de Weerd, Nepostel, April 4st 2001, The Hague.

[26] Royal PTT Nederland N.V., Annual Report, 1997.

[27] http://www.tntpost-group.com: about TPG/history, April 6th 2001.

common stock with a nominal value of NLG 1.00 has been split and redenominated into a new share with a nominal value of € 0.24.

Figure 2.3
The evolution of KPN and PTT Post Groups

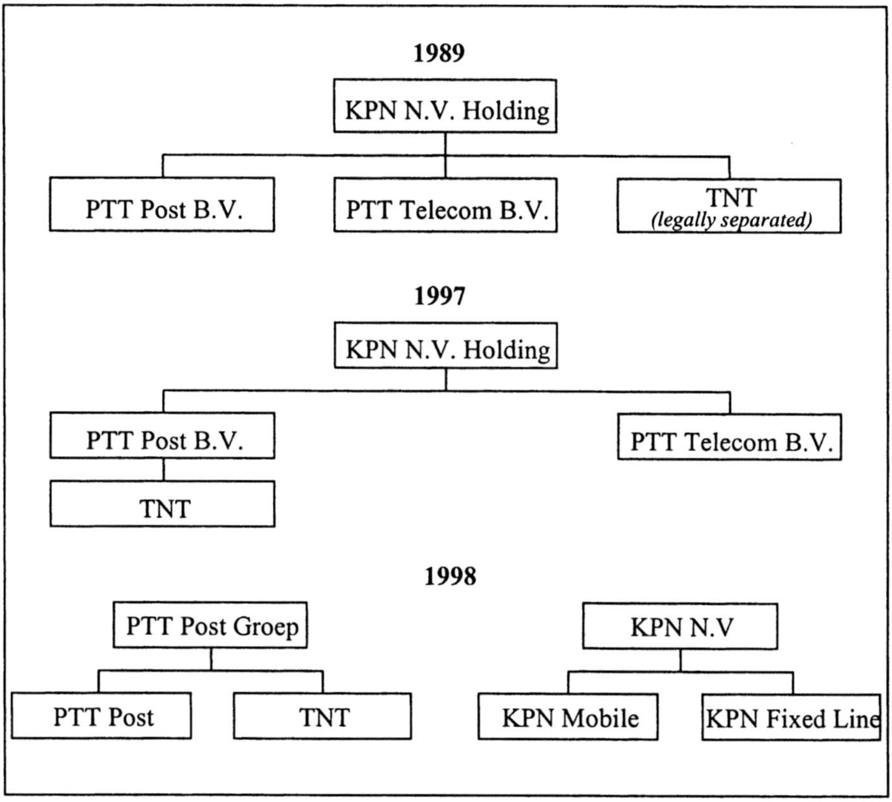

Source: interview with Mr. C. de Weerd, Nepostel, 4 April 2001, The Hague.

Table 2.2
Chronology of KPN and TPG history

January 1st 1989	The Dutch post ceased to be a state enterprise and became a private company, called PTT Nederland NV.
June 1994	KPN Floatation I: the State of the Netherlands sold 30% of its shares in PTT Nederland NV. Under its new name of Royal PTT Nederland NV (KPN), the combined postal/telecommunications company obtained a listing on the Amsterdam Stock Exchange.
October 1995	KPN listed on the New York Stock Exchange.
1996	KPN Floatation after selling another 25% of its shares, the State of the Netherlands no longer had a controlling interest in KPN. The company obtained a listing on the Frankfurt and London Stock Exchanges.
October 2nd 1996	KPN made a public bid for TNT. The friendly take – over was completed in December.
1997	KPN began the process of integrating TNT, GDEW and PTT Post
June 1998	TNT Post Group separated from KPN. TPG stock is listed independently on the stock exchanges of Amsterdam, New York, London and Frankfurt.
March 2001	The State of the Netherlands reduced its interest in TPG to 34.9% of the total shares.

Source: http://www.tntpost-group.com: about TPG/history, June 2nd 2001.

2.2.3.2 The Corporate Governance

The process of corporatisation and privatisation had led to the adoption of modern tools of corporate governance which is typical of a joint – stock company since 1989. However, as the postal delivery business is of great importance to the State for various reasons, including economic, strategic and national security reasons, the State role in corporate governance, in particular through the golden share and the right to appoint members of Supervisory Board, is significant. TPG's corporate governance mechanisms include:

Management Board and Divisions

TPG is managed by a Management Board, which is responsible for the overall results of the company as well as for corporate strategy. The Management Board consists of six members. The operational activities of TPG are divided into three divisions: Mail, Express and Logistics. In 1999 TPG further implemented the divisional structure across countries and regions. The Management Board has conducted a series of four pilot projects in different part of TPG, investigating the merits of value-based management.

Some reports on financial processes functioning are presented to the Management Board and discussed by the Audit Committee of the Supervisory Board.

Supervisory Board

The activities of the Management Board are supervised by the Supervisory Board, which may appoint and dismiss members of the Management Board. The Supervisory Board is required to notify the General Meeting of Shareholders before dismissing a member of the Management Board.

Some decisions taken by the Management Board require the approval of the Supervisory Board. These decisions include the issuance of securities, certain capital expenditures including acquisitions and the termination of the employment contracts of large numbers of employees. The Supervisory Board consists of a minimum of seven and a maximum of nine members. At present, the Supervisory Board counts eight members. The Supervisory Board has the right to appoint and dismiss members of the Supervisory Board with the exception of three members, which are appointed by the Dutch Minister of Transport, Public Works and Water Management and acts independently from the minister. The Members of the Supervisory Board are appointed for a period of four years.

Shareholders

In the General Meeting of Shareholders, the Management Board accounts for the corporate strategy it implemented, company policy and the financial results. Shareholders holding singly or as a group at least 1 percent of the outstanding shares can submit a request to the Management Board and the Supervisory Board to add points to the agenda. The State of the Netherlands owns approximately 35% of TPG shares. For certain important postal services, TPG is the exclusive holder of the postal concession granted by the State. The operation of the Postal concession is regulated by the Enabling Act. In addition, the State uses various corporate governance mechanisms to protect its mission of general economic interest. These include its ownership of the special share, options to acquire Preference Share A and a long - term equity interest in TPG.

- **Special Share**[28]. The State holds the Special Share of the Company which gives it the right to approve decisions including issuances of shares in the company's capital, restrictions on or exclusions of the pre - emptive rights of holders of Ordinary Shares, mergers, demergers and dissolution with respect to the company and PTT Post, certain capital expenditures, certain dividends and distributions and certain amendments to the articles of association. The

[28] See § 2.2.3.3 for ingoing changing in rules of corporate governance.

State has committed itself to exercising the rights attached to special share only to safeguard the general interest in having an efficiently operating postal system or to protect its financial interest as a shareholder and not solely to protect the company from shareholder influence unwanted by the company. The State is the Special Share's holder and may not transfer or encumber the Special Share without the approval of the Management Board and of the Supervisory Board. The Dutch government had this specific corporate governance mechanism to drive gradually the company from a state – owned structure to a completely market – oriented situation. This tool was used in some other experiences (e.g. in the process of KPN's privatisation) but it is due to be progressively abandoned, as mentioned in § 2.2.3.3.

- **Option to acquire Preference Shares A**. The company has granted the State an option to acquire Preference Shares A, which will have the same voting rights as ordinary shares, in order to increase its voting interest in the company to 51% in certain circumstances. The State committed itself to exercising this option only to safeguard the general interest.
- **Long-term equity interest and option to purchase Preference Shares A.** As per 31st December 2000, the State had committed not to reduce its interest in the voting capital to less than one - third before 2004. However, the State and TPG have recently discussed about a possible partial withdrawal as ordinary shareholder in due course. The State has been granted an option to subscribe for Special Shares A (see description above) during or after an increase in the share capital of the company in order to preserve voting rights equal to a minimum of one - third of the company's voting capital. The State has committed to agree that, after its equity interest is reduced to one - third of the voting capital of the company, it will not without the consent of the company transfer or encumber any shares before having agreed with the company to protective measures to be included in the articles of the association. In addition, the Minister of Transport, Public Works and Water Management has the right to appoint three of the seven to nine members of the Supervisory Board.

2.2.3.3 The Method of Share Placement and Pricing

On Monday 29th June 1998 TPG separated from its former parent company KPN. Since that date TPG stock is listed independently on the stock exchanges of Amsterdam, New York, London and Frankfurt, the same where KPN was previously floated, with a distribution of 475,173,350 Ordinary Shares[29]. The opening share prices at Euronext (Amsterdam) that day were € 33.58 (before two – for – one stock split) for KPN and € 22.46 for TPG[30].

---

[29] http://www.tntpost-group.com: about TPG/frequent question, April 1st 2001.
[30] http://www.kpn.com/br1/aboutkpn/aboutkpn, April 5th 2001.

Since it was the first time that a postal incumbent went to public through an IPO, TPG had organised road shows almost everywhere in Europe and in the US from the beginning of March 1998 to explain to shareholders and markets what would happen. As a matter of fact, shareholders had bought shares of a perceived telecom company and finally had had postal incumbent's shares plus KPN's ones.

Due to its small domestic market and to the fact KPN had already been listed on four stock exchanges, TPG started with an international placement. The main investors were the State of the Netherlands (43.3%) and institutional investors, mainly pension funds. The State of the Netherlands has been adopting different policies – more pragmatic in nature – from Italy and France regarding the existence of a "*noyau dur*".

Once the Dutch government has sold its shares, it is no longer interested in encouraging specific categories of shareholders or in trying to avoid a hostile takeover. The Government controls the activity of the Post Office through the Regulatory framework. However TPG can't be defined as a "public company", since private investors own only approximately 17% of its shares. The company did not offer any bonus share or any special clause to encourage individual shareholders. The only facility was the "Personnel Option Plan" in 1999 through which the company offered its employees working in the Netherlands under the collective labour agreement a one-time opportunity with the following characteristics:

- the employees were granted an option right for 100 of TPG's shares;
- options are awarded at the opening price (€ 27.7) as traded on the Amsterdam Stock Exchange on the date the award is made;
- the option is exercisable between the third and the fifth anniversary of the day of grant, five years after the outstanding options have been forfeited.

Members of TPG's Management Board and other senior managers were awarded company stock options in 2000 (997,425), in 1999 (828,059) and in 1998 (732,300)[31].

The main goal of this placement was to change the TPG's image from a former administration to a business company. The government hadn't influenced KPN's strategy or business decisions but the markets had a different perception. Before KPN acquired TNT, post business was not considered as high profitable and interesting. The image that Post Office gave to the public was completely different from the idea they had of more dynamic telecom business. After the merger with TNT, PTT-post and PTT-telecom had the same profitability and solidity. The problem of image was both internal and external. On one side the idea the two businesses had to be managed differently grew into the company. At the same time analysts, who had considered KPN only as a telecom company, were

[31] TPG Annual Report, 2000.

confused by the growing profitability of postal business area and found it difficult to put this "hybrid" company into a well-defined category. The splitting was favourable considered as the best solution.

As already seen in § 2.2.3.1, the corporatisation and privatisation process, which had involved KPN since 1989, led to the demerger and to the subsequent TPG's floatation. TPG's benchmark was the privatisation of Deutsche Telekom in 1996 while the condition of financial markets was not a key element to decide the date of the splitting. The goal of the Dutch government prevailed on the choice of the most favourable financial markets conditions. TPG couldn't be listed before 1998 because it wasn't fully financial independent and strong enough to go to the market. The whole re-organisation process had taken ten years with a major joint effort from employees, management and government.

The State announced on March 12th, 2001 a proposed sale of approximately 35 million of TPG outstanding ordinary shares to institutional investors in Europe. British institutional investors bought two – thirds of the stake in TNT Post Groep that the Dutch State sold[32]. The sale represents approximately 7.3% of TPG outstanding ordinary share capital excluding a green shoe option to purchase an additional 15% of the sale and assuming completion would reduce the State holdings to approximately 36% (34.9% if the additional option were exercised in full). The sale was successful (around four times over subscribed) so the green shoe option was exercised. TPG hadn't received any proceeds from the sale but the company had considered it positively, too. As a matter of fact, with the demerger in 1998, shareholders didn't decide to have postal incumbent's shares because there was a splitting on a 1:1 ratio with KPN's shares. This IPO involved only institutional investors willing to buy TPG shares to hold them on a medium – long term; so a more stable shareholder's base was created.

As already mentioned in § 2.2.3.2, the State is supposed to diminish its influence in the company changing the mechanisms of corporate governance such as the special share. In connection with the offering the State announced its intention to reduce its involvement with TPG while safeguarding the public interest of the postal concession. The agreements, which govern the relationship between TPG and the State of the Netherlands, are being amended subject to Parliamentary approval. Pursuant to this amended agreement, the Minister of Transport, Public Works and Water Management would no longer have the right to appoint three members of the Supervisory Board and the State would no longer have any option to acquire preference shares A[33]. No change is currently proposed to the status of the State's special share. The final goal of the government is to own no more than 10 % of TPG's total outstanding ordinary shares within two years and not before to avoid an excessive dilution of the value of the stocks due to the increasing number of shares coming to the markets. It is reasonable to think

[32] Dow Jones International News, April 10th 2001.

[33] In March 2001, the Dutch government wrote a letter to the Parliament asking for a larger opportunity for the Dutch State to sell more TPG's shares.

that the State will sell its shares only if, at that time, the prevailing market conditions will be favourable. The goal for further sales is to raise as much capital as possible. Golden share[34] will be explicitly diminished and limited to PTT Post brand in the Netherlands and only for those activities under the monopoly regime[35]. The State will use the Regulatory framework to control TPG and no more the ownership tool.

2.2.3.4 The Performance and the Evaluation of the Floatation

TPG has, since its demerger from KPN, successfully obtained a stock - market quotation. It obtained a Prime – 1 Moody's short term rating on the basis of a stable and efficiently managed traditional postal service, strong debt protection ratios and strong market position in European express and logistics[36].

As the first – ever quoted postal incumbent, TPG was given a tough ride on the stock exchange since analysts and markets had to understand the innovative aspects and the risks of the company and of the industrial sector. Historically, investors experience in the transport, post and logistics sector has largely been with transport companies. However, post and express delivery companies have radically different characteristics from pure transport companies. Therefore, a revision of the economic fundamentals, which drive the sector's natural market segmentation, was a first step towards the understanding of these differences and the characteristics of the "new" sector[37].

What have driven a different industry structure are the differing expectations of service which are embodied in the delivery and collection characteristics. While transport is a necessary function for post and logistics companies, it simply represents one of the several different business functions and can even be entirely outsourced without diminishing operational effectiveness. As integrators, post and logistics companies differ fundamentally from pure transport companies because of the need to operate and maintain an expensive collection, delivery and sorting infrastructure in addition to transport provision. The higher level of service is rewarded by higher prices, however, leading to much value-added than pure transport companies.

Over the first nine months TPG outperformed the Amsterdam Stock Exchange by 20%, partly because of its initial underpricing; but on the announcement of results in March 1999, which were slightly less than expected because of the

---

[34] "Het algemene beleid inzake Staatsdeelnemingen" (kamerstukken II, 1996/1997, 25, 178, hrs. 1 – 2).

[35] Interview with Mr. R. Goethart, Public Affairs, TNT Post Group N. V., April 2nd 2001, Brussels.

[36] See Pilley O., Anderloni L. (1999).

[37] See Hawkins D., Murphy S. (2000).

currency and turnover impact of the East Asian crisis, its price started falling. This falls in price was also due to regulatory uncertainties:

- deregulation was likely to be slower than expected and to be based on lowering weight and price limits across the board to avoid cherry – picking;
- the REIMS agreement was approved by the Commission and had threaten – in the short term at least – TPG's remailing businesses. The agreement links terminal dues to domestic mail tariffs in the country of destination. For example, participating countries are required to pay a minimum of 65% of the domestic tariff of the country where they are presenting mail for domestic delivery. Prior to this agreement, some European countries paid less than half that amount[38]. In addition, the quality of service provided by postal administration delivering the mail are now linked to the amount of revenue that an accepting country can collect. The agreement introduces an independently monitored quality of service standard and a penalty system that will have to be applied when the agreed standards are not met. Therefore, if post offices are not meeting the required service standards, they would not be allowed to collect the same amount of their proportionate share of revenue as would a country which was performing up to the agreed standard. REIMS agreement negatively affected TPG since it leads to higher postage costs for mailing depending on geographic mix and piece weight;
- in 1999, re-regulation, an unexpected outcome of the implementation of the first postal directive, took place in Italy and Spain barring TPG from activities it had previously exercised.

[38] http://www.dtag.de, June 3rd 2001.

Figure 2.4
Amsterdam Stock Exchange, price of TPG's share in the first month of floatation (left) and until April 2001 (right).

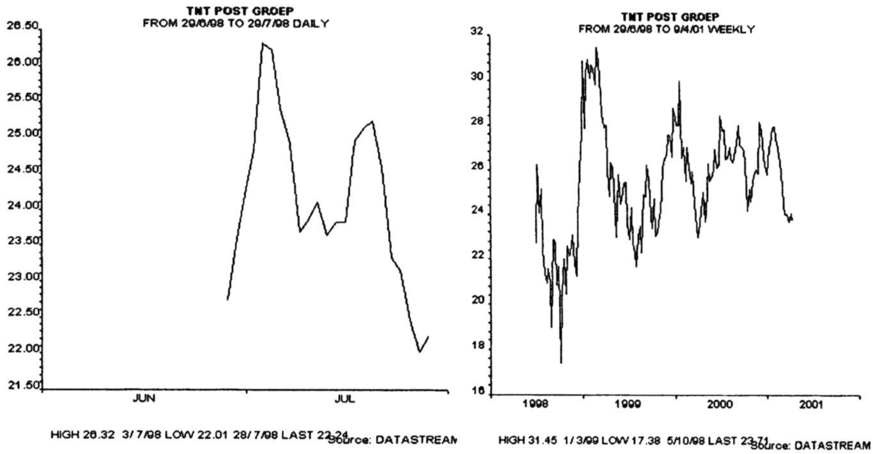

In the meantime TPG strengthened its own profitable market achieving economies of scale and developing a logistics and integrated positioning that would be hard to beat. Internationally, in view of the slower pace of deregulation in Europe, it reshifted its strategy towards the US by acquiring CTI Logistix. CTI is one of the leading third party logistics providers in the US with total sales of EUR 500m in 1999[39]. With this acquisition, TPG now belongs to the top three logistics world providers and has a major foothold in the US.

Table 2.3
Stock performance

	1998	1999	2000
Stock price High	28.04 €	35.40 €	30.70 €
Low	15.47 €	21.20 €	22.50 €
Close	27.45 €	28.45 €	25.76 €
Dividend	0.80 NLG (0.363 €)	0.80 NLG (0.363 €)	0.80 NLG (0.363 €)
Dividend %	46.2%	41.4%	33.1%
Number of Shares	475,790 932	477,584 096	479,166 412
Stock market capitalisation	13,060 bn €	13,587 bn €	12,327 bn €

Source: TPG Annual Report 2000.

[39] See Maguire R., Mons J.K. (2000).

In the third quarter of year 2000, TPG has been ill – served by Deutsche Post World Net as a valuation benchmark, since research on the latter appeared in early October 2000, ahead of its 20 November market debut.

Figure 2.5

New York Stock Exchange (left) and Frankfurter Börse (right), price and volume of TPG's share from July 1998 to April 2001.

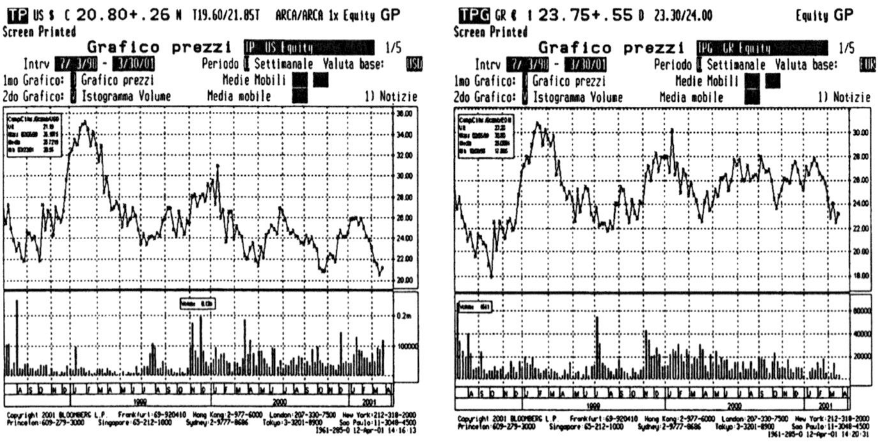

Amsterdam Stock Exchange, price and volume of TPG's share.

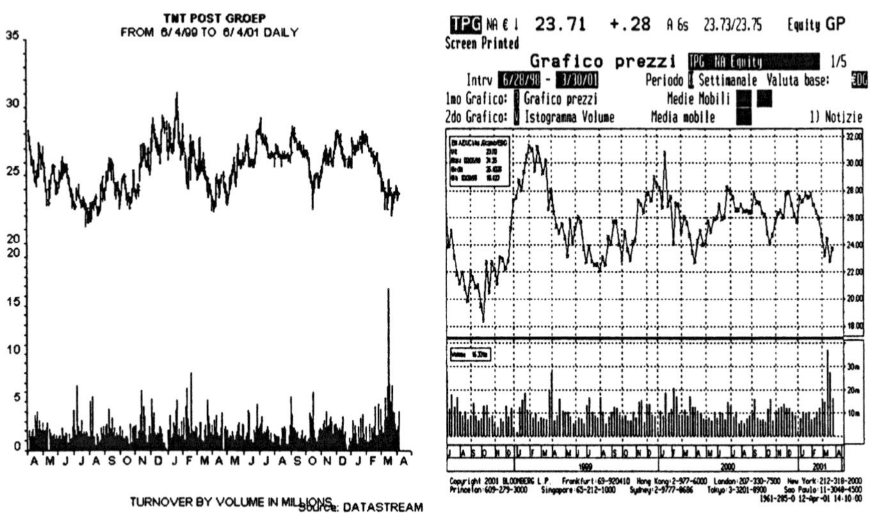

Allowing for the first (or rather, in practice, second) day premium for DPWN shares, TPG has marginally (by around 5%) under performed DPWN since DPWN's market debut (albeit with TPG under – and then outperforming in December and January)[40].

But the greater significance of DPWN – or, rather, of its being a major IPO in an increasingly difficult end – 2000 IPO market – has been in dragging TPG down towards what some analysts regarded as DPWN's technically depressed own level.

When the indicative pricing range for DPWN was implied (by syndicate sell – side research in early October 2000) to be fully 25% below suggested valuations mooted for the company in the early spring, the consequence was that TPG looked exposed. TPG shares plunged by around 15% in the first week of DPWN syndicate marketing. While they subsequently recovered – as the extent of the DPWN IPO's underpricing emerged, pointing towards a more successful offer than first feared and a useful initial premium – TPG price targets that seemed reasonable in a pre – DPWN market situation looked on December 2000 to have gone beyond reach.

Two developments should start to create more headroom for TPG shares. First having started trading at the IPO price of 21.00 € at 35% discount to TPG (on 8.5% EV/EBITDA forecast for 2002), moving to 28% after the day two premium emerged, DPWN is currently on around 25% discount. Given that in the intervening period, TPG's trading outlook has been underpinned while 2001 divisional forecasts for DPWN Express and Logistics – critical to the perception of DPWN as a successful acquisition integrator – have had to be cut, the discount has moved the wrong way. Secondly, there was the entry of DPWN to the Dax – 30 on 19 March. DPWN's arrival on a far larger number of investor radar screens should at least create a floor for DPWN and hence – given the discount – a platform for TPG.

Although TPG has presented very good figures on 12th March 2001, the positive influence on stock price has been leveraged by the announcement of the further sell of stocks from the State. The fact that more shares were coming to the market had a negative effect on share price (see graph below).

---

[40] See Ireland D., Green K., Brzeskwinski K. (2001).

Figure 2.6
Amsterdam Stock Exchange, price and volume of TPG's share from March 1 to March 30, 2001.

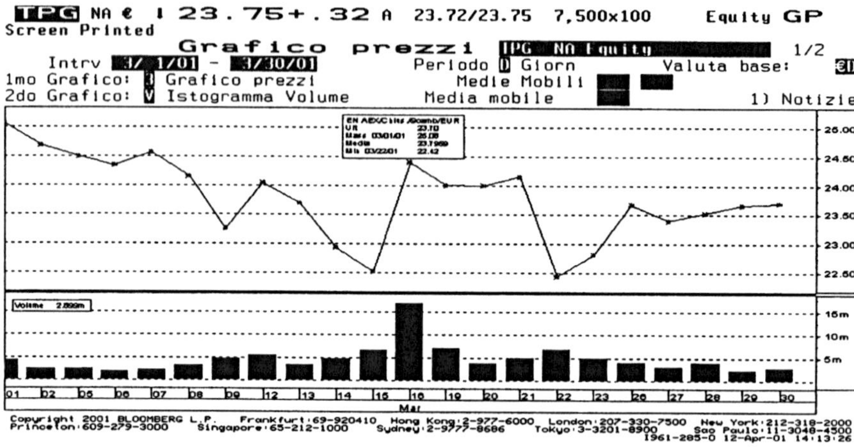

2.2.4 Conclusions

TPG unveiled its five years strategy based on value - based management principles, which should be implemented throughout the company. The company's overall strategy focuses on expansion of its Mail business into liberalised foreign markets, improving profitability in Express and Logistics and on e - business initiatives. The shift from low growth activities to higher growth activities becomes clear. TPG has managed to become less dependent on the lower growth activities of Mail.

The fair value multiple that follows the total growth of a company depends not just on the level of growth; other factors include the expected duration of growth and the cost of capital that funds the earnings stream. The group has higher growth prospects partly due to the former EU postal liberalisation and to the expansion into the US logistics arena. Its acquisition policy tends to optimise balance sheet.

Some aspects of its strategy may create ground of concern. Top line and earnings growth assumptions look aggressive so that its expansion policy mainly in Mail division into foreign markets could create a price war similar to the one that was seen in the express markets in recent years. This situation will increase the risk profile of the stock. Using a straightforward net present value model, the company's weighted average cost of capital (WACC) is applied as discount rate reflecting both risk premium and the capital structure of the company. The principal assumption is that, in the long term, a company's total earnings growth will tend to its cost of capital. Assuming a sales growth of 10% per year and an increased risk premium, the TPG share fair value could be estimated in 30 €. Therefore, at the moment, the company would be undervalued.

TPG has suffered from the slowdown in the European liberalisation. Further more, it thought the new economy process would affect more rapidly the European postal sector while opening new markets. Its lack of presence in the U.S. is another aspect of its strategy which may create concern in the long term. Reducing its stake to the minimum, the Dutch government has given more chance to move into the U.S., as the new American administration is taking a very dim view of acquisitions of U.S. companies by foreign state–owned ones.

TPG's financial structure could become more efficient through acquisitions, although it might have been wise not to go too far with acquisitions since the express business is prone to credit risk. The company seemed to have chosen the way of joint ventures and commercial agreements to improve its network and profitability. TPG established strategic alliances with China State Post, with Swiss Post, with the British Post Office and with Singapore Post. These moves appear to match two major features of TPG's strategy: international expansion and seeking diversified service offerings across previously distinct post, express and logistics.

TPG seems to have raised the bar: it is aggressively developing Web–based services, reengineering its back office and rising financial targets. The process started in 1989, which led to its floatation in 1998, was both the cause and the effect of its successful strategy. The State of the Netherlands is progressively reducing its influence and giving the company more commercial outlook. In spite of the general downturn of the markets in these last months, TPG had shown good figures. As the first postal incumbent gone public, TPG has shown a way many other Post Offices are going to follow in the next few years. However, the Dutch government pragmatic approach not to interfere in strategic decision of the company was unique and might have been one of the keys to TPG's successful floatation.

2.3 The case of Deutsche Post World Net AG

2.3.1 Foreword

2.3.1.1 Development of Privatisation in Germany

On international scale, Germany has traditionally a high share of state-owned businesses. This considerable level of average share dates back to the „inherited" stakes in companies from the German *Reich* and Prussia after World War II. Another reason was the federalist constitutional order in Germany, which allows not only the Federal Government but also the member states "the Länder" to hold stakes in companies. This dual stakeholder situation can lead to conflicts when both parties have a stake in a company and both have conflicting interests connected to the company's privatisation, leading to postponement of privatisation or even ending in stalemate.

These reasons lead to a postponement of privatisation in Germany, compared to other European countries like the UK, which had a consequent policy of privatising state-owned businesses. First major sales of stakes in industrial companies like Preussag AG, Veba AG and Volkswagen AG took place in the '60s by issuing so called „people's shares". Smaller transfers into private ownership followed.

After these partial privatisations there were no major industrial state-owned companies left. Many of the existing state-owned companies ran at a loss, especially the Deutsche Bundespost. Therefore the national finances were restructured with the aim of sustainable consolidation. This restructuring phase ended in the early 80's.

One important decision was the passing of the Programme for the privatisation and stake holding policy of the Federal Government in 1985, which redefined the future of further stakes in companies by the Federal Government. The new programme and the increasing pressure of European neighbour countries led to disinvestments of formerly state-owned businesses, which had become profitable. In 1982, the Federal Government had direct or indirect stakes in 808 companies, six years later only 309 companies were totally or partially state-owned[41]. In the first phase, primarily stakes in industrial companies were transferred into private ownership like Volkswagen or Viag. The second phase in the 90's added service and financial companies like Depfa Bank AG in 1991[42].

The third phase – the long-time untouched sector of logistics, telecommunications and postal services started in 1994 with the privatisation of Deutsche Lufthansa. In 1996 Deutsche Telecom AG went public – it is one of the three companies constituted after the privatisation of Deutsche Bundespost.

November 20th 2000 marked the end of more than 400-years, in which the German postal sector was exclusively in state hands. On this day, the initial public offering of the Deutsche Post World Net Aktiengesellschaft[43] was initiated at the German stock exchange. The comparison of the IPO with other IPOs in the postal sector can lead to very satisfactory results. We focus our research on the question if previous IPOs, like the privatisation of TNT Post Groep, influence to most recent public offering in the postal sector.

---

[41] See Schogs F. (1988).

[42] For further information about Banking Privatisation in Germany see Gruber D., von Stein J.H. (1999).

[43] Abbreviated: DPWN AG.

2.3.1.2 Outline of this Section

The analysis of an IPO is not confined to mere technical indicators – a thorough analysis of the company is important to have. In particular, the setting up of the company and the process of transfer into private ownership are important milestones to analyse the public offering and the future prospects of the company.

This article has two main sections: each study of an Initial Public Offering (IPO) starts with an analysis of the company (§ 2.3.2). The formation of the DPWN AG and its development from a state-controlled authority to a privately owned logistic affiliated group is discussed in § 2.3.2.1. The following § 2.3.2.2 analyses the current situation with some actual data. § 2.3.2.3 is an overview of the most important operating activities, which is useful for a comparison with other postal companies. The main focus is on non-traditional post activities like logistics and financial services.

The second focus of this article is on the IPO itself. § 2.3.3.1 shows the objectives, while § 2.3.3.2 addresses the condition of financial markets at the time of offering. §§ 2.3.3.3 and 2.3.3.4 describe the terms of the offer and the method of share placement and pricing. § 2.3.3.5 analyses the performances in the short and long run. In this particular framework, it is important to consider the problems of a monopoly, federal regulatory authorities and their effects on stock performance. The study ends with a short conclusion and an outlook on future developments.

2.3.2 Deutsche Post World Net AG

2.3.2.1 Privatisation in the Postal Sector – Three Postal Reforms

The history of the postal system in Germany dates back to the 15th century. The postal service was state controlled since 1595. Recent history started in 1949 when the German constitution was enacted - this represents the cornerstone of the Federal Republic of Germany. At that time the German federal postal service "Deutsche Bundespost" had been founded to control the whole sector of postal and telecommunication services. Additionally, it was designed as a bank called "Postbank". The federal postal service was subordinate to the Department of Postal and Telecommunication Services. The head of the Department also ran the Department's businesses.

The state-owned company was build upon these bureaucratic structures and was in a bad condition in the early 80's. An analysis of the company hasled to the following results[44]: Deutsche Bundespost was not market-oriented, the production processes were complex and very expensive. There was no transparency of the

---

[44] See Zumwinkel K. (1998).

company's activities. There was no bookkeeping, no cost accounting[45], no product accounting. Marketing and sales were run without any guidance, a general controlling department was non-existent.

Considering these facts it was not surprising, that the company produced heavy losses year after year. In 1990 alone the deficit of the German Post (Federal Republic of Germany) was € 320 millions. Additionally, some € 750 millions liabilities of the German Post (German Democratic Republic) had to be taken into account. In the late 80's the German Federal Postal Service was deep into the red figures and a case for restoration to profitability[46].

Postal Reform I in 1989

The postal reform I from July, 1st 1989 divided the former German Postal Service into three separate state-owned companies in the sectors Telecommunication Services, Postbank and Federal Postal Services. The Department of Postal and Telecommunication services was responsible for the federal tasks, but for each sector a CEO was assigned for running the company. The main goal of this reform was to streamline and restructure the company from a market-based perspective. This meant also the restructuring of the rigid internal bureaucracy.

Postal Reform II in 1995

On the basis of a resolution of the European Union in November 17th 1994, the EU Member States were obliged to open completely their national telecommunications markets and their postal markets partially to competition until January 1st 1998. The Postal Reform I was primarily a company-restructuring programme, the Postal Reform II, however, sets the framework for financial and competitive structures.

To fulfil their obligation, the three companies were transformed into independent private companies[47] – some six years after the postal services in the Netherlands[48].

The company was completely owned by the Federal Republic of Germany. A material privatisation did not take place[49].

---

[45] Until 1990 the Deutsche Bundespost has a governmental accounting.

[46] See Zumwinkel K. (1998).

[47] Based on "the Law about the reorganization of companies of the Deutsche Bundespost into a limited company" which also resulted in a change of the fundamental law of the Federal Republic of Germany.

[48] Basis of this transformation was a law, which also evoked a change in the federal constitution.

The highly profitable telecommunication services branch of the German Federal Post – which became Deutsche Telekom AG after the reform – had its IPO on November 11th 1996 and became one of most important shares in Germany. The second branch – financial services – became the new Deutsche Postbank AG. The third sector – national postal services – became Deutsche Post AG.

Telecommunication and postal services still had an extended monopoly. This led to the creation of regulatory authorities, which supervised the companies and could dictate prices – a development parallel to privatisation.

Despite these far reaching reforms, it was evident that another reform would become necessary. The EU resolution was incorporated only on a very limited extent; some important parts of the resolution were postponed until the end of 1999.

Postal Reform III

The Postal Reform III deregulated the markets, especially the telecommunication services market, which was opened for competitors for the first time. The postal market has been opened in 1998 formally, but there are still far-reaching regulations. Especially the monopoly of Deutsche Post AG in one of the most attractive market segments (letters<200g, mass mailings <50g and mail-order catalogues <200g) is curbing competition. For other market segments a so-called „licence market model" was established, which enables competitors in these sectors to operate on local markets. The total liberalization of the postal markets was originally scheduled for January 1st 2003 (Postal Reform III). The German legislative chamber "Bundestag", however, extended the national monopoly of DPNW AG until 2007. This means, the company will still take advantage from its monopoly position. This special situation has to be included in the analysis of the company and the IPO.

2.3.2.2 Deutsche Post World Net AG today

The far-reaching effects of Postal Reform III on the national monopoly and the national markets incensed the management to an aggressive move into new markets. The goal was the formation of an international logistics company. First, Deutsche Postbank AG[50] was again integrated into the affiliated group. Subsequently, several international companies were acquired, which helped

---

[49] There are two kinds of privatisations: „Formal" means transfer from public to private law. „Material" refers to the transfer of publicly held stakes into private ownership. For additional explanation see Anderloni L. (1999).

[50] Deutsche Postbank AG was reintegrated on January 1st 1999 into the Deutsche Post AG.

Deutsche Post to move into one of the top spots of European logistics companies. The large network of stakes and joint-ventures encompasses 75 national and 222 foreign companies[51], mainly in the logistics sector. Today roughly 70% of the total turnover are national.

The transformation from national postal service to international affiliated group is also visible in the name of the company: Deutsche Post World Net AG. The IPO took place on November 20th 2000.

This means, DPNW is a logistics and financial service company under private law, but still dependent on the German government, because the main shareholder is still the Federal Republic of Germany. In 2000 49,9% of the shares (514.98 mil.) were issued to the Kreditanstalt für Wiederaufbau[52] to prepare the IPO. Today only 31% or 319.93 mil. shares are privately held after exercising the greenshoe-option.

Only a partial material privatisation followed the formal privatisation in 1995. A material privatisation to such an extent that the government's stake is less than 50% is possible within five years according to Dr. Klaus Zumwinkel Chief Executing Officer (CEO) of DPWN AG[53]. It is questionable though if the government wants this.

Table 2.4
Development of the German postal system

1949	Formation Deutsche Bundespost
1989	Postal Reform I: dividing of Deutsche Bundespost into three fields: telecommunications, postal services and Postbank
1995	Postal Reform II: formation of three independent stock companies: Deutsche Telekom AG, Deutsche Post AG, Postbank AG
1996	IPO Deutsche Telekom AG
1998	Postal Reform III: partial liberalisation of postal and telecommunication markets.
1999	Re-integration Deutsche Postbank AG
1999-2000	Several acquisitions, formation of international logistics company, renaming in Deutsche Post World Net AG
November 11th 2000	IPO Deutsche Post AG

[51] Annual Report 1999, p. 104.

[52] The "KfW" is the operative bank of the Federal Government and the German Länder. It organises programmes supporting German economy, financing export and projects and development aid. The "KfW" is also participated in Deutsche Telekom AG. The Federal Government holds 80% of the KfW-shares, the member states participate with 20%.

[53] Reuters News Service, Zumwinkel – In fünf Jahren Post-Vollprivatisierung möglich, 29/10/2000.

Figure 2.7
Changes in ownership of Deutsche Post World Net AG

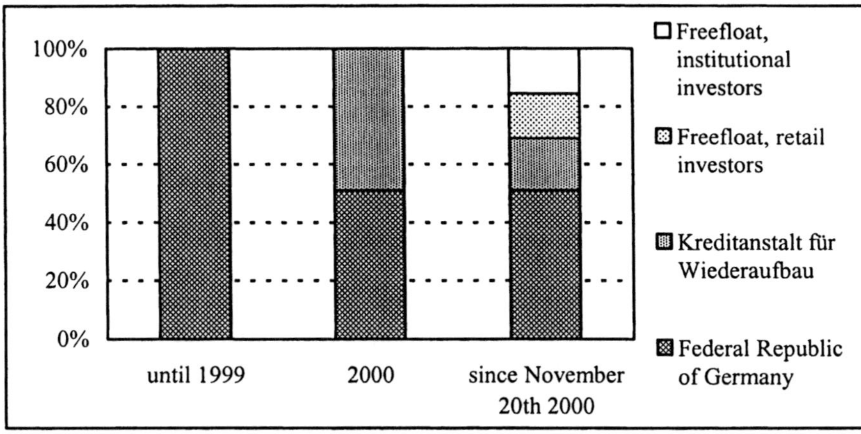

Source: Deutsche Post World Net, Annual Report 2000.

Some financial data

The company transformation can be illustrated by several figures. The turnover of DPNW AG is actually € 32,708 mil., compared to € 9,500 mil. in 1990, the year after the first Postal Reform. The major share of this growth results from the new business units logistics and financial services. The company earned € 1,500 mil.[54].

Within this context the development of employment is notable. Since the postal reforms in 1989 and 1995 employment was reduced, but raise steeply in 1999 because of several acquisitions. Today, roughly 324,000 are employed[55], after employment took a dive in to 220,000 in 1998. Since 1995 newly employed persons are no longer civil servants.

2.3.2.3 Business Units

DPNW AG is focused on services in the fields of communication, transport and logistics, especially postal services and financial services. The company is internally structured into four independent strategic business units: Express, Logistics and Letters (formerly the national postal service) and Financial Services

---

[54] By December 31st 2000.

[55] Because of the acquisition of the "Deutsche Postbank AG" and other companies. Otherwise the number of employees would have been decreased.

with the Deutsche Postbank AG as core competence. The business units are divided into three specific markets.

Business Units Letters, Express and Logistics

The business unit Letters is the core competence of the DPNW AG. This unit is the biggest postal service in Europe, which transports around 70 million letters every day to around 35 million private and 2.8 million business clients.

In Germany, this business area is strengthened by the still existent monopoly on letter transportation. Since there is a monopoly, the prices for services in the sector "letter" have to be regulated by the regulatory authority for postal services. The monopoly on letters was limited until December 31st 2002, but an extension until 2007 was resolved[56]. Figure 1 shows, how much this business unit contributes to companies overall success. The difference between the share of turnover and the share of EBITA[57] shows the gains from the monopoly position of the DPWN AG.

The business units express and logistics are primarily focused on international markets, while letters is predominately nationally oriented. They are not as big as the letter unit and are not as profitable, because they do not have a monopoly position. The business unit Express covers national and international parcel- and express deliveries as well as international letter services.

The business unit logistics was created with the acquisition of the logistics company Danzas in January 1999. DPNW AG acquired additional companies in this sector and offers today tailored logistic solutions as well as worldwide logistics by air and sea and transports by road or rail within Europe.

Business Unit Financial Services and Postbank AG

The business unit FINANCIAL SERVICES is composed of Postbank AG and the pension service[58] and has a special position within the Deutsche Post AG. It is the only business unit outside the core competence transport/logistics. At the core of this business unit is the Deutsche Postbank AG, the third part of the former Deutsche Bundespost. The financial services offer standardised banking and financial services in retail banking, in corporate banking, as well as parts of investment banking. The core competence is still in classic retail banking. After the privatisation of the Deutsche Postbank AG in 1990 Postbank moved from former governmental administration to one of the leading retail banks in Europe.

---

[56] Süddeutsche Zeitung, Liberalisierung der EU-Postmärkte rückt in weite Ferne – Briefmonopol wird verlängert, 10/11/02/2001, # 34, p. 27.

[57] Earnings before interest and taxes.

[58] This contains pension services.

This was made possible by strategic acquisitions. A network of 138,000 branch offices in Germany[59] allows exhaustive customer-oriented service[60].

By integrating telephone and Internet banking Postbank positioned itself as multi-channel and leading direct bank in Europe. With these core competences Deutsche Postbank AG is the market leader in Germany and Europe. Sight deposits in Germany had a total volume of about € 204 billion on December 31st 1999, whereof Postbank AG held 6.1%. In the category of single banks[61] the Postbank AG was immediately ranked after the leader Deutsche Bank AG. In savings deposits the leadership is more obvious. Here, Deutsche Postbank AG is on the top of the single banks. With about € 34 billion its part is 3,9%[62]. Measured on the number of customers Deutsche Postbank AG is on rank five in Europe after Crédit Agricole, Crédit Mutuel-CIC, La Poste and Lloyds TSB. These figures explain why Deutsche Postbank AG has a leading role as retail-bank in Germany[63]. Since 1995 it has the licence of a regular bank. By December 31st 2000 Deutsche Postbank AG has 11,299 employees and contributes 23.5% of the consolidated revenues and 21.2% of the EBITA.

Figure 2.8
Distribution of turnover, EBITA and employment in business units

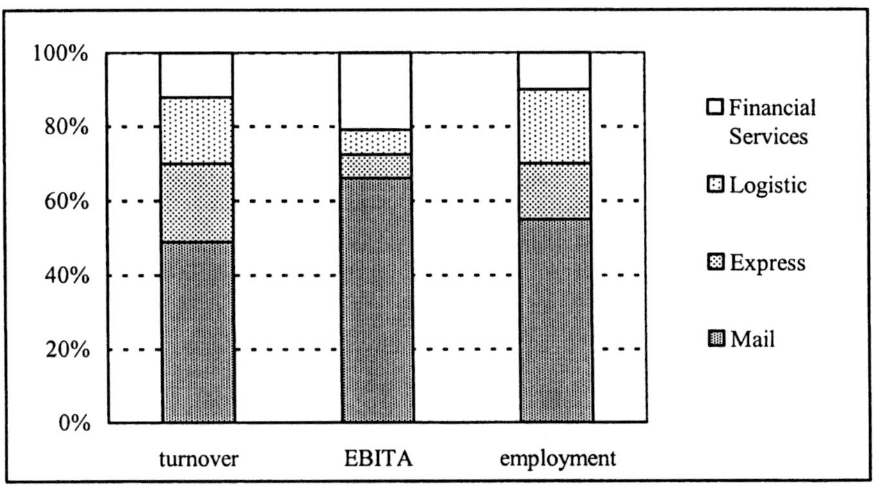

Source: Deutsche Post World Net, Annual Report 2000.

[59] By June 30th 2000.
[60] Comparison: the largest German Bank (measured at the balance sheet total) Deutsche Bank AG has got only 1,400 agencies in Germany.
[61] Referred to a bank not belonging to a group.
[62] By December 31st 1999.
[63] By December 31st 1998.

2.3.3 Initial Public Offering of Deutsche Post AG

2.3.3.1 Reasons and Objectives

§ 2.3.2.1 described the main microeconomic, macroeconomic and political drivers of the formal privatisation in 1995. For the Initial Public Offering (IPO), meaning partial material privatisation, the Ministry of Finance had similar objectives[64]. The improvement of the economical efficiency is still the main goal. The listing on the stock exchange and the interests of shareholder intensified the pressure on the company to act economically and entrepreneurial.

The Deutsche Post AG was forced to move from a former public authority to an international logistic corporation as soon as possible. This restructuring would have taken much more time if the federal government had sole ownership of the corporation. The federal government reasoned that a formerly state-controlled company prepares much better for the opening of the markets as an incorporated company. Thus, it is prepared to compete on national and international scope. Being competitive is necessary to make sure that the company can exist after the market for postal services has been opened: only a healthy and competitive corporation will save jobs in within the former state-controlled monopoly market in Germany. To improve the economic efficiency, employment will be cut in the initial phase of the IPO. The remaining jobs will undoubtedly benefit from better conditions and will be preserved by the fact the company will generate no more losses. The competitive environment would endanger the remaining jobs if no precaution is taken.

Another goal of the IPO was the budget consolidation by the earnings of the privatisation. The earnings of the privatisation have been used to cover pension obligations and to repay the debt from the state-owned company. So at the time of the IPO Deutsche Post AG did not have any old debts of the time when it had been a public authority. At the same time the federal budget was discharged from these obligations.

2.3.3.2 Condition of the Financial Markets

If the whole year of the Initial Public Offering of Deutsche Post World Net AG is considered, it must be admitted that all in all it was not a good year for shareholders. Since January 2000 stock indices declined worldwide. The Dow Jones, which has always had a significant influence on the German stock exchanges, reached an all time high in January. But the Dow lost 11.2% of its value until November 20th 2000 when the Deutsche Post World Net AG was listed for the first time.

---

64 See Department of Finance (1995).

The German stock exchanges were hit even harder. The German stock market index DAX which includes the 30 most important stocks had an all time high on March 7th 2000 but lost 18% of its value until November 20th 2000. Compared over the year[65] the index lost 5% of its value. Since 1994, the year 2000 was the first year where the market made losses from the beginning to the end of the year. Worth mentioning in this context is the fact that within the DAX Deutsche Telekom AG had been the main loser. In 2000 it lost 55% of its value.

The year 2000 did not start badly. In January the Dow Jones reached a new all time high and in the first quarter the DAX gained significantly. There was still a high number of IPOs. Many of them produced high gains within a very short time. Especially the IPOs of the technological sector got high gains. However climate changed. Until September 2000 prices nearly stayed the same. Many shareholders saw this development as a consolidation that was necessary. Then prices dropped again. Reasons were the slight weakening of the US economy and the crisis in the technology sector. Besides, in Germany the optimistic rates of growth that had been predicted for the national economy had to be adjusted. Many shareholders lost trust in highly valued stocks. Significant interest rate cuts in the United States and in Europe supported the markets only for a short time. When prices fell in the United States, the prices in Germany fell as well.

Many of the IPOs that had been very successful in the beginning lost much of their valuation and some fell below the IPO price. Other IPOs that had been planned for the fourth quarter of 2000 have been shifted to a later time. First insolvencies in the technology sector evoked a negative attitude of shareholders towards the whole market. After a short rally in the beginning of November the DAX became weaker and weaker. Earning warnings in all sectors forced prices down.

The transport and logistics sector, which includes DPWN AG, was affected by this market weakness. Compared with the whole transport market (measured by the CDAX-Transport[66]) from the beginning of 2000 until the IPO on November 20th 2000 the DPWN AG gained about 1% . At the time of the IPO the market environment was pessimistic. Since prices went down all shareholders acted market wide very carefully. Performance problems and the postponement of IPOs had a negative effect on the remaining IPOs. Altogether the sector developed positively because it was relatively stable despite all uncertainties.

As mentioned before, the general market outlook at the time of the IPO was difficult. But the Federal Government of Germany stickled to the original timeline – it would have been very costly to discontinue the IPO-Campaign and to reschedule the IPO. Analysts of the banks of the consortium were optimistic about the logistics sector. The government was convinced of the quality of the stock and disregarded other influencing factors – besides that, the earnings of the IPO were

---

[65] January 3rd 2000 – December 29th 2000.

[66] This index contains all German stocks of the transport and logistic sector.

already booked in the federal budget. A postponement would have been quite expensive. But the losses and the overall negative stock market led to a loss in the share price of Deutsche Post World Net AG of roughly 25% in the time from March 2000 until November 2000.

2.3.3.3 Terms of Offer and some Figures

The IPO of the Deutsche Post World Net AG included the sale of 278.20 million to 319.93 million[67] shares that were in the possession of the "Kreditanstalt für Wiederaufbau". So 25% to 29% of the shares were listed at all German, but not at foreign stock exchanges. The remaining 71% are still held by the Federal Republic of Germany and the Kreditanstalt für Wiederaufbau. All shares participate on earnings since January 1st 2000.

Several points of the offer are remarkable: first, the Federal Republic of Germany is still controlling Deutsche Post World Net AG. Second, the shares are only listed at German stock-exchanged – this makes sense, because the international turnover of Deutsche Post is only 30% of its total turnover. On an international scale, the company is relatively unknown and not attractive for international investors. A further international expansion will also lead to a higher attractiveness of the company for international investors. This goal might be achieved with the complete privatisation in about 5 years.

Additionally, employee's participation was developed and the banks of the consortium had a greenshoe-option.

One objective of the former owner, the Federal Republic, was to attract individual shareholders with special terms of the offer. The German government wanted to ensure that the former state-owned company would still be in the hands of the German people. To achieve that objective the terms of the offer were similar to the terms that attracted a large number of individual shareholders at the IPO of Deutsche Telekom AG. This very successful IPO was the reason why many people in Germany discovered shares as an attractive new investment. Today, the free floating shares are still widely in the possession of individual private shareholders.

Offering for private investors

First there has to be mentioned the so-called "early order discount". This is the most common term to attract individual shareholders. It includes a discount of €

---

[67] If the Greenshoe-Option is fully exercised.

0,5 per share for all private investors who made an early commitment to order shares in the time from October 30th 2000 to November 10th 2000[68].

Additionally there was a "bonus share plan" which guarantees all private shareholders one bonus share per 15 shares if they subscribed shares in the early period and held them at least until November 30th 2002. In another program, customers of the Deutsche Postbank AG had the chance to get additional 35% of the shares in favour. These different terms of the offer achieved the intentional objective: roughly 50% of the shares were issued to private investors[69], making it one of the most widely held stocks in Germany.

Employee and management participation plan

Even for the 244,000 employees there were possibilities to get special shares using the so called "employee participation plan" which has become a recent trend in IPOs. Employees of the DPWN AG could purchase shares in a three-column-model until an amount of € 6.953. The first column included the purchase of up to € 306 in shares. If these shares were held longer than six years the purchase would be tax-free. For each share purchased in the second column each employee got one call-option. This entitled the holder after two years to buy additional stocks at the issue price. The shares from this column have to be held longer than two years otherwise the option expires[70]. Column three made possible to purchase stocks up to an amount of € 5,114. These possibilities to participate in the own company were widely used by the employees because they guaranteed the investors to get at least a few stocks[71].

For a very limited circle, about 1,000 manager of the DPWN AG, there was an additional program called "management participation plan". This included options to purchase 50 millions additional stocks. The allocation will take place in four different stages respectively on the first trading day in July, beginning with the year 2001. Entitled to benefit are only managers who purchase stocks with their own money. The amount of these purchases has to be at least 10% of their yearly personal earnings. The stock-options can be exercised three years after the purchase. The amount of these options is coupled with the stock performance. The higher the stock price, the more options could be exercised by the management to secure profits. Today the employees and the management own about 6% of the company.

---

[68] The regular subscription period lasted from 30th October to 16th November 2000 (for private investors) and 17th November 2000 (for institutional investors).

[69] See Frankfurter Allgemeine Zeitung, Die Post stellt schon für 2000 eine Dividende in Aussicht, October 31st 2000, # 250, p. 20.

[70] This also happens if the employee leaves the company.

[71] See Frankfurter Allgemeine Zeitung, Aus Postlern werden Aktionäre, November 20th 2000, # 267, p. 22.

50 mil. shares (around 6% of the total amount of shares of DPWN) were issued to the employees.

- Up to 3.5 mil. shares to the members of the managing board;
- Up to 7 mil. shares to the members of the boards of co-operating companies;
- Up to 22 mil. shares to managers below the top management level;
- Up to 17.5 mil. shares to managers at associated companies;

Some 145,000 employees received shares using the programmes.

The Greenshoe-Option

The banks of the consortium had the greenshoe-option. This makes possible to buy additional 47.9 mil. stocks from the KfW to stabilise the rate of the shares. This option was fully exercised[72], which means that today 319.93 mil. stocks are publicly traded.

Lock-up-Agreements

Besides the mentioned lock-up-agreements of the "employee participation plan" and the "management participation plan" there were further agreements. The Federal Republic of Germany and the KfW agreed not to offer any new stocks directly or indirectly before November 20th 2001 without the permission of the global consortial banks. The Deutsche Post World Net AG agreed not to increase its capital stock.

Table 2.5
The Terms Of The Offer

Symbol/Number	**DPW.FSE/555200**
Offered shares	278.20 mil. (25%)
Greenshoe-Option	41.73 mil. (4%)
Total	319.93 mil. (29%)
Listed stock-exchanges	All German stock exchanges, no foreign stock exchanges.
Dividend starting	January 1st 2000

[72] See Börsen-Zeitung, Greenshoe bei Post-IPO voll ausgeübt, December 19th 2000, # 243, p. 24.

Table 2.6
Special Offers

Offers for private investors

Early Order Discount	All investors pre-ordering in the time frame of October 30th 2000 until 10/11/2000 received a rebate of € 0.5 per share.
Bonus shares	For every 15 shares not sold until November 30th 2002 every investor receives one bonus share.
Programme for customers of Postbank AG	35% additional shares

Employee offers (roughly 244,000 persons)

Column I	Acquisition of shares up to € 307. The acquisition becomes tax-free, if the shares are being held until December 31st 2005.
Column II	Acquisition of shares up to € 1,534 and the same number of call-options.
Column III	Guaranteed acquisition of shares up to € 5,113
Combined	Preferred acquisition of shares up to € 6,954

Offers for the management (roughly 1.000 persons)

Management Participation Plan	Four step plan of additional shares and call-options.

Source: DEUTSCHE POST WORLD NET AG (2000): Global Offering.

2.3.3.4 Method of Share Placement and Pricing

The following methods of share placement and pricing[73] are used most often: public offer at a fixed price, public offer with auction, placement with book-building, private placement and public offer for subscription.

In the case of the DPWN AG the method was a classic book building process. This method is used on most IPOs all over the world and in recent years even more in Germany. The advantage of this method of share placement is that the investors are more involved in the pricing-process. It is even possible to prefer predetermined types of investors. This makes it possible for the former owner, the Federal Republic of Germany to prefer private, long term orientated investors. The typical timetable of a book building process is shown in Figure 2.9.

---

[73] For further information see Anderloni L. (1999).

Figure 2.9
Book-building

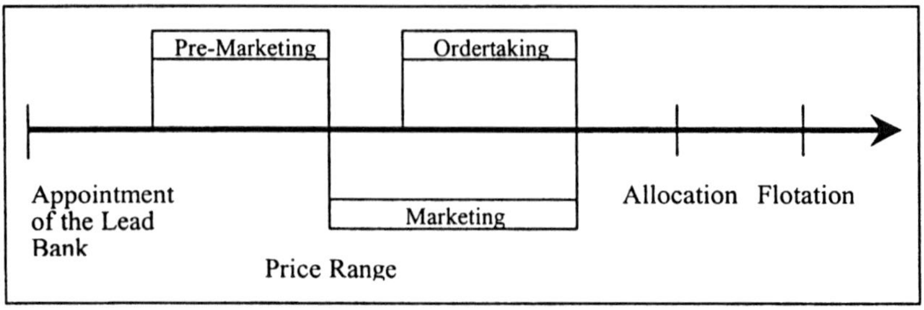

Source: Voigt, H.-W. (1995)

Appointment of the Lead Bank

In the broader sense a book building process starts with the appointment of the consortium of banks and the lead bank. In our case, the consortium of banks contained 23 international banks. The Deutsche Bank AG and UBS Warburg were lead banks. With this consortium private and institutional investors from the most important European countries, the USA and Japan could subscribe shares.

Pre-Marketing and Marketing-Phase

The «pre-marketing-phase» and the «marketing-phase» of the process follow the appointment. The pre-marketing includes a first outreach to potential investors and the presentation of the company's specific risk-profile. This is supported by the consortium of banks' research, including a detailed valuation of the company. The real marketing-phase starts with the announcement of the price-range for the issue price that is determined by the evaluation of the company. The pricing range was from € 18 - € 23 and roughly 25% below the expectations of spring 2000. The reasons for this devaluation were primarily the sliding stock markets. An increasing number of analysts pointed out that the slow growth rates and the loss of the national monopoly on letter transport could steer the company into problems.

In our case, major marketing-activities like TV-spots, road shows and one-on-one meetings began months before the November 20th 2000. Similarly to the case of Deutsche Telekom AG, many of these activities were especially for private investors.

Pre-marketing and marketing period were important for the IPO of DPWN AG. A campaign to improve the image of the company was introduced in early 1999. At this stage the company was perceived by the population as being slow, unreliable and the staff as unfriendly and not customer focused. The campaign was aimed at changing these perceptions. Especially the sponsoring of the widely popular Formula 1 racing team was one method. The message was clear: Deutsche Post is fast, modern, risk-taking – in total the complete opposite of the former German postal service. A series of TV spots aimed at the IPO were featuring a widely popular entertainer and his brother. The brothers accompanied the television audience half a year prior to the IPO and explained the company, its functions and strengths. The brother of the entertainer was introduced as savvy investor, who incorporated the most important advantages of the share for private investors: security, constant growth and focused on the future. The marketing effort totalled around € 55 mil.

Order Taking and Price fixing

Only a few days after the announcement of the price-range the phase of "order taking" started on October 30th 2000. The investors get the opportunity to subscribe shares of the company at one bank of the consortium. The demand is collected and permanently transmitted to the lead bank. Though no names of investors have to be reported it is possible to determine the distribution of demand by types of investors, quality of investors, regions etc.. In the case of the DPWN AG the "regular" subscription period began October 30th 2000 and lasted respectively until November 16th 2000 for private investors, November 17th 2000 for institutional investors. Even at this stage the demand was extremely high.

At the end of the order taking period the lead bank analyses the wishes for subscription on the basis of a scoring-model. The possibility of demand being higher than supply is quite high. In our case it was eight times higher[74]. After the determination of the demand the consortium of banks and the issuer agree on an uniform issuing price. The Deutsche Post World Net AG's issue price was € 21.00.

Allocation and Initial Public Offering

Finally the shares were issued. The demand was analysed and shares were distributed according to a fixed ratio to investors. The day of the first listing was November 20th 2000.

This process led to an equal distribution of shares to private and institutional national investors. First research showed that foreign private investors did subscribe to the share on a very small basis. Institutional investors were more interested, because the share was predicted to become part of the DAX, the index for the 30 most important shares in Germany. As a whole the international demand was rather weak.

---

[74] See Reuters News Service, Post-Aktie zum Börsendebüt leicht über Ausgabekurs, November 20th 2000.

Overall the flotation generated earnings of € 6.6 billion for the Federal Republic, which were used to reduce debts from the time the "Post" was state-owned.

2.3.3.5 Performance in the Short Run and Long Term Prognoses

Short term performance

Deutsche Post World Net AG started trading with € 21.40, a raise of +1.9% compared with the subscription price of € 21.00[75]. Figure 4 and 5 illustrate the good performance of the stock. It did outperform the DAX by nearly 10% and reached its all time high on February 2nd 2001 at € 24.20.

This performance mirrors a high demand of the share coupled with a high volume of trading in the first days. Especially institutional investors acquired the stock for their portfolios. But there were rumours, that the consortium of banks did try to support the stock price by massive purchases. Without this supportive measures the stock would have suffered even more in the difficult market environment.

Within this context the performance a comparison with TNT Poest Group is interesting: since the start of the book-building phase of DPNW AG in summer 2000 TNT was losing value. The stock price started to recover only after the high demand in DPWN shares could not be satisfied by the markets. This process shows clearly the international arbitrage of the most important postal and logistics shares in Europe. A comparison of the stock performance of both stocks will be at the end of the section.

The original enthusiasm was followed by downturn. DPNW lost ground hand in hand with the DAX by nearly 28%, reaching the all-time-low of € 17.5. While the markets recovered, DPNW AG was moving sideboards. Main reasons were new rumours on a weak growth prospects especially of the company as well as the weak markets, hit by the crisis in the high-tech sector. Another reason were disappointing interim results of the parcel service EXPRESS in spring 2001.

After rumors on the general meeting of the DPWN AG on June 27th about good earnings in the 2. Quarter of the year 2001 the share recovered and is currently traded – like the DAX – roughly 10% lower than in November 2000. It is interesting to note the performance of the relative-strength-index[76] of DPNW AG: the first figure is quoted at around 70, a sign for an "oversold" market, which points to an exceptional high demand of the stock and in a medium term perspective to lower prices. In January 2001 the chart technique showed a buying signal, because the RSI crossed the line of the oversold segment into positive territory. This was followed by a short rally with the already mentioned all-time-

[75] All rates from the Frankfurt stock exchange.

[76] For more information see Murphy (2000).

high late February. Currently the stock is again in the oversold segment. The development for the next few months point more to a downward trend.

Additionally, the overall weak correlation with the DAX of 0,07 is remarkable. The IPOs are more dynamic in the short-run after the first listing because of the specific characteristics of the company. Therefore a weak correlation with the overall market evolve. However, the correlation is increasing over a longer period. There is a much higher correlation with the sector index of 0,71, which shows the clear domination of DPNW AG in this sector in Germany.

Figure 2.10

Performance of DPWN AG and Relative Strength Index

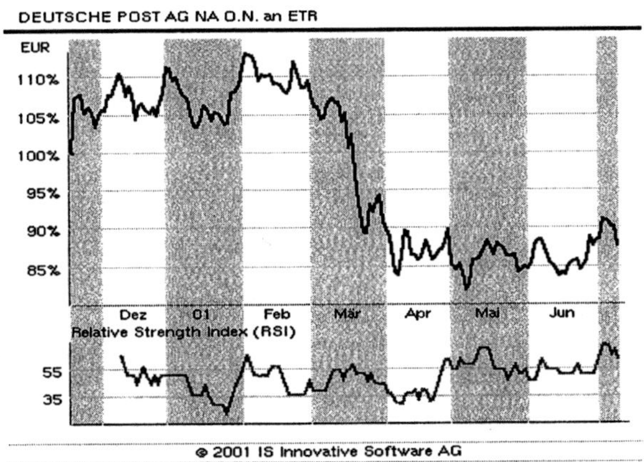

Source: http://www.consors.de

Figure 2.11

DPNW AG and DAX in comparison

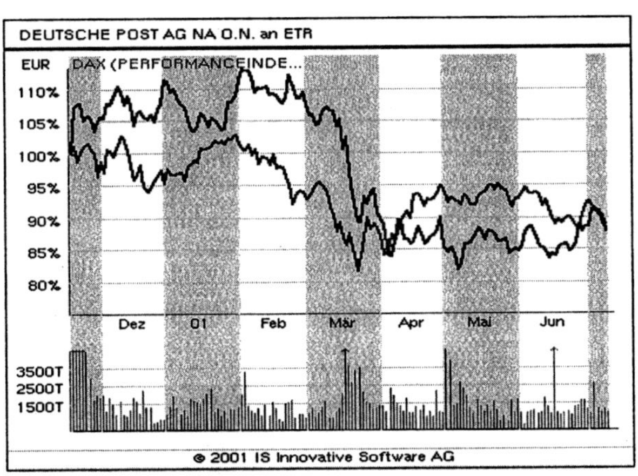

Source: http://www.consors.de

Outlook and criteria for prognosis

The operational activities of the DPWN AG mail, logistic or even financial services are typically no sectors with a very high or very volatile rate of economic growth like Internet or biotechnology. In contrast, they promise constant growth which is better to anticipate for the stockholders. Because of that the stock should have a lower volatility compared to the overall market, other than high-tech companies where expectations are very difficult to anticipate. Thus the stock is rather a long-term investment in contrast to a speculative one. Another positive development is the early integration of the share into the DAX on March 19th 2001[77]. This should support the performance because it increases the visibility and importance of the stock and attracts more foreign investors.

A problem of the long-term development is the monopoly of the DPWN on the national postal market and the existence of a regulatory authority. With the fixing and changing of prices in the monopoly market the authority affects the revenues and the EBIT of a privately owned company. Besides the political problems of that construction, it directly affects the value of the company. The MAIL sector is the most important sector in revenues and EBIT for the Deutsche Post World Net AG. Therefore, news like the extension of the monopoly on letter transport affect the stock price. If a company - like the DPWN AG - now has earnings from a monopoly position, the state will stop this by intervention. This could result in a reduction of the monopoly price, fixed by the state. In our case, a present discussion addresses a reduction of the postage of about 9%[78]. Such a decision has a significant effect on the revenues and the company's EBIT. The company itself is not responsible for external influences neither can it exercise any influence on the decision-making process. Thus, for a long term prognosis the investor has to consider such political effects. In our case ,these effects are more important than in other sectors. If we presume that the long term objective consists of a fully open postal market in Germany the monopoly will vanish and the revenues and the value of the company would decline. Therefore, it is particularly important for DPNW to use its time of state protection to develop strong international activities. If not, the stock will come under pressure in the long run.

As an overview of the general outlook on DPNW AG and its stock performance a SWOT analysis can be useful.

---

[77] See Frankfurter Allgemeine Zeitung, Mühsamer Start der Post-Aktie im DAX, March 20th 2001, # 66, p. 33.

[78] See Süddeutsche Zeitung, Liberalisierung der EU-Postmärkte rückt in weite Ferne – Briefmonopol wird verlängert, February 10th, 11th 2001, # 34, p. 27.

Table 2.7
SWOT Analysis

Strengths	Weaknesses
• Large company with good market position and excellent branch structure. • Past change processes were successful.	• Focused mostly on national business • Depended on national monopoly in letter transportation services • Little customer focus in some parts of the business
Opportunities	**Threats**
• Possibility to use the profits from national postal monopoly to facilitate international strategy. • Existing cooperations offer big international possibilities.	• Failure of internationalisation strategy and loss of national monopoly are possible threats. • Federal Government has direct influence on the profits of the company.

The key for further development of DPNW AG is an internationalisation strategy, which includes important advances in Internet and e-business technology. If this strategy fails, the company will not be able to compete with internationally highly successful postal companies like TNT Post Group. The future performance of the stock and the chance of a complete privatisation – i.e. the listing of all shares at national and especially foreign stock-exchanges – are dependent on the success of this strategy.

2.3.3.6 Evaluation of the IPO

This study was written only nine months after the IPO. Since many aspects of the IPO can only be evaluated in the long run the evaluation cannot be finished.

For a short time evaluation it is now important to distinguish the motivations and goals of the participants.

For the Federal Republic of Germany, the evaluation should consists of the fulfilment of the objectives explained in § 2.3.3.1. Today, the main objective for IPO, namely a better efficiency and therefore the preparation for international competition can not be fully evaluated. However, an historic comparison can help. At first, the postal reform the "Deutsche Bundespost" was a state-owned authority with negative earnings. Many processes were not efficiently organised, the number of employees was too large. These circumstances changed after the reforms in 1989 and 1995. The organisation was restructured, the number of employees was reduced. The company became a logistic corporation with positive earnings. The objectives of the reforms were achieved. This does not mean that the objectives of the IPO will also be achieved but it shows the flexibility and the development of the DPWN AG. further objective, namely the reduction of the debt of the former state-owned Post, was achieved. The flotation generated earnings of € 6.6 bill. for the Federal Government which was nearly enough to completely cancel the debt. Additionally it has to be mentioned that many shares could be given to private investors, also a very important objective. For the Federal Republic the minister of finance spoke of a "successful" IPO[79].

For the consortium of banks the IPO could be evaluated positively. Many new private investors subscribed the stock during the book building. For that reason large earnings were generated. Overall the IPO of the DPWN AG was the third largest IPO of the year 2000 in Germany.

From the investor's perspective, the main aspect of an evaluation is the stock performance. In our case the prices were – compared to other IPOs – lower in the beginning. They never got the large gains of other stocks from the Internet sector. Reasons were the difficult conditions of financial markets at time of the IPO and especially the operative activities, which had no high growth rates. In contrast the stable prices are positive for long-term orientated investors. Although the consortium of banks enacted supporting measures for the stock, it has become one of the most important ones in Germany.

2.3.4 Conclusion and Outlook

By the already mentioned postal reforms, Deutsche Post World Net AG was transformed from a state-owned authority to a performance-oriented logistics company. A huge success factor was the deceleration of European privatisation policy and subsequently the national monopoly on letter transportation, which protects the company from internationally successful competitors like the TNT Post Group. But this is only a momentary slowdown; Germany will have liberated markets. To build sufficient defences and a competitive position in the market against international competitors the IPO was an important step. The IPO forced DPNW AG to implement the necessary restructuring efforts, especially the implementation of an internationalisation strategy.

The third largest share placement in 2000 resulted from a classic book building process. In this system, the Federal Republic was able to encourage individual shareholders to subscription with specific offers such as bonus shares and rebates

[79] Vwd Vereinigte Wirtschaftsdienste GmbH, Aktie Gelb gibt solides Börsendebüt, November 20th 2000.

for early subscribing. Especially private investors hold today 50% of all free floating shares. In comparison with TNT Post Group this IPO stressed employee participation programs. By using four different methods the 145,000 employees bought together 50 mil. shares.

The condition of the financial markets during the IPO was quite difficult. Worldwide stock prices fell and the economic growth was small. Nevertheless the performance of the DPWN AG stock was relatively solid. If the short-term objectives like encouraging individual shareholders or recent stock performance are analysed, the IPO must be considered "successful". Long-term objectives like the opening of the company and the improvement of efficiency can not be evaluated at this point. A further significant step for the company will be the abolition of the postal monopoly in Germany. Although this was recently cancelled[80], there will be an open postal market within the next decade. The problems resulting from this constellation affects the IPO and can only be resolved by an internationalisation of the company.

Another important step for the company will be the abolition of the national monopoly on letter transportation, which has been recently postponed. The resulting problems are affecting the IPO and can only be solved by an internationalisation strategy of the company. Further restructuring is necessary in the future. New markets like e-commerce need to be entered. Other postal companies like the TNT Post Group already lay out the roadmap.

After the successful IPO of the Deutsche Telekom AG in 1996 the IPO of the Deutsche Post World Net AG was an important step in the process of privatisation in Germany. More companies are likely to follow. First there has to be mentioned the Deutsche Bahn AG, the German publicly owned railway company, which was in the focus of the privatisation debate. Because of the pressure of the European Union the German public banking sector is also destined to broad restructuring measures. But the structures cannot and should not be broken up too fast. The success of the IPO of Deutsche Post World Net AG is a tribute to this careful policy.

2.4 Conclusion

Powerful global trends are combining to enhance investment appeals of the post, express and logistics sector. Globalisation is well underway. The leading global integrators FedEx, UPS, TNT and Deutsche Post are in a pivotal position as the industry seeks to expand and globalise. EU Postal Liberalisation has stimulated industry consolidation. TPG and Deutsche Post's floatation has shown a way many other post office in Europe would follow in the next few years.

---

[80] See Süddeutsche Zeitung, Liberalisierung der EU-Postmärkte rückt in weite Ferne – Briefmonopol wird verlängert, February 10th, 11th 2001, # 34, p. 27.

Some elements of similarity between the two-privatisation processes can be underlined. Both companies had chosen an international placement even if they were moved by different reasons. The Dutch market is smaller than the German and the openness to international exchanges, which had characterised the Netherlands since ages, was reflected in this experience, too. Besides DPWN has chosen an IPO but it has excluded some countries (for example France) from sale.

Both companies did not follow the French theoretical approach of having a "*noyau dur*" in their investors. TPG had shown a strong preference for institutional investors, having only 17% of its shares owned by private shareholders. DPWN was interested in having a strong retail investors' base. Consequently, it had clauses to encourage them, such as bonus shares. About 145,000 DPWN employees acquired shares through an employee share program[81]. Nothing similar could be found in Dutch experience even in spite of the adoption of an option plan for workers.

Both companies regarded financial markets conditions as marginal factors to their floatation. TPG's placement followed the steps fixed by the Dutch government which main goal was to achieve a better management of the company through the markets. TPG went to public when the re-organisational process, started in 1989, was concluded. The Deutsche Post was involved in a long process, too, which drove from a state – owned entity generating losses to high profitable joint – stock company. TPG's floatation was a benchmark for DPWN and it had increased the pace of the privatisation process.

One of the major differences between the two privatisation was the fact that TPG started to be floatated from a splitting on a 1:1 ratio of KPN's shares, while Deutsche Post had been already separated from the telecom company before the floatation. DPWN went public when the market was already used to the performance of a postal incumbent but it had to introduce itself to the potential investors. When KPN's shares were splitted, the main goal of the road-shows was to explain the reason why a new company was going to be floated separately since the investors were already used to KPN's performances. German investors were positively influenced by the successful quotation of Deutsche Telekom and autonomously decided to buy shares of a postal incumbent. That was not the case of KPN's shareholders who had shares of TPG from one day to the other without having decided to buy them. As it could be understood from the initial situation the goals of the road – show were different.

Besides the reason which led to the floatation of TPG and DPWN partially differs. In 1990, after the re-unification of Eastern and Western Germany, the government didn't want the German post office to generate losses anymore. The government's attitude drove the privatisation process cutting debts of the post office of East Germany.

---

[81] See Elliott R., Flower S. (2001).

In the Dutch case, the impact of new technologies on labour intensive activity and the acquisition of TNT paved the way to a strong re-engineering process. The EU legislation undoubtly played a role but mainly in the final period, since it was a political issue subjected to slowdown by Member States to protect national interest.

Both TPG and DPWN face regulatory risk. At a domestic level rules become tough as the Regulatory Authority's control becomes more severe. At an international level in the medium term they face the threat of USPS, the US Post Office, which would move to other countries strong of its monopoly position in the domestic market.

Global post, express and logistics companies are entering a period of rapid revenue growth, concentrated towards the major players. Both FedEx and UPS have found the going tough in trying to establish solid market position in Europe to add to their core US strengths. This reflects both differences in the marketplace (customer need for services, geographical and demographic differences) and an aggressively combative response by European competitors seeking to defend their home turf.

TPG and DPWN, as integrators, differ from express operators such as FedEx and UPS and telecom company, as KPN or DT, since they link different business areas and are not specialized on single markets.

First analysing global express operators, Federal Express Corporation's initial public offering was on April 12, 1978 at $24.00 per share. Federal Express began trading on the New York Stock Exchange on December 28, 1978. FedEx Corp. common shares have split five times with a ratio 2 for 1 in 1978, 1980, 1983, 1996 and 1999[82]. United Parcel Service went public through an IPO with the issuance of 109,400,000 shares of Class B common stock on November 10, 1999 on the New York Stock Exchange. The offering price was $50.00 per share[83] and it was under priced.

Since start of this year, both express operators and logistics plays have seen their valuation multiples contract on the expectation of a more prolonged and deeper U.S. slowdown. TPG and DPWN benefit from their greater exposure to the higher growth European market.

---

[82] http://www.fedex.com, June 3rd, 2001.
[83] http://www.corporate-ir.net, June 2nd, 2001.

Figure 2.12

New York Stock Exchange, price of UPS' and FedEx's shares since November 1999.

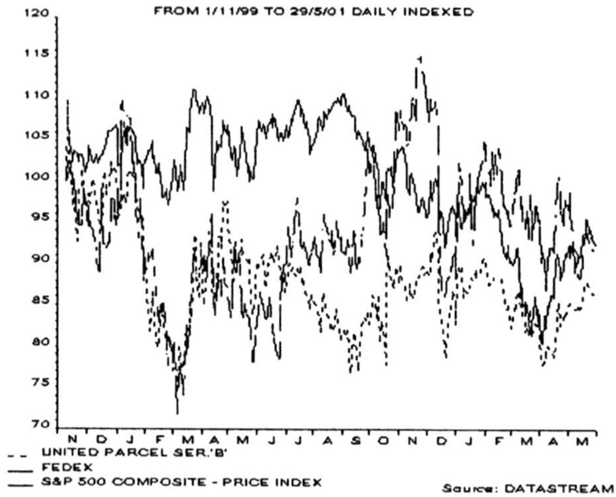

From the analysis of the performance of telecom and postal companies' floatation, KPN and Deutsche Telekom looks to have far over performed TPG, DPWN, AEX and DAX during year 2000. In the same year KPN had debt amounting to € 21.9bn[84]. Subsequently, the slowdown of U.S. economy and the crisis of Internet related sector, the postal incumbents have recently benefited from being considered as a defensive growth stock due to the utility like characteristics of the mail business. While in the Dutch case, the government informed the Parliament that it considered the State's withdrawal from KPN desirable, in view of the changed circumstances in the telecommunications market, the State of Germany still own 43% of shares.

TPG and DPWN show less volatility than telecom shares, with a stronger financial position. However TPG's mail activities contain a higher proportion of higher growth direct and international mail activities compared to DPWN's. TPG also operates in the faster growth, higher barrier to entry areas of express and logistics[85]. The task of integrating DPWN's acquired logistics and express assets remains difficult. Danzas AEI has lost some significant managerial staff in the first half of year 2001. In addition, with the liberalisation process in Europe potentially getting more impetus, some concerning regards the revenue outlook for DPWN's mail activities[86].

---

[84] See KPN Annual Report 2000.

[85] See Allchurch D., Bennett R., Cater J., Crawley O., Kent R. (2001).

[86] See Allchurch D., Borghetto M., Kent R. (2001).

Figure 2.13
Amsterdam Stock Exchange, price of KPN and TPG shares starting from the split (on the left); Frankurter Börse price of DT and DPWN shares starting from DPWN floatation (on the right).

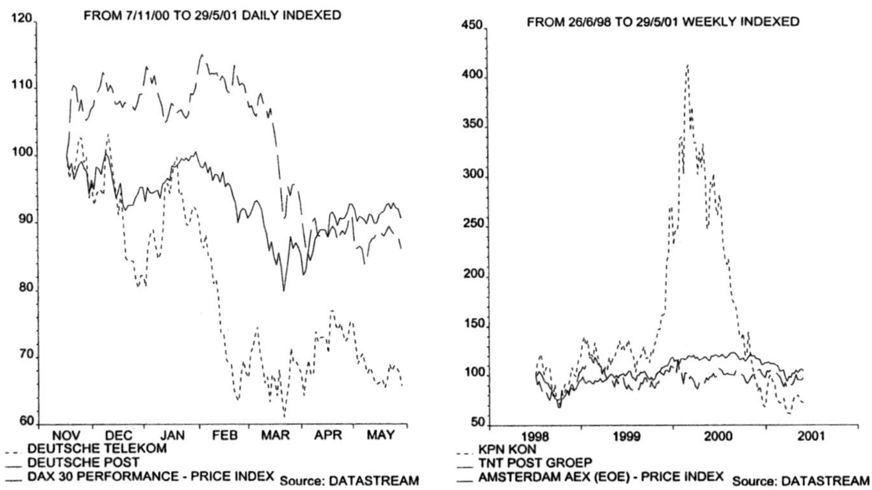

However, the link between telecom and postal companies is still present. KPN Telecom is partner of Postkantoren, the 50:50 joint venture between TPG and Postbank, for mobile and fixed-line phone products and phone-cards[87]. DPWN reached an agreement on July 4th 2000 with Deutsche Telekom to outsource corporate activities to each other. DPWN transfers IT and network operations to Deutsche Telekom, while it transfers the areas of logistics and printing services to DPWN[88].

2.5 References

Anderloni L. (1999), Methods of Privatisation. Optimisation of the Objectives of Sellers and Investors, and the Role of Financial Institutions, in Ruozi R.,

[87] See Allchurch D., Bennett R., Cater J., Crawley O., Kent R. (2001).
[88] See Allchurch D., Borghetto M., Kent R. (2001).

Anderloni L. (eds) (1999): Banking Privatisation in Europe, Springer, Heidelberg.

ALLCHURCH D., BORGHETTO M., KENT R., (2001): Deutsche Post World Net, Morgan Stanley Dean Witter Equity Research, April 6.

ALLCHURCH D., BENNETT R., CATER J., CRAWLEY O., KENT R. (2001): TNT Post Group, Morgan Stanley Dean Witter Equity Research, March 16.

BÖRSE ONLINE (2000): Rückblick auf die Börsenwoche, 47/00, p. 27.

BÖRSE ONLINE (2001): Das war 2000, 02/01, pp. 12-15.

BÖRSE ONLINE (2001): DAX mit zwei Gesichtern, 02/01, pp. 18-20.

BÖRSENBERICHT (2000): Deutsche Post World Net AG: Ziel Weltmarktführerschaft, 12/00, p. 6, BfG Bank.

BÖRSENBRIEF (2000), Baden-Württembergische Bank, Nr. 18, 04.10.2000.

BÖRSENBRIEF (2000), Baden-Württembergische Bank, Nr. 19, 16.10.2000.

BÖRSENBRIEF (2000), Baden-Württembergische Bank, Nr. 20, 02.11.2000.

BÖRSENBRIEF (2000), Baden-Württembergische Bank, Nr. 21, 15.11.2000.

BÖRSENBRIEF (2000), Baden-Württembergische Bank, Nr. 22, 04.12.2000.

BÖRSENZEITUNG (2000): Greenshoe bei Post-IPO voll ausgeübt, 19/12/2000.

BUNDESMINISTERIUM DER FINANZEN (Federal Ministry of Finance), (1995): Bericht zur Verringerung von Beteiligungen des Bundes (report on reducing the Federal Republic's stake in Companies), Bonn.

BUNDESMINISTERIUM DER FINANZEN (Federal Ministry of Finance), (2000): Perspektiven der Privatisierungspolitik des Bundes (perspectives of the Federal Republic's privatisation policy), Bonn.

BUNDESMINISTERIUM FÜR WIRTSCHAFT UND TECHNOLOGIE (Federal Ministry of Economics and Technology), (1995): Orientierungen für eine Postreform III: Gutachten des Wissenschaftlichen Beirats beim Bundesministerium für Wirtschaft, Bonn.

BÜSCHGEN, H. E. (ed.), (1998): Bankbetriebslehre, Wiesbaden, 5th.

DEIPENBROCK, G. (1991): Die Deutsche Bundespost auf dem europäischen Binnenmarkt, Baden-Baden.

DEUTSCHE POST WORLD NET AG (1999): Annual Report 1999, Bonn.

DEUTSCHE POST WORLD NET AG (2000): Interim Report 01.01.2000-30.06.2000, Bonn.

DEUTSCHE POST WORLD NET AG (2000): Verkaufsprospekt (Global Offering), 18/11/2000 Bonn.

DIE TELEBÖRSE (2000): Die Post kommt, 40/00, pp. 44-48.

ELLIOTT R., FLOWER S. (2000): European Postal Companies in the Spotlight, Schroder Salomon Smith Barney Equity Research, January 19th.

FRANKFURTER ALLGEMEINE ZEITUNG (2000): Treueaktien für private Post-Aktionäre, 07/10/2000.

FRANKFURTER ALLGEMEINE ZEITUNG (2000): Die Post stellt schon für 2000 eine Dividende in Aussicht, 31/10/2000.

FRANKFURTER ALLGEMEINE ZEITUNG (2000): Aus Postlern werden Aktionäre, 20/11/2000.

FRANKFURTER ALLGEMEINE ZEITUNG (2001): Mühsamer Start der Post-Aktie im Dax, 20/03/2001.

GROßFELD B. (1990): Deutsche Post Postbank - Struktur und Aufgaben, Tübingen.

GRUBER D., VON STEIN J.H. (1999): Privatisation in the German Banking Sector, in in Ruozi R., Anderloni L. (eds) (1999): Banking Privatisation in Europe, Springer, Heidelberg.
HANDELSBLATT (2000): Post lockt mit Treue-Aktien und Rabatten für Privatanleger, 09/10/2000.
HAWKINS D., MURPHY S. (2001a): Deutsche Post World Net, Nomura Equity Research, January 10th.
HAWKINS D., MURPHY S. (2001b): Deutsche Post World Net, Nomura Equity Research, January 25th.
HAWKINS D., MURPHY S. (2000): Global post, express and logistics, e-fulfilment accelerates growth, Nomura Equity Research, May 12nd.
HERRMANN E. (1986): Die Deutsche Bundespost – Kommunikationsunternehmen zwischen Staat und Wirtschaft, Baden-Baden.
IRELAND D., GREEN K., BRZESKWINSKI K. (2001): TPG, ABN-AMRO Equity Research, February 23rd.
JÄGER B. (1994): Postreform I und II, Köln.
KIRCHHOF F. (1990): Tätigkeitsfelder der Deutschen Bundespost Postbank, Berlin.
KPN Annual Report 2000.
MAGUIRE R., MONS J.K. (2000): TNT Post Groep, UBS Warburg Global Equity Research, September 15th.
OECD (1993): Methods of Privatising Large Enterprises, OECD, Parigi.
PILLEY O., ANDERLONI L. (1999): European Post Offices in Financial Services. Competitors or Strategic Partners ? Lafferty Publications Ltd., Dublin.
PARKER D. (1998): Privatisation in the European Union, Routledge.
REUTERS NEWS SERVICE (2000): Post-Emission bereits überzeichnet, 05/11/2000.
REUTERS NEWS SERVICE (2000): Post-Aktie zum Börsendebüt leicht über Ausgabekurs, 20/11/2000.
REUTERS NEWS SERVICE (2000): Zumwinkel – In fünf Jahren Post-Vollprivatisierung möglich, 20/12/2000.
RUOZI R., ANDERLONI L. (eds) (1999): Banking Privatisation in Europe, Springer, Heidelberg.
SANDERSE M., RIPPER A., STEEGERS P. (2001): TNT Post Group, Merrill Lynch Equity Research, January 3rd.
SPELTHAHN, S. (1994): Privatisierung natürlicher Monopole, Berlin.
STOLZ, C. (1998): Nachfrageorientierte Emissionspolitik mit Bookbuilding, Bern.
SÜDDEUTSCHE ZEITUNG (2001): Liberalisierung der EU-Postmärkte rückt in weite Ferne – Briefmonopol wird verlängert, 10, 11/02/2001.
TNT POST GROUP, Annual Reports 1997, 1998, 1999, 2000.
VOIGT, H.-W. (1995): Bookbuilding – Der andere Weg zum Emissionskurs, in Die Bank, 6/95, pp. 339-343.
VWD Vereinigte Wirtschaftsdienste GmbH, „Aktie Gelb" gibt solides Börsendebüt", 20/11/2000.
WINDISCH, R. (Ed.), (1987): Privatisierung natürlicher Monopole im Bereich von Bahn, Post und Telekommunikation, Tübingen.

Interviews

Mr. R. Goethart, Public Affairs, TNT Post Group N. V., 2 April 2001, Brussels.
Mr. C. de Weerd, Nepostel, 4 April 2001, The Hague.

Data bank

Bloomberg
DataStream
Il Sole 24 Ore

Web sites

TNT Post Group: http://www.tntpost-group.com.
PTT – Post: http://www.ptt-post.nl.
TNT Group: http://www.tnt.com.
KPN: http://www.kpn.com.
Deutsche Telekom: http://www.dtag.de.
ING: http://www.ing.com.
Postbank: http://www.postbank.nl.
Fedex: http://www.fedex.com.
UPS: http://www.ups.com.
UBS Warburg: http://www.ubswarburg.com/researchweb.
Amsterdam Stock Exchange: http://www.aex.nl.
Frankfurter Börse: http://kurse.exchange.de.
London Stock Exchange: http://londonstockexchange.com.
New York Stock Exchange: http://cgi.nyse.com.

3

The Posts: Role and Position in the Financial Services Industry

Luisa Anderloni

3.1 Foreword

In the European countries' tradition the postal system plays, or used to play up until recently, an important role in the supply of retail payment banking services and deposit collection. The presence of a capillary network of branches, i.e. of contact points with the general public, has been an important factor which, alongside the image of trust and safety the institution conveyed, initially encouraged the Post to choose these activity areas and later supported their development. In many situations, however, the potential of this network is starting to be questioned, in the sense that some are beginning to wonder whether it represents a strategic opportunity or, on the contrary, an obsolete channel by now, too economically intensive in terms of management costs in many locations. This also leads to questioning the role of the Post for the future in the supply of financial services.

One of the factors which supported, in the past, the development of the Posts in the area of payment service activities, mention should also be made of the public service vocation of postal systems which meant that Post Offices were naturally regarded as "cash desk service" for the reception of payment in favour of public administration and organisations.

Mention should also be made, in other situations, of the social aim of promoting savings among less wealthy social groups and the channelling of resources thus collected for the financing of the public sector, to support the State treasury or to the benefit of investment for social purposes. There is no doubt that the development of economic systems and the structure of modern financial systems have changed the operational perspectives with respect to the past.

The historical experience is no doubt useful to understand the development of the Posts in Europe as far as financial services are concerned, even though institutional and market changes in the 90's led to a reflection on the appropriateness of traditional intervention strategies, and in some cases, even to questioning the continuing of activities in the sector. The strengths and weaknesses of the Posts in the different areas of financial intermediation and in the different market segments are undergoing unceasing changes and the very development in the structure of financial systems and operational methods requires a kind of updating which is not always easy task.

Therefore, in order to evaluate the Post's potential within the financial service system, first of all an analysis of the general background needs to be carried out, and this on the basis of some considerations related to:

1. the on-going changes in the banking sector as a whole, considering the growing inter-connection and overlapping between banking, financial and insurance activities;
2. the competitive pressures and institutional changes with reference to the postal sector.

The analysis of the position of the Post in the supply of financial services in Europe and of on-going trends is divided into the following issues: the historical experience acquired by the Post in banking activities in Europe (§ 3.2); the drivers for change in banking systems (§3.3)[1] in order to acquire the necessary tools to understand the strategic choices for the new market conditions (§ 3.4).

3.2 The Historical Models of the Post Banking Services Supply

3.2.1 Introduction

The origin of access and development of the European postal systems in the financial sector are in some cases common to one another and in other cases they are diversified, with subsequent developments which led to typical development paths. Generally speaking, a distinction can be made in Europe between two different models which establish themselves over the years: the banking and the administrative model.

In the banking model, the activities related to the provision of financial services are controlled by an entity other than the public administration, which deals with the postal activity per se. They are attributed to an ad hoc juridical subject - often a private-law company - belonging to the Government or, more rarely, to the postal Administration. In some cases, public shareholding was later eliminated or reduced with the transfer of shares to private subjects. This means that the financial services supplied by Post Offices are run by banking subjects, which adopt the status of a bank and are thus subject to the norms for this category of operators. Therefore they are on the same level as other banking operators in terms of operations and competitiveness. This model does not involve the participation of postal institutions in the financing of public requirements. The lending activity

[1] The institutional changes in the postal activity are analysed in detail in Chapter 1 of this volume.

is carried out on the free market, usually giving priority to retail-type market segments, in line with the nature of the customers served on the deposit taking side and of the payment instruments on offer.

This is the model which is typically found in the United Kingdom, in the Netherlands and in the Postbanks of the Nordic countries.

In the administrative model, on the other hand, the activities related to the provision of services in the financial sector are related to the public administration. This means that they are part of public functions and in particular the funds raised by the Posts are devoted to the financing of public utility works and to covering the Government expenditures. The financial services supplied by the Posts are not subject to banking legislation and are run following different rules than those related to banking institutions. In particular, administrative criteria are followed for the definition of applicable products and prices.

The administrative model prevailed in France, in Italy and initially in Germany.

As will be shown by the following analysis, origins are often common in all countries and can be traced back to the same pattern, whereas in the twentieth century the experiences became more diverse and organised according to the two above mentioned models. It is also worth mentioning that the financial activity of postal systems started and was consolidated with norms and statutes designed as part of financial market regulations which were radically different from those of the 90's and of the beginning of this century. In particular, up until the end of the 70's, competition in European banking systems was generally regarded as a threat systems stability. The entry and chartered regulation, the separation between market sectors and the setting up of special regimes for credit institutions with specific missions were all subordinated to the main objective of stability. Market surveillance was of a structural type, with political-administrative intervention to direct credit and, in many cases, public ownership was widespread also in the banking sector. Efficiency was not regarded as a priority because, in any case, it was subordinated to the stability of the system and functionality with respect to the need of mobilising saving and financing the economy.

This explains the reason why administrative and banking models for the organisation of the Post banking activity were both developed by generally applying special regimes with respect to the organisation of similar activities performed by other subjects. Only recently has the situation become more homogeneous, following the establishment of a market culture.

3.2.2 The Experiences Inspired by the Banking Model

The experience in Great Britain

The experience in Great Britain is really unique. As a matter of fact, the Commonwealth reality is such that the postal system has been obliged to manage an international network of relationships world-wide. Therefore, the positioning of the bank model seems not to match with the other subjects of the same type. Nevertheless, provided some simplifications, we can consider this positioning as an appropriate choice.

In Great Britain the Post started its banking activities at the end of the eighteenth century with payment services. The aim was that of facilitating the transfer, in a safe and convenient way, of small sums to soldiers and sailors. This is how operations started up and, at the end of the nineteenth century, the system was also used by the British Government to provide pensions as well as other subsidies and contributions. Furthermore, the postal system could also be used to pay taxes without any commission being applied.

At the same time, the experience in the collection of savings through Post Office branches was being developed. In 1861, the British Government set up the "Post Office Saving Bank", which was simply a brand name for a saving scheme, aimed at promoting saving by workers so that they could "*provide for themselves against adversity and ill health*" and to channel it through the Ministry of Treasury in order to finance public spending. The capillary distribution of the postal network made it possible to reach the least favoured social groups and to offer the product throughout the national territory, while the guarantee from the Government was an important strength. The two aims survived over time and the range of products on offer was expanded in 1916 with the Savings Certificates and then in 1956 with the Premium Bonds.

In 1969 the first important structural change took place: the Post Office Savings Department became a separate Government department, controlled by the Ministry of Treasury and it was renamed "National Savings". Therefore, the Post Office was entrusted with a distribution function, while the product range started to be expanded in order to satisfy and meet the requirements expressed by the market, both in terms of saving / investing and from the side of the Treasury[2].

On 1st July 1996, the second relevant structural change took place, when the National Savings took on the status of Executive Agency for the Chancellor of the Exchequer. The guarantee of the Treasury was preserved, but the status of agency guaranteed greater autonomy in ordinary management. The strategic role of the Post was confirmed by the critical revision completed in the year 2000, on the occasion of the five-year Treasury evaluation which underlined the potential of the network to meet market requirements, while on the other hand setting the aim of cost reduction for the purpose of debt reduction[3].

---

[2] At the time there were 10 different saving and investment products on offer dedicated to the private saver segment including tax-free Savings Certificates, Premium bonds with a monthly premium of £ 1 million and Pensioners Bonds designed for customers who are over 60 years old, guaranteeing a monthly revenue.

[3] The products of the National Savings will continue to be guaranteed by the Government which is still in charge of key decisions, including those concerning interest rates and conditions for new products. In the same way the Chief Executive of the National Savings Agency will still be fully responsible towards Government and Parliament.

What is to be stressed is the fact that the operations of the postal branches were traditionally paper-based and oriented towards transactions rather than customer relations. The technological updating activity of the National Savings was started in 1999, by means of a fifteen-year agreement with Siemens Business Services. It is aimed at providing computer support to financial operations and to tax payment, with more rapid response times, greater flexibility in products and their commercialisation also through channels such as the telephone and the Internet.

From the payment services point of view, at the end of the '60s, important structural and organisational changes got under way with an expansion of the service range. In 1968 the National Giro was opened, which was meant to be a new postal service for funds transfer where all accounts were centralised and managed by the Giro-centre in Lancashire. The aim was to offer alternative channels, at a low cost, rapid and available in a capillary way on the territory as a means of contrasting the monopoly of the main clearing banks[4]. Initially the service was used for the provision of "Unemployment Benefit Payments", but was later extended to other areas: in 1970 a Business Deposit service was introduced for corporate customers; in 1971 a first report on the experience was drawn up which led the Government to support the continuation of the service and, in the same year, the Local Authority Rent Collection was introduced. At the same time, using the instrument of advantageous conditions, the payments of salaries and wages through the Giro was promoted. From an organisational point of view, once the activity was started in 1972, the Giro gradually became more independent, being managed as a separate business within the Post Office, and in 1973 also the administration of postal orders was transferred from the Post Office to the Giro.

As far as the range of services supplied by the Giro is concerned, the operational possibilities are extended because the business customers can make deposits with mixed transaction purposes, in cash and with cheques; international giro operations are also introduced thanks to the inter-operation with other countries. In 1976 the Post Office Banking Service Act opened up the competition between the Giro systems and the banks for fund transfer services on behalf of the Treasury. At the same time, the Giro system was authorised to grant loans and to pay interest on deposits. On this basis the possibility was introduced, for some segments of the private clientele and for selected customers consisting of companies, to use a limited amount of overdraft. Also from a formal point of view the transformation of the activities into those of a bank was continued: in 1978 the name was changed from National Giro to Nationalgirobank, in 1979 the status of bank was adopted and the postcheque service introduced. In 1980, then, the extension of the service range went through the preparation of loan packages for smaller enterprises for sub-postmasters and the introduction of debit orders on the account as well as with the possibility of transfers to other banks. In 1983, with the admission of Girobank as associate member of the Committee of London Clearing Bank, the complete integration was obtained between postal payment

---

[4] See Channon D.F. (1977), p. 38.

circuits, managed by the Girobank, and the banking circuits of the four clearing banks. In 1985 the network LINK was also launched, with Girobank among its founding members, and the BP/EFTPOS service was started in 1987.

In 1985 the private legal form (plc) was adopted, emphasised in later years with a campaign to promote the brand; this paved the way for substantial privatisation of the system. In 1988, in view of a particularly brilliant balance sheet result of 23.5 million £, the intention was announced to dispose of the bank. The offer chosen was that of Alliance & Leicester Building Societies, because the Building provided the best opportunities to exploit the synergies between the two banking groups and the best opportunities for the agreement to use the network of postal branches. Initially the agreement also included the exclusive use of the postal channel to supply the Girobank services. Later on with the new agreement signed in 1998 for a duration of 8 years, the basic operation areas were confirmed, including the handing out of cash, the payment of subsidies and pensions, standing orders, as well as personal transactions although not exclusively, whereas the exclusive relation is confirmed for the operations with corporate customers.

So, the Post Office was able to establish business relations for the distribution from post branches of services also from other banks, including those of Co-operative Bank, Lloyds TSB and Abbey National. According to the provisions in these agreements, customer relations are usually started at the bank agency, while day-to-day operations can also be performed at Post Offices. This type of organisation clearly gives banks greater flexibility in the rational use of their own branch network, because they can also avail themselves of support from the Post Offices.

From the point of view of the payment of bills in Great Britain the competition is really very keen, not only from the banking sector but also through agreements with the providers of the utilities themselves who adopt pre-paid cards or debit cards which can be used at the terminals located in retail outlets.

Girobank and Post Office play an essential role in the passage of cash, especially of commercial distribution, therefore they are essential partners for the supply of ATMs. The ATM cash dispenser network is expected to increase significantly as a consequence of the rationalisation strategies of the bank network which will lead to the closing of a large number of agencies and to the promotion of self-service operations.

It is also worth mentioning that in 1997 Alliance & Leicester abandoned the status of mutual benefit society, choosing the legal form of plc and started to be quoted, entering soon in the FTSE 100 index. Rumours occasionally circulate about other commercial banks' intention to try to take-over Alliance & Leicester: the access to the postal network and to the customer relation portfolio of Girobank looks particularly appealing from a strategic point of view.

At the moment, Girobank plc has its own network with about 300 branches and customers can have access to account services through the whole network of the

Post Office. As part of the banking group it performs the function of specialist for relations with corporate customers[5].

The delays in the automation of the Post Office, due to the absence of investment in this area during the70's and 80's and to the subsequent slowdown experienced by the Horizon project, started in 1996[6], also had repercussions on the development of financial services. Its volumes are decreasing[7] and the Benefits Agency has terminated the agreement for the payment of pensions at Post Offices; this means that as of 2005 all operations will be carried out through direct crediting on the account. This will have a significant economic impact because this activity accounted for as much as 40% of the revenues generated from the branch network.

As for the extension of the range of financial services supplied from the Post Office, for the offer of insurance products, the adopted solution is the commercial agreement with the company Royal & Sun Alliance. The offer consists of standardised life insurance products (an experiment was started in 1995) and of some elementary damage areas such as personal accidents, protection of the household income, payment of bills, risk management for the house (since 1998).

Generally speaking for the supply of financial services at the Post Office the market target is the lower customer segment, people who have no other relation with financial institutions, pay particular attention to prices, clear conditions, and favour face-to-face relations with the sales and assistance staff.

[5] On its web site the parent company refers visitors to Alliance-Leicester, for products and services devoted to personal customers, and to the Girobank in the case of those designed for business customers. The latter distinguishes between the following service categories: Business banking (customers divided into smaller businesses, large businesses and clubs & societies as well as underlining the supply of electronic banking), Paybill; Sovereign and Revenue Collection Services.

[6] See also Chapter 1, § 1.4 in this volume.

[7] As shown in Table 3.1, since 1996 there has been a marked downward trend, with current values being lower than those registered in 1994.

Table 3.1

Transaction volumes at Post Office branches (data in million £)

	1994*	**1995***	**1996***	**1997***	**1998***	**1999***
Girobank	258	271	321	247	225	207
Pensions and Allowances	896	887	962	898	863	831
National Savings	26	24	23	22	20	19
Telephone Bill Paid	39	39	39	39	38	38
Bureau de Change	--	--	--	1	2	2

* Fiscal year ending March 31st

Source: The Post Office Annual Report.

The experience in the Netherlands

In the Dutch experience the activity of postal deposit collection through a banking structure dates back to 1881 with the creation of the State Postal Savings Bank (Rijkspostsspaarbank), while the activity of fund transfer and postal payment systems was started in 1918 through the Postcheque-en-Girodienst. A few years later, in 1927, another State owned bank was created, the Nederlandese Middenstands Bank-NMB, for the financing of small and medium-sized enterprises.

Both Postal Saving Bank and Postcheque-en-Girodienst operated using Post Office branches as distribution channels, but due to the constraints imposed also by existing regulations they could offer a limited range of services which even partly overlapped; therefore, in 1986, the two entities were merged to create Postbank, a commercial bank still subject to some limitations (for example it could not act as stockbroker and it did not have access to the wholesale market). From a juridical point of view Postbank adopts the private law structure, even though its only shareholder is the Government. The distribution through Post Office branches, continues on the basis of a commercial agreement. In order to allow the bank to operate in a comprehensive way like all other commercial banks, it is decided to find a bank with a complementary profile in terms of operations. The NMB-Bank mentioned above had the potential to be the third bank in the country, but its penetration into the personal customer segment was limited. This meant that it had the necessary complementary requirements.

In 1989 the concentration between the two groups with a public base was completed with the creation of the NMB-Postbank Group. At the beginning the two brand names were kept and the two entities continued to operate as independent business units, in spite of the problems encountered due to the different managerial cultures. The advantages were related to the possibility for NMB to gain access to cheaper financing sources through Postbank and for Postbank to use the NMB expertise for the lending activities. The two together were able to take advantage of the economies of scale for the management of payment services.

In 1992 NMB Bank changed its name and became ING Bank.

At the same time the insurance sector history with a public base developed with the merger, in 1963, between the Netherlands Insurance Company and the National Life Insurance Bank. Both the companies reached a consolidated experience and tradition, the former created in 1845 and the latter in 1863. By the merge the Nationale-Nederlanden has been created. The results were satisfactory and the new entity achieved substantial growth both domestically and through external acquisitions; it reached the top position in the insurance sector in the Netherlands, heading a multinational group with subsidiaries in the United States, Canada and Australia, which was able to generate more than half of its revenues abroad. The distribution of insurance products was developed mainly by means of agreements with independent brokers.

During the second half of the 80's the distinction between banking and insurance activities started to become less clear-cut with the first experiences of bank-insurance. On the basis of this vision of a development of the markets towards banking-insurance groups, in 1991 an important group was created combining an insurance component (National-Nederlanden) with a banking element (NMB-Postbank Group) under the denomination International Nederlanden Group-ING with a lion in its brand. At the time of the creation of the group, the shareholding of the Dutch Government in NMB Postbank Group had gone down to 49% and dropped to 8.2% with the merger[8]. Following subsequent dismissal operations, the shareholding of the State decreased even further below 1%.

During the time the Postbank developed its own commercial functions through direct marketing and long-distance channels as a distinctive feature. About 60% of Dutch households has an account with Postbank, whereby the contacts are kept by mail, telephone and, more recently, via Internet[9]. This distribution strategy is by now well-established, being at least ten years in advance with respect to other banking experience. It has been designed with a far-sighted approach, taking advance of the connection with the public telephone group providing remote services (call centres, telephone kiosks inside the branches, internal telephone network, remote communication infrastructures and ATMs), as well as the link with the postal company for the exchange of documents by mail. Postbank has a substantial market share also in the management of payment services for small and medium-sized companies in the Netherlands.

The Postbank brand name was strengthened with campaigns to promote the image and communicate the gradual expansion of the supply range; these initiatives have consolidated the already stable, efficient and convenient image of the financial services provided by the group. As for the pricing policies, they are geared towards reducing transaction costs, which was made possible by taking advantage of the economies of scale in a period when the postal system held a monopoly position in the management of the giro system as well as through the standardisation of services. With the advent of the direct channel, the pricing principle adopted was that of uniformity, regardless of the channel used for the transaction.

The range of products and services on offer is wide, covering the whole brokerage spectrum, from traditional to innovative payment systems, to deposit accounts and mutual investment funds, from credit to consumption and personal

---

[8] Since the regulations forbid the same subject from carrying out banking and insurance activities, the group structure was chosen with ING N.V. holding controlling ING Bank N.V. and ING Insurance. NV. and, in multiple stages, the other product and specialised companies by geographical market.

[9] The telephone connection structure is by far the most frequently used, while PC banking is still lagging behind in second position. The latter channel of communication is used mainly by young people and by people who are older than fifty and have a university-level education.

loans - the latter granted very quickly by means of a scoring system - and to mortgages. The offer is completed by life insurance products, property-causality insurance products and by the new discount securities brokerage service, which does not include advice services and is therefore the cheapest on the Dutch market.

In more recent times Postbank had to face the competition in the lower-market segment from Rabobank, a co-operative bank present especially in rural areas which has managed to penetrate the market segment where customers are less used to direct channels and prefer face-to-face relations.

Mention should finally be made of the fact that the network of Post Office branches is managed by Postkantoren, a joint venture between the postal company and Postbank. In this way the two partners are equally responsible for the elaboration of strategies to promote the economic management of the network in a framework of direct operation. The strategic answers are based on the modernisation of the structures, on choosing locations in high circulation areas and, especially, on expanding the range of services on offer, in close co-operation with KPN Telecom and with numerous public agencies (for example for the management of car documents, the elaboration of information on public services, the handling of statements from the Chambers of Commerce, as a ticket office and more)[10]. In the Dutch experience the postal-financial partnership is very successful and none of the conflicts that emerged in other countries between the postal and financial aspect have appeared.

The experiences in Nordic countries

Generally speaking Nordic countries have adopted the banking model. Postbanks were set up a long time ago in Sweden, Norway and Finland. A similar experience exists in Denmark with Postgiro, set up in 1920, which changed its name in 1991 to Girobank A/B and in 1996 merged with Sparkasse Bikuben, creating BG Bank. As of March 2001 it has become part of a major banking group and the relation with Post Denmark is developed on the basis of a commercial relation.

In Sweden two banking entities with a postal base have been set up over the years. In 1925 Postgirot was created with the aim of providing payment services in the Post Office circuit. In 1994, when Posten was transformed into a joint stock company, it took on the status of a bank, the new name Postgirot Bank AB and became subject to banking laws.

Actually the bank still keeps its original specialisation in the management of payment services, especially through the instrument of giro which is used for the settlement of utility bills. The giro service system can be traditional or electronic, in the latter case the payment order is passed on to Postgirot by telephone or via the Internet. It is worth mentioning at this stage that the Internet is widespread

---

[10] See Chapter 1, § 1.4 in this volume.

particularly in Nordic countries due to geographical and climate reasons, as well as to the economic development of the country and to the far-sighted approach adopted by employers for its dissemination. This means that banks have accessed this important business area and, in their turn, started a banking compensation system (giro) which also involves Postgirot as a bank. The price competition is extremely keen making it necessary to adopt more economical processes and to gain in terms of efficiency. For this reason also the Post started to discourage the traditional solution of payments in cash at the Post Office, by applying commissions that are relatively higher[11]. Postgirot has a substantial share in the market of bank transfers amounting to about 60-65% of the annual volume. About 90-95% of companies uses Postgirot for customer invoicing. In the past the Postbank managed cash desk services on behalf of the Government, but at the beginning of 1999 the RSV (Swedish National Tax Board) introduced a special tax account which meant that a substantial part of the tax payment flow was carried out by bank transfer, thus by-passing the Postgirot mediation, while the agreement for other treasury services for the Government was extended only until the end of 1999. There are still numerous agreements, however, for the supply of cash desk services to municipalities and regions.

The distribution of the Postgirot products took place on the basis of a commercial agreement which remained in place until July 2000, through the network of Post Office branches and through the travelling staff in rural areas belonging to Posten Sverige AB[12].

The second experience in postal banking is that of the postal Savings Banks, which at the end of the 70's merged with another public bank, Kreditbank, thus creating Bank PK. The Government decided to partially privatise the bank, keeping a 66% control share. Towards the end of the 80's PK merged with Nordbanken, another extremely dynamic Swedish bank which was also created through concentration processes. Later on the crisis of the bank, caused by the property sector, was solved also thanks to a disputed intervention by the Government which in 1992 took over its full control. In 1996, also following further merging processes, the recovery was successfully completed.

The commercial agreement, dating back to 1974, between Nordbanken and Posten AB aimed at selling savings products at Post Office branches was also kept in place. These are standardised products, dedicated to the middle market segment[13]. In 1996 a new partnership agreement was signed for a duration of five years aimed at modernising the banking services offered by the branch both in

---

[11] A study carried out by TEMO and commissioned by the National Agency for Post and Telecommunication concerning the way the giro service is used showed that 70% uses transfer communication by mail, 5% goes personally to the post office, 1% goes to the bank and 9% uses the Internet.

[12] Subsidiary of Posten AB in charge of managing the network.

[13] By means of indication it should be pointed out that, in 1995, the share in the turnover of current accounts, loans and savings products remunerated on the basis of the number of transactions amounted to 17% of the network management costs.

terms of cash and of saving, and also of financing using the Post brand name, i.e. "Postbanken". The offer takes place through the interaction between Post Office branches, with improved face-to-face services and with the support of telephone connections and call centres, and of Nordbanken banking branches. The customer segmentation strategy involves the migration of the more sophisticated clientele from Postbanken to Merita-Nordbanken, and on the other hand of the customers who require products that are standardised, easy to understand and cheap from Merita-Nordbanken to Postbanken. The support to the commercial function performed by Post Office branches is provided by staff training initiatives. The strategy proved to be successful, eroding market shares from the Savings Banks which traditionally served this market segment.

The agreement, however, was terminated in 1999 following a unilateral decision by Posten, so that the co-operation ended in March 2001.

The contribution to the turnover of the Posten AB group was significant[14], but the margins were becoming smaller[15]. The growing competition in the banking sector, the reduction of margins and the strategic approach focussing on the postal core business which involved the reduction of the branches[16] were the factors behind the decision taken by the management, and supported by the approval of the Government, to dismiss Postgirotbank AB[17].

The above mentioned decision by Posten to abandon the financial sector leads back to the question of a basic banking service supply in the country[18]. The agreement between Posten and the Swedish Government, renewed until March 2001, laid down that the Post should offer a cash service on a daily basis, known as basic offer[19], separate from the one available on a commercial basis. It also laid

---

[14] The share in the turnover (net of the infra-group services) was 14.1% in 1998 and 15.8% in 1999.

[15] The profit margin went down from 8% to 7.2%, as against 7.8% of the postal activity in 1999.

[16] The regulation and controls Authority for Post and Telecommunication in Sweden laid down that by 2005, the post office network should be reduced to a number of branches between 300 and 700.

[17] The range of potential candidates was wide, among them also GE Capital: Postgirot automatically offers access to an important market segment, in particular in the case of corporate customers. In June 2000 the buyer was found and the price set at 4 billion SEK. The choice fell on Bankgirot, which as already seen was the banking payment system that already competed with Postgirot on the market of fund transfers by giro. This competitive solution was basically neutral in the country because Bankgirot is controlled jointly by the four largest Swedish banks, while it consolidated the banking monopoly. As for the other banking activities managed by Postgirot, they will be sold because the four banks no longer have any interest in having joint control over them. The operation was subject to the approval of the Swedish Commission on Competition (KKB) and the outcome could be either the transfer to GE Capital or the introduction of a control system on prices to prevent the wrongful use ensuing from a monopoly position.

[18] For more details see Chapter 5 in this volume.

[19] It includes: payment operations originated or domiciled on a post office account, the paying-in and withdrawal of cash, as well as forms of payment for those who do not have an account (orders and giro supplied in cash).

down the prices applied to customers and the public contribution which the Post could benefit from for the commitment to keep branches open even if their operational levels were not satisfactory and, therefore at a loss.

The compensation mechanism actually dates back to the beginning of the 90's and it originally consisted of the two-day delay granted to Postgirot for the payment of the fiscality paid at its branches. This delay was later reduced to only one day; with the gradual reduction of interest rates, the indirect contribution thus supplied proved to be insufficient and therefore had to be integrated by a monetary flow[20].

In January 2000, the Government announced its decision to sell Postgirot and, upon termination of the distribution agreement with Merita-Nordbanken, the Post withdrew from the supply of financial services. In a country where particular attention was always paid to consumer needs, the decision was also examined by the authority for consumer protection which basically approved it. Taking into account the development in telecommunications and automation combined with the level of familiarity of the general population with the latter, it was decided to reduce the opening days of some branches to one a week or five a month and to reorganise the "luxury service", represented by the Post Office staff paying house visits in some rural areas. The above mentioned contribution allowed by the State, which was granted to the Post in the past, should be used more effectively in order to develop distribution channels in co-operation with other commercial entities, thus increasing the welfare of the population in low-density areas[21].

The Norwegian experience is somewhat similar, in the sense that the Norway Post Bank, set up in 1932, was transferred in 1999 to Den Norske Bank, a private bank which for a short time had entered the public area, as part of a rescue and recovery operation. Later on it was privatised and quoted on the stock exchange. However the brand name of the Postbank was kept separate, as were the operations geared towards the retail market segment. With the transfer of the Postbank to a private bank, therefore, there was no longer any right/duty to offer at least a basic service through the Post Office branch network. On the other hand a commercial agreement ending in May 2002 was signed with Den Norske Bank for the sale of financial products and services at Post Office branches, on the basis of a commercial logic. In this way Norway Post was allowed greater freedom in restructuring its branch networks, with a more widespread use of outsourcing solutions for the management of the network[22] combined with the possibility to develop the new postal strategy[23] as integrator for the offer of E-commerce

---

[20] The amount is about 300 mln SEK, later reduced 200 mln SEK in the years 1998-1999.

[21] The "Kassaservice" study was promoted by the Government in co-operation with the consumer Association Konsumentverket; it also provides alternative partnership scenarios between financial institutions, retail commerce distributors and other organisations whose activity is based also on the use of a network of contact points with customers. Mention should also be made of the fact that MeritaNordbanken has started a project for cash desk payment services at food stores and petrol stations.

[22] See Chapter 1 in this volume.

[23] See Hurlen J. (2001).

solutions. It will play the role of provider of communication, transport services, managing payment services and the certification of digital signatures. In the meantime it will reduce the weight of those branch services that have a lower added value.

In the Finnish experience the Post's banking activities started at the end of the nineteenth century under the Russian empire, with the aim of promoting saving and investment. In 1970 Postipankki, the public institution, adopted the bank status of commercial banks, even though it was still controlled by the Ministry of Finance and enjoyed unlimited guarantees by the Government. In 1996 it was transformed into a joint stock company, still controlled by the Government and ranked second on the market. All Finnish companies have an account with it.

In 1997, the merger of Postipankki and Finnish Export Credit produced Leonia, the second bank in Finland after the Swedish-Finnish group Meritanordbanken[24] which, in turn, also includes a post banking experience in Sweden as seen above. It is still fully owned by the Government, but after the merger with the insurance group Sampo, the Government shareholding went down to 43%, while the remaining 57% is owned by shareholders of the Sampo group, quoted on the stock exchange. Traditionally, Postpankki distributes its own products at Post Office branches on the basis of a commercial agreement, which later included Leonia with the concentration process[25].

The commercial agreement terminated in 2001, as a consequence of problems related to overlapping between the commercial network of Leonia and that of the Post. There was also a reduction in the profit margins for operations performed through the postal channels. Over time there also emerged difficulties in the commercialisation of more sophisticated and profitable products at Post Office branches, so that Leonia decided to open a dozen new agencies in the more densely populated areas and to focus on strengthening its virtual network. As far as the Post is concerned, it expects to be able to rationalise and downsize the branch network, because there are no constraints imposed on the geographical coverage to meet the financial requirements of customers for the provision of a universal service. The solutions suggested to meet the requirements related to the provision of basic banking services are similar to those presented in Sweden, while new agreements are being developed for the sale at Post Office branches of insurance; in particular negotiations are under way with the British insurance company CFI, the GE Capital group, interested in the postal channel also in other countries.

---

[24] In 2000 Meritanordbanken merged with Unidenmark, the second bank in Denmark in terms of size, thus confirming its interest in regional development in Northern Europe.

[25] By means of indication it should be pointed out that in 1998 Leonia paid the Finnish Post 480 million FIM for the use of Post Office branches as commercial channel, 300 million FIM in 1999 and 225 million FIM in the year 2000.

The Austrian experience

As for Austria, mentioned should be made of the experience of the Oesterreichische Postsparkasse (PSK), a bank which up until recently was entirely controlled by the Government. In the past it was a public-law institution guaranteed by the Government whose operations were limited to the household sector and payment services. Its activities included Government financing, providing credit to regional bodies, granting credits guaranteed by the Government, provinces and by the Vienna municipality, provided this was done in pool with other commercial banks. It also had the function of Government treasurer and could grant overdraft facilities for requirements in cash. In 1997 the bank was transformed into a joint stock company and took on the status of fully operational commercial bank. PSK currently sells its products and services through its network of 2,325 Post Office branches and with its own agents. The agreement with the Austrian Post is negotiated on a contractual basis and includes the supply of all basic services in every Post Office, whereas more sophisticated services with the assistance of financial advisors are provided only at the branches with more operations. Through the subsidiary Oesterreichische Post AG it participates in the supply of other financial services, including credit to enterprises. The group also created an insurance company, Postversicherung Ag, active since 1996 in the life and accident sectors, distributing mainly through the Post. It had been laid down that the Government could hand over up to 49% of the capital of Oesterreichische Postsparkasse and over time different dismissal options had been formulated. Indeed in the spring of 2000 the new Government decided in favour of complete privatisation and started taking the necessary legal steps in this direction, including changing the statute. The offer was made following the call for tender procedure and at the beginning there were four potential candidates: Bawag, Volksbanken, Raiffeisenbank and the German Deutsche Postbank. Only Bawag and Volksbanken then actually made an offer. The tender was won on the basis of the price: 17.6 billion ATS (Euro 1.29 billion) offered by a group led by Bawag[26] which thus gained entry to 2,300 Post Office branches with a portfolio of 600,000 customers.

The Belgian experience

Also Belgium recently started to look more carefully at the Postbank services. In this country, La Poste offered payment services through the instrument of the Giro and of Postcheques, brand names of products managed by the same post company. It also commercialised savings products from the CGER (the public social

[26] Bawag is the fourth Austrian bank and is partially controlled by the Trade Unions and by the German Bayerische Landesbank. PSK therefore has the following corporate structure: 75% Bawag and 25% a holding which includes the association of Austrian Trade Unions, Bayerische Landesbank, the travel agency Ruefa and the American Refco.

security's institutions). In 1995 a Postbank was established, under the name Banque de La Poste, in order to offer a wider range of services, with a joint partnership between La Poste and Fortis Bank, selected through a call for tender.

The intervention of the Post in the offer of financial services is included in the management agreement between the Government and the Post. The following services are mentioned when defining the mission of the postal institution aimed at meeting public interest requirements:

- deposits and payments on behalf of other financial institutions[27];
- offer of a current account service, without cash desk facilities, with debit card use and access to transfer services, domiciliation, standing orders and ATMs of the postal network[28].

These services are regarded as "public universal services" of a general nature, in the sense that they are not exclusively entrusted to the Post. On the other hand, there are "reserved public services", alongside the running postal services, which also include financial postal services, that is a range of payment services regulated by specific laws[29]. In April 1998 the integration of the Postcheque account into the Postbank was completed and since then current accounts, as happened in other instances, have been extremely successful.

The Banque de La Poste distributes its own products through a network of 1,400 Post Office branches on the basis of a commercial agreement and addresses the retail segment. This distribution policy has been accompanied, since 1999, by direct marketing actions. The Postbank has a lean structure: for its administrative activities the service provider is "La Poste" on the basis of an agreement which is regularly renewed, while for financial engineering and the design of new products it avails itself of the competence of Fortis Bank.

Also in this case, however, some competition problems are emerging owing to the overlapping of the services provided by Fortis Bank and the Postbank supply, at least in some sites. The situation is made more difficult in this case by the fact that the Banque de La Poste is still young and has not been able to give value to its own brand. Recently some rumors seems to indicate Fortis Bank willingness to acquire the remaining 50% of Postbank from La Poste. It would confirm the existence of problems mentioned before.

---

[27] Laid down by the law of 26 December 1956, art.3, par. f.

[28] The service in question is provided upon simple presentation of some form of identification and upon condition that the applicant is at least twelve years old. Considering that this is a social banking service, it can obviously be supplied only free of charge.

[29] See also art.2, §2, 2° which lays down: a) the issuing and payment of postal orders; b) the payment at home of old-age and survival pensions; c) the payment of attendance fees during elections; d) the printing and sale of licence stamps on behalf of the mixed Belgium-Luxembourg administrative Commission; e) the book-keeping of funds and papers of road fines; f) the distribution and payment of the papers from the Office national des vacances annuelles; g) the printing, sale, reimbursement, replacement and changing of fishing permits.

Also the Belgian group has entered the insurance sector with the participation in Assurances de La Post S.A. and Assurances de La Poste-Vie S.A in joint venture with the Axa group, which takes care of all back office activities[30], while the distribution function is entrusted exclusively to Banque de La Poste, through the Post Office branches.

The development model based on partnership solutions presents some difficulties due to the difference in strategies and corporate and market culture of the different institutions.

The German experience

At the beginning Germany followed the path of the administrative models, which it later rejected in order to reposition itself on the banking model.

In the case of Germany, the entry into the financial sector was relatively recent, with the "launching" in 1908 of the Giro service in 13 specialised offices, in spite of the strong opposition from the banking system. The crisis in the years of the great depression affecting the banking payment system also involved the Giro system which started to take off again in the period after 1932. The outcome of the Second World War and the division of the territory into the four occupied areas led to a fragmentation of the postal system as well as of financial services. At the beginning of the 50s Deutsche Bundespost was turned into a special administration of the Federal Republic. The offer of financial services was limited to payment services, deposits and to traditional postal savings books.

With the postal Reform of 1989 the Deutsche Bundespost was organised into three divisions: Deutsche Post, Deutsche Telekom and Postbank, each of them with joint aims of economic balance.

The operation system of Postbank was criticised by banks for the difference in regulations and the ensuing competition advantages. Even though in 1995 the Federal Court of appeal acknowledged that Postbank did not engage in anti-competitive activities, in the same year the second postal law was approved in Germany and as a consequence Postbank took on the full status of a bank.

This marked the shift towards the banking model of intervention by the Post in the supply of financial services.

Having thus solved, at least from a formal point of view, the contrast with the banking system because Postbank became a full member of the latter, there emerged the differences between Deutsche Post and Postbank. The former, aimed at increasing the profitability of the network, thought that in order to exploit to the full the synergies in the use of branches it was necessary to have full control and to introduce the banking company within the structure of the postal group; the

[30] The product policy is based on standardised products with a wide range of supply which includes life insurance also with specific plans for children's future, capitalisation products, saving-pension insurance, car insurance, person & vehicle insurance, house insurance and insurance against accidents.

latter maintained that the economic conditions of postal distribution were not in line with costs and the success strategy could be found in the development of alternative channels. The division of the postal activity on the one hand and of the banking-financial activity on the other without a shared and agreed strategy for the management of the branches, has therefore become an element of strategic weakness preventing the implementation of successful business policies.

In the autumn of 1995 Deutsche Post, together with Deutsche Bank and with the insurance group Swiss Re, tried to take over 75% of the capital with an offer of 3 billion DM. This was done in order to try and replicate the ING model, that is the setting up of an important banking-insurance group with pan-European development potential.

The question appeared to be complex, also from a political point of view because both organisations belonged to the German federal government.

A first step towards the solution of the dispute was the reduction of the payment made by Postbank to Deutsche Post for carrying out commercial branch function, while Deutsche Post was "remunerated" with the transfer, free of charge, of a 17.5% shareholding in Postbank. At the same time Postbank started to create its own network of bank branches, in order to increase its commercial autonomy, alongside the development of direct channels.

With the 1998 general elections the new Government found the strength to solve the problem for which, in spite of numerous rumours of different partnerships on the market, it had not been able to find a concrete solution. Following the recommendations made by international investment banks acting as advisors, it was acknowledged that the combination between Deutsche Post and Deutsche Postbank was strategically the best in the medium term and it was decided to transfer the remaining 82.5% to Deutsche Post against a payment of 4.325 billion DM (2,211 billion Euro), with the aim of quoting on the stock exchange in the medium term a share amounting to 50% minus one of the voting rights.

Deutsche Postbank is one of the largest banks operating in the retail segment in Germany[31] and has thus become part of the DWPN group. Within this framework, the Financial Services division was therefore created, with the main mission of providing a wide range of products, from standardised payment products to savings products, to insurance and investment. The strategic significance of the Financial Services division is shown by its division into three business areas: Private customers, Corporate customers and Financial markets. Postbank offers its services to all the offices of Deutsche Post and has a substantial portfolio of customers who take advantage of its telephone banking and on-line banking service (about 1.9 million accounts at the end of 1999)[32].

---

[31] At the end of 1999 the customer portfolio had 19.1 million savings accounts, 3.9 million current accounts, 1.9 million on-line/telephone accounts, for a total of 24.9 million accounts overall (Annual report 1999).

[32] The balance sheet structure shows, on the liability side, a greater weight of savings deposits with respect to other commercial banks, even though this trend is decreasing, and

In the area of mortgage credit, Postbank has been active since 1997 also as a broker on the basis of a commercial agreement with Wüstenrot, one of the oldest mortgage banks in the country which is still independent. The latter was about to become a commercial bank and in spite of the high capitalisation and productivity found difficulties in terms of marketing. Wüstenrot later created, with Württembergische Insurance, the insurance banking group W&W.

For the offer of insurance services in 1999 joint ventures were created with HDI[33] and PB Lebenversicherung and PB Versicherung were set up. These products are commercialised under the Post Bank brand name.

The portfolio management is entrusted to specialised units, entirely controlled by Deutsche Postbank[34].

At the beginning of the year 2000 Postbank acquired DSL Bank, thus replacing the federal Government and integrating the branch network with those of DSL Bank, more suitable for customer relations which require greater customisation.

---

on the asset side reduced loans to customers and substantial investments to other banks and to the security portfolio (See Table 3.2).

Table 3.2
The balance sheet structure of Deutsche Postbank

ASSETS	1995	1996	1997	1998	1999
Liquid funds	5,399	4,741	7,234	3,954	2,983
Due from banks	40,347	59,529	59,863	63,309	52,796
Due from customers	4,953	5,961	3,522	5,653	6,977
Securities	44,705	33,096	37,200	37,416	45,740
Other assets	3,817	3,461	3,636	3,747	8,794
Total	**99,221**	**106,788**	**111,455**	**114,079**	**117,291**
LIABILITIES & SHAREHOLDERS' EQUITY	**1995**	**1996**	**1997**	**1998**	**1999**
Savings deposits	57,055	59,799	60,723	62,699	57,600
Savings certificates, term deposits	5,962	9,584	9,615	10,808	15,743
Demand deposits	28,603	27,942	26,786	28,371	30,375
Capital and reserves	4,318	3,104	3,131	3,147	4,077
Other Liabilities and shareholders' equity	3,283	6,359	11,200	9,054	9,496
Total	**99,221**	**106,788**	**111,455**	**114,079**	**117,291**

In million DM.

[33] HDI – Haftpflichtverband der Deutschen Industrie is the fifth insurance group in Germany, specialising in the market segment for low-cost standardised products. The joint ventures with Postbank are on an equal standing. The range of products supplied includes pension coverage, car and home accidents, life insurance to cover credit facilities.

[34] Some with offices in Luxembourg (Deutsche Postbank Asset-Management S.A., Deutsche Postbank Capital-Management S.A, Deutsche Postbank Vermoegens-Management S.A), others in Bonn (Deutsche Postbank Investment Kapitalanlagegesellschaft mbH and Deutsche Postbank Privat Investment Kapitalanlagegesellschaft mbH).

Furthermore DSL within the postal group is able to develop its distinctive competencies in the area of mortgages, loans to companies and financial brokerage[35]. The on-line brokerage service was successfully started[36], with Postbank EasyTrade AG.

The strategy in the financial sector is to consolidate its position as a primary bank – also through commercial agreements and partnerships - in the retail segment and to develop the multi-channel activity through the expansion of the loan activity and of services to private customers, through the expansion of the product range for business customers, finally by strengthening the multi-channel orientation by strengthening direct channels, reducing overheads and increasing efficiency[37].

The Spanish experience

Also in Spain, initially, the Caja Postal de Ahorros belonged to the Public Administration[38] and only in 1977 did it become an independent body of financial nature, part of the public administration system. In July 1991 it took on the legal form of joint stock company, with the status of a bank. As of that date, for statistical purposes, it is therefore classified among private banks, rather than Savings Bank, even though it is 100% controlled by the Government and performs the typical operations of a Savings Bank geared towards retail collection and mortgage credit, being provided with a widespread banking network (more than 500 branches) in addition to postal branches. The adoption of the bank status was instrumental for the creation of the public banking structure set up in the Spring of 1991[39] and completed in the same year through the creation of the Corporation

---

[35] The shareholding thus increased from 81.3% to full control. DSL is the holding of a group which apart from the bank with offices in Bonn, owns a bank with offices in Luxembourg and one financial institution in Amsterdam.

[36] See Annual reports 1999 and 2000.

[37] The strategic restructuring led to a slow but steady downsizing of staff which from 17,156 (full and part-time overall average) in 1994 decreased to 11,796 in 1999 with a similar proportion of full time e part-time employees. The cost of the occupational element therefore went down from 1,843 million DM in 1995 to 1,354 million DM in 1999.

[38] The Decree of 19 March 1960 approved the Ordenanza Postal with character of Ley Delegante which confirmed the current structure of the Spanish Post. The postal service is defined as "public service under the Government's sovereignty" and the postal Administration is a specific branch of the central Administration of the State. The postal service is divided into two units: postal and banking services respectively. The latter include among others: Giro Postal, Cobro de efectos, Cheque Postal e Caja Postal de Ahorros.

[39] On the basis of the Royal Decree-Law of 3 May 1991 which was aimed at giving a new organisational structure to public banks in order to prevent the continuation of a public-type management approach and to create a diversified and well co-ordinated banking group. Later on the public shareholding in the group was reduced following privatisation after four public offerings. See Del Burgo S.S. – Turnabell Carrió R.(1999).

Bancaria de España group, later renamed Grupo Argentaria. The model initially adopted was a bank federation with a divisional structure for the management of the three macro areas of activity: banking, para-banking (financial, leasing and consumer credit) and non-banking (insurance, property and industrial shareholding). As a consequence the Caja Postal was a specialised bank, alongside four other banking institutions[40], characterised by a greater specialisation for lending to economic sectors and apart from the Banco Exterior de España, much smaller in size[41].

The stated aim was to turn the Argentaria group into an efficient and competitive financial structure, highly diversified with its specialised divisions, and to develop in a gradual but very steady fashion on international markets in view of privatisation. Indeed with four subsequent public offerings between April 1993 and February 1998 all the shares of the Grupo Argentaria were placed on the Spanish Stock Exchange, in New York and in London. In June 1998 Caja Postal, Banco Hipotecario, Banco de Crédito Local and Banco Exterior de España merged into a single institution in order to reduce costs and increase operational efficiency. At the time Caja Postal accounted for 26% of the overall profits of the group.

In 1992 the agreement between Caja Postal and Argentaria and Correos y Telegrafos, known as "Proyecto Nexus" was launched. Its aim was to commercialise banking and para-banking products of the Caja Postal through its network of 1600 Post Office branches throughout the country and introduce an investment plan for the modernisation of branches, started in 1994. The Nexus commercial agreement in 1996 caused a stir in the banking world and was criticised especially by the Confederación de la Cajas de Ahorro and by the Cooperativas de crédito rurales. The latter, feeling threatened by competition, questioned:

- the absence of a public tender for the granting of the co-operation which took place through direct attribution[42];
- the violation of Law 12 of 27 May 1992 on agency contracts because none of the agreements between Correos and Caja Postal could qualify as agency contract;
- violating the provisions in law 25/1991 because different conditions had been applied with respect to other banking and financial institutions.

---

[40] The others were Banco de Crédito Agricola, Banco de Crédito Local, Banco Hipotecario de Espana and Banco Exterior de Espana.

[41] At the end of 1993 the total assets of Caja Postal amounted to 2,341,644 million Pesetas and deposits and savings from customers 1,460,683 million Pesetas. The collection by Banco Exterior de España amounted to 1,640,776 million Pesetas out of a total 4,522,649 million Pesetas, while the collections from the other units in the group were substantially lower (Banco Hipotecario de España 152,248 million Pesetas, Banco de Credito Local 199,256 million Pesetas and Banco de Credito Agricola 56,921 million Pesetas).

[42] Therefore violating art. 15 of the Statute of the Post which talks about a call for tender.

As a consequence of the above mentioned substantiated comments, the Nexus Programme, signed in 1992, could not be automatically extended for ten more years after December 1996, as initially expected, because the banking partner had to be chosen through a public tender. In February 1997 a tender was called for the wholesale management service of postal payment accounts by large enterprises and public bodies[43] which was won by the Bilbao Vizcaya BBV group. On July 18, 1997 there was a call for tender related to the supply of banking and financial services to Post Office branches featuring 6 participants, representing the main banking groups in the country. The Grupo Argentaria, in spite of the criticism and continuing controversy, was chosen once again for the agreement, known as Red Nexus[44]. A development strategy then began to be elaborated for the partnership relation which was mainly centred on equal payment for staff in Post Offices dealing with the financial service offer and bank employees.

In November 1998 the agreement was terminated, allegedly due to diverging views on the interpretation of contract clauses related to staff management[45]. With this termination of the agreement the parties explicitly renounced any claim, both in court and out of court, as well as any form of refund. For Banco Argentaria this marked the beginning of the phase aimed at designing strategies to keep the advantages of the commercial investment made[46], while the Post started the

---

[43] The service had been previously managed by Argentaria through the Caja Postal.

[44] The offers included a compensation for the Post divided into a fixed and a variable part and an investment plan, while the Post made available their branch network (1,692 offices plus 11,000 other contact points) and part of the staff to help in banking activities. The content of the offers (related to a ten-year duration of the agreement) is summarised in the following table.

Table 3.3

The offers for the Red Nexus

Tender	Fixed rate	Variable rate	Total
Argentaria	32,500	28,099	60,599
Caja Madrid	33,997	20,166	54,113
Banco Santander	21,617	15,199	36,816
BBV	23,182	2,283	2,.465
La Caixa	The offer is not comparable		
Bankinter	The offer is not comparable		

(Data in million Pesetas)

Argentaria undertook to invest a further 34,800 million Pesetas in computer projects (10,800 million), staff training (1,800 million) and promotion.

[45] The official explanation given for the difficulty was that for the banking partner it was impossible to provide suitable training for the staff in the Post Office branches for the promotion of financial services because of their insufficient background.

[46] With the termination of the agreement it lost 50% of its contact points with customers, represented by the 1,700 Post Offices alongside the same number of bank branches managed by the group.

selection process for a new banking partner. Several banking institutions competed, three of them making an official offer: Bankinter, Deutsche Bank and Citybank España. In Spring 1999 Deutsche Bank was selected, which thus expanded its own network of 300 branches in Spain with about 1700 Post Office branches. These were the criteria adopted for selection: nation-wide coverage, technological and operational capacity, competence in managing investment, the available infrastructure and the strategic plan for the joint development with Correos of the branch network. The agreement is based on an association formula for the promotion of Post Office branches network managed by the public body and its key points can be summarised as follows:

1. duration of the agreement: 10 years;
2. investment in infrastructure by Deutsche Bank for 11,596 million Pesetas in computer equipment, cash dispensers, training, marketing and advertising;
3. division of the profits from financial operations carried out at Post Office branches at 50% between the two partners, both with reference to customers at the Post Office branch and to banking customers for operations carried out at the Post Office branch. From this point of view, when choosing the partner, the importance of Spain as a tourist destination was taken into account because the German group has a portfolio of about nine million customers who are able to operate through the Post Office branches if they travel to Spain;
4. commercialisation at Post Office branches of the whole range of banking and financial products of the Deutsche Bank group. In this way postal customers will have access to phone banking and services via the Internet;
5. at Post Office branches areas known as "Oficina Directa" will be set up for the banking and financial operations mentioned above with the participation of staff from the postal Administration and Deutsche Bank.

Therefore, the Spanish postal company is set to supply a wide range of financial products (for payment, saving and investment, loans and insurance coverage) with the Deutsche Bank brand name and experience.

3.2.3 The Experiences Based on the Administrative Model

As for administrative models, the most significant examples are those provided by France and Italy.

The French experience

The French postal system is one of the main operators on the domestic market as supplier of financial services and, in particular, as collector of savings from the low and medium-low customer segments.

The Caisse d'Epargne Postale was established on April 9, 1881, under the aegis of postal administration and according to the functional model of the Caisse d'Epargne et de Prévoyance, set up in 1818. Later on its name was changed to CNE-Caisse Nationale d'Epargne et de Prévoyance: it does not have an independent juridical structure, but from the commercial point of view it is managed by La Poste, whose branches it uses and, from a financial point of view by the Caisse des Dépots et Consignations[47], which is in charge of postal collection. The postal savings are mostly used to finance investment for public purposes. More recently, policies have changed and the collection is no longer aimed at specific forms of investment. The savings products are therefore created on the basis of the requirements of the various market segments of savers, regardless of the type of investment. There is an ad hoc fund which ensures high solvability, so that the possibility of having to pay the guarantee, which is in any case offered by the Government, remains remote.

The savings products offered by CDC are divided into three categories: 1) *livret A* for Savings Banks and the postal collection by CNE and the *livret bleus* for the Crédit mutuel, which are tax-free; 2) the *livret d'epargne populaire (LEP)* and *Codevi*, always tax-free and which can also be issued by other financial institutions and are not obliged to centralise the management at CDC, 3) the *livret B*, the *Comptes d'Epargne Logement (CEL)* and the *Plans d'Epargne Logement* (PEL) which can also be issued by other financial institutions which do not have to centralise the management of investments at CDC, with the exception of the postal savings. The interest rates are set administratively by the Ministry of Finance. Since these instruments are so widespread among the population[48] the issue of the variation of rates is politically sensitive. For the activities related to the placing of savings books, La Poste receives a compensation based on the management volumes[49].

La Poste also offers current account deposits, whose collection was transferred on a daily basis to the Treasury. Since the middle of the 90's la Poste started asking to manage these resources directly so as to have greater direct operation ability and more substantial profit margins.

The role played by La Poste in the supply of payment and saving services is important due to the market shares it controls and to the extension of the institutional mission which places it within the core business of the group. Indeed, in the Cahier de charge de La Poste of 1990[50], when defining the mission of the Post, two separate areas are indicated: running services and financial services[51].

---

[47] CDC is an independent public body.

[48] The *Livret A* is the most popular savings instrument: in 1997 there were 51 million savings books on the market, corresponding to 80% of the population. However, due to the performance differentials, the flow of funds collected with the *Livret A* is decreasing to the advantage of savings products to finance the house and of popular savings books.

[49] In 1998 the commissions paid to the network amounted to 4.6 billion FF for the placing of *Livrets A* and *B* by La Poste-CNE (4.4 in 1997 and 4.5 in 1996).

[50] See Decree n° 90-1214 of 29 December 1990.

[51] Regulated respectively by articles 1-7 and by articles 8-13.

For the latter area of activity a detailed list is given which includes payment services, savings collection, financial operations and distribution of insurance products[52].

With the "launching" of the new Cahier de charge de La Poste[53] the area was still wide-ranging, but the management of the resources collected by customers through current accounts is entrusted to La Poste itself, by means of the creation of an ad hoc company with the status of investment company and whose capital is controlled by the same postal company, known as Efiposte. Furthermore Law n° 96–597 of July 2, 1996, which implemented the community Directive on financial services, includes La Poste among subjects explicitly authorised to operate on the market of security placement.

This means that La Poste has developed its own operations in the financial sector with product companies.

As for managing mutual investment funds, La Poste and CDC have set up a subsidiary - with a 51% shareholding by La Poste and 49% by CDC - called Sogepost. The latter, managing 23 open-end investment companies and 77 funds commercialised by the postal network, has an important market share in managed savings and its growth rates are still substantial. CDC is the second asset manager in Europe and La Poste has a good distribution network. As mentioned above, it has an excellent image and a large customer base for the placing of insurance products. As for the financial products supplied, since 1868 its partner has been CNP, a public entity managed by CDC until 1987, when it was transformed into a joint stock company, in which La Poste has an 18% shareholding[54]. The distribution is based on a commercial agreement between La Poste and CNP, which has been modified several times over the years and will be valid until the end of 2009. More recent developments include the creation of Préviposte – 100% controlled by La Poste - for the provision of insurance products which could not be supplied by CNP and Assureposte – in partnership with CNP – for the development of products in the life sector and related to individuals such as disability insurance or risk coverage for sanitary expenses.

From the point of view of the product range on offer and of the extension of the customer base, La Poste is the third French financial group in terms of brokerage activity volumes.

---

[52] These are indicated as follows: fund raising from the general public and supply of the following services and products: payment instruments and transfer operations of national and international funds, regardless of the support or technological procedure used, including accounts on demand related to services of postal cheques, currency exchange, accounts, savings books and bonds from La Poste and other savings products; placement, subscription, purchase, administrative management, safekeeping, sale of securities and of all financial investment products; asset management, management of portfolios, as well as advice and assistance in all these areas; all types of insurance products; loans related to saving aimed at buying a house .

[53] See Decree n° 2000-165 of 28 February 2000, issued in compliance with the financial Law for 1999 (Law n° 98-1266 of 30 December 1998), art. 126.

[54] The other partners, apart from the government, are CDC and the Caisse d'Epargne.

The Italian experience

From several viewpoints, the Italian experience reflects the French situation which inspired it.

With the Italian Unification it became necessary to reorganise the liquidation of debts of the pre-existing States: in various cases *Casse* (i.e. a sort of savings bank) had been created in order to collect voluntary and statutory deposits to be invested for public purposes[55]. As a consequence of the unification process, in 1870 the different *Casse* were grouped together in the *Cassa Centrale* operating at the central directorate for public debt. Later on the substantial growth in collection made it necessary to go back to more decentralised solution. This led to the setting up, in 1875, of the Postal Savings Banks[56], which from a financial point of view were controlled by the *Cassa Depositi e Prestiti - CDDPP*. Each Post Office thus becomes a branch for the collection of deposits which are transferred to the CDDPP[57]; in this way its territorial coverage is unique in terms of dissemination and capillary extension.

The CDDPP is not an independent legal entity, but has autonomous accounting and administration[58]. The Treasury Ministry determines lending and borrowing rates of interest granted respectively on loans and on the different forms of savings products. The issuing is on demand and the characteristics of the securities combined with the absence of a secondary market make them appealing to private investors but not to institutional investors[59]. The following postal savings instruments have remained basically unchanged over time: i) Post Office savings books; ii) interest-bearing postal bonds and iii) non-interest bearing judicial

---

[55] With the law of June 1857, the *Parlamento Subalpino* had set up a *Cassa Depositi e Prestiti – CDDPP* at the General Directorate of public debt which was followed by other experiences in other states. With the law of 17 May 1863 the institutional context of the Casse was redefined and it was decided that the funds raised should be used by local bodies and charitable institutions for social purposes.

[56] See Law 27 May 1875 which laid down that the service provided by the Casse di Risparmio Postale should be part of the cash services offered by the Post and Telecommunication Ministry, managed by the Direction of the bank-post services.

[57] In order to regulate the collection of resources for public purposes, over time various laws and several regulations were passed which were all brought together with the Single Text on CDDPP of 1913; their operations are governed by the Regulations of 1916 and of 1919 which are still the regulatory framework today.

[58] It is divided into 8 different management structures including that of the Casse di Risparmio Postale which provides the most substantial amount of funds. It has its own special and independent legislation because it does not operate with Government funds, but with funding from individuals paid into the Cassa through the postal structure.

[59] These took an interest in postal savings instrument in the 1990s during a phase of rapid decrease of market rates, while the paperwork related to setting the rates and communication time along the line made performance differentials of postal saving particularly advantageous for investors if compared to market rates.

deposits[60]. These instruments are particularly advantageous from a fiscal point of view, for the obligations undertaken guaranteed by the Government and for the particular monetary regime of postal collection. The success features include reimbursing on demand of both savings books and bonds at a fixed price, known at the moment of subscribing them and without losses, guaranteed by the Treasury[61].

In 1917 the postal current account service was inaugurated with a payment activity based on issuing and managing means of payment (orders and cheques) and procedures (postal notes and giro), especially managing the cashing in and payment services for Government, public bodies and utilities. Unlike savings collection through savings books and deposits, current account collection is carried out on its own behalf[62], but all funds collected are transferred to CDDPP on an ad hoc interest-bearing account opened in favour of the Central Government Treasury[63].

The financial service activity for collection and payment on demand is regarded and perceived mainly in terms of public service.

The regulatory framework was redefined and regulated in recent years[64].

With the transformation, in 1994, of the Post and Telecommunication Administration into a public economic entity, with the new statute of the organisation and the programme agreement, some of the historic constraints

---

[60] The law sets limits on the paying-in and withdrawal operations, differentiated depending on the importance of the issuing Post Office. The following diagram provides an indication of the volumes mediated by postal saving, through the trend in postal collection

Table 3.4

Trend in postal savings

	Postal savings books	Interest-bearing postal bonds	Total
1945	20	72	92
1955	164	1,198	1,362
1965	831	2,797	3,628
1975	2,841	9,007	11,848

Source: Report on the service of the Casse di Risparmio Postali, various years and Bank of Italy, various years.

[61] For more details see the report by the Director of the CDDPP, Salvemini M.T. (1999).

[62] This is why Poste Italiane, in their balance sheet, register among liabilities debts towards current account holders

[63] There is therefore a 100% reserve obligation to guarantee solvibility as a safeguard for customers with a current account.

[64] See Single Text with the legal provisions on postal matters, bank-post and telecommunications, approved with Presidential Decree (DPR) 29 March 1973, n° 156 and the implementation regulation on bank-post matters, approved with Presidential Decree 1 June 1989, n° 256, and Law Decree 30 July 1999, n° 284, concerning the restructuring of the *Cassa Depositi e Prestiti* and art. 40, par. 4, of Law 23 December 1998, n° 448 which delegated the Government to make suitable provisions for the changing of the single text related to legal provisions on postal matters, bank-post and telecommunications approved with DPR 29 March 1973, n° 156 and DPR 14 March 2001, n° 144.

imposed on the operation of bank-post have been removed because they were outdated and hindered the products from meeting the requirements of the customers. By means of example the innovations include the possibility of joint heading of deposits, the right of independently setting interest rates on collection and to differentiate them depending on the customer segments[65].

In 1994 the Post was authorised to carry out subscription and reimbursement operations on government securities at the branches, thus starting the placement firstly of all monetary market securities (BOT) and in 1995, gradually, of long term securities (CCT and BTP). In 1996 the range of financial instruments which the Post is entitled to distribute is expanded by including the securities issued by local public bodies and joint stock companies, upon condition that part of their capital is owned directly or indirectly by the Government[66]. So, the Italian Post was able to proceed to the placing on securities on the stock exchange in the second half of the 1990s following the privatisation processes.

In 2001 the regulations on the Bancoposta services offered by Poste Italiane s.p.a. has been updated[67], in particular extending the range of services to the area of investment services, excluding the negotiation activity on its own behalf and the management on an individual basis of investment portfolios. Furthermore it does not have the possibility of granting any loans to customers on its own[68].

The above mentioned activities are carried out without the need to be included in any register or list; generally speaking the provisions applied are those contained in the Single banking text and in the Single text on finance. In this way Poste Italiane are placed on the same level as banks from the viewpoint of controls on the financial service activity. From the organisational point of view, for the management of bank-post activities it has been laid down that the postal company should avail itself of independent organisational structures and that it should set up

---

[65] This was laid down by the financial Law for 1997, whereas in the past, as already mentioned, the rates were set administratively through a Decree by the ministry of the Treasury.

[66] It should be noted, however, that those who subscribed securities at Post Offices could not divest before the expiry date because the authorisation to placement did not cover subsequent brokerage which implied agreements with other authorised brokers, or the setting up of an independent stock brokerage company.

[67] See the DPR of 14 March 2001, n° 144 mentioned above approving the Regulation of Bancoposta's activities, art. 2.

[68] The operational areas are identified as follows: a) savings collection from the general public [as defined in art.11, par. 1, of the single banking text] and related or instrumental activities; b) collection of postal savings; c) payment services, including the issuing, management and sale of pre-paid cards and other payment instruments [as mentioned in art. 1, par. 2, lett. f) numbers 4 and 5 of the single banking text]; d) exchange brokerage services; e) promoting and placing with the general public loans granted by banks and authorised financial intermediaries; f) investment and ancillary services [in compliance with art.12 below, i.e. with the reference to art.1, par. 5, letters b), c) and e) and to art. 1, par. 6, letters a), b), d), e), f), g) of the single text on finance], as well as activities related and instrumental to investment services.

a system of accounting for the bank-post activities separate from the other activities[69].

With the 1998-2002 Corporate Plan, the organisational structure has been redefined adopting the divisional model with the creation of the Financial Service Division, alongside the Postal Service Division and the Network Division. The aims of the Corporate Plan in the financial field include the following points:

1. rationalise and strengthen its own activity in the collection of savings through the postal current account;
2. carry out in the most efficient way possible the collection of postal savings on behalf of the CDDPP;
3. rationalise the operation of investment services;
4. increase its own activity in the payment system.

Bancoposta is therefore still an important part of the activities of Poste Italiane; this brand name has been recently launched commercially again, by proposing a strategy to boost the image and expand the range of services. The Bancoposta brand includes both services provided on behalf of third *parties (Cassa Depositi e Prestiti*), and directly on its own (payment and current account services), but also on its own indirectly through product companies (Postevita for insurance products, Bancoposta Fondi Sgr for mutual investment funds), and as a broker on the basis of commercial agreements signed on the market (like the one with Deutsche Bank for the loans and consumer credit facilities and with San Paolo-Imi for the placing of securities).

The Irish experience

Similarities with the administrative model can also be found in Ireland.

The Post Office Saving Bank is the financial arm of the Irish Post operating in the area of payments and savings collection. It is not legally autonomous and is controlled by the Treasury. The collection through the Post contributes to the financing of the National Treasury Management Agency-NTMA, which acts on behalf of the Ministry of Finance and in this way has a capillary network of branches for the placing of debt instruments on demand. In the past this network was regarded as essential but now, with the reduction of public debt as a consequence of the need to follow the parameters of the Monetary Union and with the better conditions obtained on the financial market, its strategic relevance has decreased and the future of the financial service supply is still under discussion. The postal distribution channel has proved effective for the placing of privatised companies, including the Telecom Eireann. An Post continues to operate as the

---

[69] Obviously this was done in order to prevent cross subsidisation between the various activities and to allow for the supervision system in place for financial activities.

main agent for the Department of Social, Community and Family Affairs[70] and this activity gives an essential contribution to the economics of the branch network. Another important operation area is the one generated by BillPay, a payment system for bills and invoices by mail and through call centres, which provide information to companies about the sums paid in an electronic format.

An Post also launched a very successful initiative as Internet service provider through PostGem and its subsidiary Ireland On-Line which could have been, for the first time on the Irish market, a starting point for the development of the e-commerce business area. However the excellent performance of these initiatives on the market supported the strategy of selling to Esat Telecom Group thus producing net earnings amounting to 93.3 million IR£ for An Post[71] as well as raising sufficient cash to support the investment in infrastructures necessary to modernise the postal company.

In 1999, An Post also successfully entered the market of standardised insurance products with its motor insurance, home insurance, life insurance products, and serious illness plan. This activity was started by An Post Direct Limited and by An Post Direct Management Services Limited One Direct, both subsidiaries fully controlled by the postal Company. They took on the status of insurance brokers, operating exclusively through the direct channel with call centres. The Post Office and the network of post employees are in charge of delivering documents and getting the contracts signed. The insurance policies are produced by a partner insurance company on the market, smaller in size and commercialised under the new postal brand name One Direct.

According to official reports the Post Office Division is the operative arm of An Post in the retail postal activity and financial service supply business, both of which are part of its core business together with the provision of services to the Government. However the efficiency of the banking sector, its capillary distribution and in particular the substantial resources available to the main competitors (in particular the Credit Unions) are jeopardising the strength of the financial service offered by An Post. This means that future strategies aimed at keeping An Post active in the financial sector are being questioned.

---

[70] In February 1999 the question was raised whether, according to EU law, this activity should be attributed on the basis of a call for tender. The Government decided that, in view of the social value of the service provided by the branches, this was not necessary and the agreement has been renewed for the three years 2000-2002.

[71] An Post also agreed to reinvest 24 million IR£ through the purchase of ordinary shares from ESAT and the latter was subsequently bought by British Telecom plc, the value of the subscribed shares went up to 65.1 million IR£, thus creating a increase in value amounting to 41.1mln IR£ during the year 2000.

3.3 The Drivers for Change within Banks Systems

In the 90's, the European financial systems, similarly to the ones of other economically advanced systems, are confronted to deep changes in the structures and operational modalities, in the business models and therefore also in the competitive dynamics[72].

From the structural point of view, special attention deserve:

- the concentration processes with consequent reduction of operators. The consequences of the restructuring processes are to be felt also in the reduction of personnel and the rationalisation of branches networks as well as in the closing up of the non-profitable branches[73];
- the growing integration between financial intermediation activities with inter-sectorial concentrations (bank-insurances, commercial banks-investment banks, credit intermediaries – securities firms, in particular);
- a new relative importance of the main financial services areas, with growing bank disintermediation and securitisation, spread of different forms of savings and of insurance and social security products;
- the coming of new competitors, namely operators from non financial sectors.

Furthermore, the different categories of banks – which, in the past, took advantage of an artificial market segmentation owing to particular privileges and exclusive operational fields – tend more and more to be homogenised one another from the institutional point of view.

As a consequence of that, market imperfections have been reduced and have become more and more disputable. In addition, a more lively competition has arisen.

On the demand side, a stronger differentiation of the most important segments is to be highlighted:

---

[72] Llewellyn D.T. (1999) identifies, as "secular pressures on the banking industry" the following elements: *i*) competition; *ii*) banking markets have become more contestable; *iii*) globalisation; *iv*) declining entry barriers; *v*) exit barriers; *vi*) deconstruction; *vii*) asymmetric competition; *viii*) regulation; *ix*) technology; *x*) excess capacity; *xi*) erosion of cross-subsidies; *xii*) consumer trends; *xiii*) cost structures; *xiv*) capital markets and securitisation; *xv*) capital market pressures. These trends' implications are then summed up in: *i*) structure of the financial system; *ii*) capital markets and securitisation and *iii*) consolidation of structure. As far as the strategic reactions are concerned, their impact is to be felt in the new setting up of the bank business itself, which can be analysed on the base of the following key points: *i*) the fundamentals of banking; *ii*) use of core competencies; *iii*) cost strategies; *iv*) pricing and cross-subsidies; *v*) delivery/access channels; *vi*) further securitisation; *vii*) off-balance sheet business.

[73] The differences in time and intensity of restructuring and in the economic impact depend, on one side, upon institutional constraints for jobs preservation and, on the other side, upon social issues for the non impoverishment of the socially and economically less favourite areas.

- the *corporate* market; with its growing sophistication and awareness of the importance of the financial area for business competition and for managing crucial transition phases of a company's life-cycle, needs growing levels of specialisation. Demand, in addition to traditional banking services, calls for investment banking services, corporate finance, innovative credit and risk management. Also those markets which used to have several bank relationships are experiencing a major trend to housebank models with closer relationships with a limited number of intermediaries, or even with just one of them. These intermediaries are then supposed to be able to meet, at the same time, all the clients' needs. In this market segment, the middle market companies' demand is to be satisfied, too. In response to that, market segmentation strategies are implemented in order to guarantee a proper offer differentiation comprising products and prices, in order to meet the different needs;
- the *retail* market, which consists of families and of small and medium enterprises, feels the consequences of a wider competition on the market. This category takes advantage of the availability of a better information, a bigger transparency of conditions and, in general terms, of a higher economic culture. Nevertheless, at the same time, it shows a bigger volatility than in the past. This mobility is made possible also by making good use of the new technologies and the innovations in the distribution channels. Moreover, it concentrates more and more its customers to a single intermediary able to meet all their financial needs, combining the best price-quality ratio, similarly to what happens even more widely in the *corporate* segment, as above mentioned.
- the *private banking* market, which is destined to highly sophisticated demand, needs specialised higher and higher management competencies in order to reach high level performances in the financial market whose major trend's name is globalisation. In Europe, the introduction of Euro, on one side, and the reduction of income yields, on the other side, pave the way to a rapid development of the market which presents favourable growth perspectives and interesting margins, provided that high level performances are guaranteed and high added value services are concretely offered.

Furthermore, in the different market segments, clients are much more volatile and demanding in terms of quality-price ratio, practical access, rapid service delivery and level of advice. In general, the demand is reactive to the new powerful marketing instruments[74], and this is a relatively new condition for the financial sector.

---

[74] Harker and Zenios state: "Perhaps the strongest force of change, however, is the consumer. Consumers are demanding anytime-anywhere delivery of financial services, while demonstrating a rapid evolution of their needs and desires". See Harker P.T.-Zenios S.A. (1998), p. 4.

Besides securitisation, a further aspect to be highlighted is the growing demand for insurances and pensions. This is in line with the present crisis in the traditional pension systems that are confronted to rapidly ageing population, to precarious work conditions and to the growing use of temporary workers, not always covered by public or obligatory insurance, as well as with the reduction of welfare and presence of the public sector in the social security area. That means then that these markets have great potentials.

Finally, the macro trends of economy, namely globalisation and market internationalisation are to be registered also in the demand for financial services. The introduction of Euro speeds up and accentuates the impact of these trends.

Other relevant factors connected with changing are:

- deregulation, considering the impact owing to the markets enlargement after the elimination of artificial segmentations, the possible implementation of universal banking models as well as financial conglomerates, which are considerably diversified and very much present in the different market segments and considering also that the access is now subject to a lesser number of entry barriers. In general terms, this causes weaker monopolist's profits, stronger price-competition and margins erosion;
- the privatisation of state-owned banks and the normalisation of special corporate structures (such as the co-operative ones). This allow a more incisive shareholders view in the bank sector, the search for financial performance conditions which are in line with the financial market's expectations and able to sanction and not to support development policies without suitable yields potentials, and a better transparency in the companies choices as well as clearer setting up of strategies;
- the impact of technology that revolutionises the production processes and makes new business setting up and organisational solutions economically favourable - by changing the processes themselves. Also the coming of new competitors in the financial area – already mentioned with reference to the structural evolution of banks systems – is partially a consequence of the new information technology applications to the financial services industry. Moreover, the information technology offers the opportunity to modify the traditional branches up to automatic channels, without any direct contact with the bank personnel (remote banking). The choice of suitable channels become then, on one side, important factors for succeeding and, on the other side, it might expose to the risk of failure in a evolving framework with contradictory signs. The non homogenous level of presence and use of different channels for the different services (see Table 3.5) show the crucial importance of this choice.

Further more, the level of presence of computers is different in Europe (see Tables 3.6 and 3.7). This fact can help understanding the different use of remote banking in Europe as well as the different perspectives of the traditional post-banking activities.

Table 3.5
Bank services delivered through remote channels

Channels / Services	Branches	Kiosk banking	Telephone Banking (person to person)	Telephone Banking (tone or voice-activated)	Online PC Banking	Internet banking
Cash withdrawals	Yes	Yes	No	No	No	No
Loading of prepaid cards	No	Yes	Yes	Yes	Yes	Yes
Loading of network money	No	No	Not usually	Not usually	Yes	Yes
General information on bank products and market developments	Yes	Yes	Yes	Yes	Yes	Yes
Account balance information	Yes	Yes	Yes	Yes	Yes	Yes
Money transfers	Yes	Yes	Yes	Yes	Yes	Yes
Directs debits and standing orders	Yes	Yes	Yes	Yes	Yes	Yes
Credits and debits card request	Yes	Yes	Yes	No	Yes	Yes
No cheque books orders	Yes	Yes	Yes	Yes	Yes	Yes
Investment advice	Yes	No	Yes	No	Yes (for standard products)	Yes (for standard products)
Securities transactions	Yes	No	Yes	No	Yes	Yes
Loans (standardised)	Yes		Yes 4)	No	Yes	Not yet
Deposit business	Yes 1) 2)	Yes 1) 2)	Yes 2)	No	Yes 2)	Yes 2) 3)
Non-standardised banking Transactions	Yes	No	No	No	No	Not yet
Insurance products	Yes	No	Yes	No	Yes	Yes

1) Paid-in cash 2) Via transfer from another account 3) Via transfer from other means of payment (e-money, credit card, etc) 4) Up to certain limits.
Source: ECB (1999).

Table 3.6
Penetration of telephone banking in some EU countries

Belgium [1) 2)]	5%
Germany [3)]	6%
Spain [1)]	6%
France [1) 4)]	10%
Ireland [1)]	5%
Italy [3)]	3%
Netherlands [5)]	5%
Finland [1)]	2%
Sweden [5)]	4%
United Kingdom [1)]	10%

Data refer either to 1998 or to 1997. 1) Percentage of the retail customer base; 2) 1996 figure; 3) Percentage of retail bank accounts; 4) Minitel users; 5) Percentage of payment transactions.
Source: EU supervisory authorities represented in the Banking Supervision Committee, ECB (1999).

Table 3.7
Pc and Internet diffusion in the EU

	Personal Computers *per 1,000 people* **(1999)**	**Internet users** *thousands* **(1999)**
Austria	256.8	1,840
Belgium	315.2	1,400
Denmark	414.0	1,500
Finland	360.1	2,143
France	221.8	5,370
Germany	297.0	14,400
Greece	60.2	750
Ireland	404.9	679
Italy	191.8	7,000
Netherlands	359.9	3,000
Portugal	93.0	700
Spain	119.4	4,652
Sweden	451.4	3,666
United Kingdom	302.5	12,500

Source: World Bank (2001) on data from the International Telecommunication Union - ITU.

Structural changes and innovative general factors have an impact on the different sectors' business and competition strategies. Consequently, the traditional business models are put in a difficult position, the gaps in terms of economic positioning become bigger and bigger and a wide range of choices for specialisation in the different phases of the value chain becomes available[75]. The bank is able to exploiting the competitive advantages it has in particular phases and by overcoming the negative positioning gaps in others. If a selective positioning is done along the different phases[76], so that these strengths can be exploited and enhanced, it is possible to avoid the risk to see global positioning strategies -which are not supported by optimal conditions in all phases of the value chain – to spread the impact of their weakness all over and lead to the progressive expulsion from the market.

In practical terms, before choosing the positioning, it is important not only to evaluate the bank's weakness and its future perspectives but also to start from the concrete impact of competition onto the margins erosion and, in more particular terms, on their distribution along the value chain and on the force relationships, in a middle term perspective, between manufacturers and distributors within a scenario where the two functions are separated. Through the *contract banking* model, deriving from *deconstruction* processes, some banks are able to assume the special role to supply to some other banks a "sub-component" of a service and some other banks become "*contract co-ordinator*". At the same time, referring to different products lines, a bank can be "*contract co-ordinator*" and acquire from outside the products that are needed to satisfy the terms of the contract the bank has to respect to meet its clients' demands for services and products with a

[75] The de-construction of production and distribution processes of the different bank's business areas is a relatively recent phenomenon which combines outsourcing to some phases of the value chain also for the activities that traditionally belong to the core business of the bank. These processes are to be found mostly in the industrial sectors, while the bank, which offers a wide range of services and products, is generally perceived as a vertically and horizontally integrated firm that addresses the growing complexity of specialised processes and products with specialised firms which are integrated within a group structure. See Llewellyn D.T. (1997) who very clearly statues " While technological innovation develops the economies of scale in the field of bank operational processes, the same innovation allows the banks to split their own products in sub-components or elementary processes and to externalise a part of them. Doing so, also the small companies will be able to realise economies of scale and become competitive. A further advantage of this phenomenon is the possibility to modify the business costs' structure which becomes more variable. For companies this brings bigger operational flexibility".

[76] Llewelling D.T. (1999) identifies the following key roles within the bank activity: *i*) a customer interface and the management of customer relationships; *ii*) the supply of a range of products and services; *iii*) a range of ancillary services (services which are not explicitly demanded by the customer but which are an integral part of what is demanded, e.g., risk analysis and administration); and *iv*) a supplier of alternative delivery mechanisms. Harker P.T. and Zenios S. A. (1998) perceive that the bank's retail activity is being structuring upon three different stages: *i*) product origination, *ii*) retail servicing e *iii*) back office operations.

specific standard. It can also be "*sub-contractor*" for some products by transferring its products to third parties, so that it will make a good use of the know how it has developed and its exceeding production capacity.

About the predictions of future possible scenarios, uncertainty is to be felt as for the spread of on-line financial services. The on-line operations are pulled by three major propellants, namely the computers infrastructure and the technology with the development of standards encouraging interoperativity, easy access and high mobility, stronger segmentation policies and sharper marketing initiatives and, finally, the need for cost reduction related to the supply of services, offering solutions that are able to offer bigger flexibility and use of economies of scale and to go beyond space issues. So, the distribution on the territory could be improved. With its three above mentioned propellants, this on-line operativity has no doubt conquered the most advanced segments, which are also the most open to innovation. Moreover, it has also attracted – on experimental base – the clients that are mostly moving and difficult to be conquered. It still shows different levels of penetration in different markets and has already experienced some standstill. In the United States as well as in some Euro-zone countries, from the offer side, the innovators were often the new comers (the so-called e-specialists), while the traditional banks was obliged to react against this competitive sharpening, which was jeopardising their traditional prerogatives, such as the presence on the territory, the proximity of the client and the personalisation of the relationship within face-to-face relationships[77]. However, it is not clear yet what can be the best mixture between *direct marketing - distance assistance* and *face to face* relationship in the different market segments. From their side, the new comers have based their success by considering each single part of the value line of the traditional activity as an individual market. Several new professional profiles have arisen: specialised producers, integrators, aggregators, brokers, non financial actors (among which telephone operators and large retailers), with a constant evolution in terms of choices for high specialisation, diversification and incoming into business areas closed to each other.

The clients with a preference for on-line transactions show to have high potentials, have a consumption function which enhances the volume of real transactions and covers a wide range of services. Therefore, thanks to these clients, very interesting margins are possible. Nevertheless, they are also more volatile. It is not unjustified to doubt about the fact that, the success of on-line financing depends also from a cyclic factor. Therefore, it would be wrong to react by implementing strategies based on structural hypothesis. For example, it is difficult to evaluate how much the success of on-line trading at the end of the 90's is the result of the market's exceptional performances.

Whether the banks are able to raise their demand or whether the existing demand is subdivided between traditional and remote channels: this is a very

---

[77] Nevertheless, in Europe, most of integral remote banks belong to bank groups. See ECB (1999), p. 10.

difficult question to be answered, too. As a matter of fact, in the second hypothesis, no solution is given to the problem of excessive capacity; on the contrary, it becomes even more serious[78].

The so-called "proximity banks", in particular, that have taken advantage of the competitive advantages of their penetration of the market's geographical areas, with personalised relationships with the clients, see then this advantage as being questioned. In some situations, the articulated branches network and their personnel for *face-to-face* relations and assisted operativity become an economical charge instead of self-service with ATMs – POS or via Internet or by phone. At present, proximity is rather measured in terms of easy access with the most developed means of communication or, in other terms, of convenience within the relationship.

Consequently to the de-construction of production processes and the dissociation between production and distribution functions, the new comers are in a favourite position while choosing their positioning along the value and distribution chain. As a matter fact, they have now the possibility to prepare them ad hoc rather than to engage themselves into restructuring plans that need to take different stakeholders' needs in consideration (clients, employees and social parts, in particular). With the deregulation in the financial sector and the globalisation and internationalisation of economies, the new comers are not only foreign financial intermediaries but different subjects of different origin (mainly large retailers[79] and telecommunications) among which also the postal incumbents. These postal operators are traditionally present in the offer of payment services and in the market of savings collection or even also with "Postbank" which have consolidated retail banking experiences, but are re-inventing their positioning.

3.4 The Strategic Choices for the 21st Century

The radical transformations that are under way in postal systems on the one hand and the equally important trends in banking and financial markets on the other hand have led to strategic thinking about the future role of the Post in the delivery of financial services and on the ways in which this action can be implemented.

The essential question is whether to be present or not on the supply side and, subsequently, with what range of products and services, addressed to which market target, using what technologies and delivery channels.

As previously mentioned, on the financial market there are operators covering a wide spectrum of intermediation activities and service provision. Also for the postal groups the option is open between limiting themselves to certain areas of activity or being present in all areas (see Table 3.8). In the light of the trends described above towards the deconstruction of the chain of value in the financial

[78] See ECB (1999), p. 29.

[79] For alliances banks and retailers, see ECB (1999), pp. 32-33. More generally on the entry of large retailers into the financial sector, see Pilley O. (1998).

sector, the choice remains whether to become specialised only in some specific phases of the production and distribution process or to position oneself in the areas where the greatest strength is.

Table 3.8
The operation areas of the Posts in the supply of financial services

Banking			**Financial**	**Insurance and social security**
Payments	**Deposits taking**	**Lending**		
Payments in cash: orders, transfers Delivery of pensions and subsidies Debiting on credit accounts: giro and cheques ATM withdrawing Credit card and POS Currency exchange E-payment and digital signature certification	Savings deposits Deposits on current accounts Postal bonds	Mortgages Consumer credit (credit cards) Personal loans Cash desk facilities and current accounts overdrafts	Security placement Mutual funds placement Pension plans Securities brokerage Trading on-line	Life products and social security saving Property-causality insurances (car, travels, house) Pensions

The relevant factors from the point of view of the choice of positioning are the priorities chosen in terms of redefinition and implementation of the strategies in the core business of the postal activity, as well as the level reached in approaching the goals that have been set in this area, and finally the operational prospects for the branch network. In some countries, for demographic or geographical reasons, there are lots of Post Office branches that do not have many customers and therefore their profit margins are negative. The supply of financial services based on transaction relations of a traditional type and on *face-to-face* relations here can be seen as an opportunity or, on the contrary, as an economic constraint. The revenue generated by financial services is a very positive element, this means that the latter certainly play an essential role in the management of the network, creating important synergies. In this particular area the main strengths, in many cases, apart from the capillary distribution and closeness to customers, are longer opening hours, combined with the image of soundness, transparency and user friendliness of the service pricing systems.

The natural market target is the medium-low, or sometimes also the higher cultural segment, consisting of those customers who are interested in cost reduction. The availability of resources in some cases might not be particularly limited, but the management approach gives priority to the choice of standardised products and proposes offer conditions that are easy to understand. The combination with the postal activity also allows for service provision "at home", which is seen as an extension of the branch activity. The market potential in this particular segment can be particularly appealing also due to the new emerging business areas, including the various forms of asset management, social security and insurance coverage of elementary branches, in the development phase of the mass market. Although the product simplicity and the standardisation, as well as the customers' attitude itself reduce the area of application for advisory activities, it is true that the Post Office branch is not always suitable to perform these functions. The proposed solutions vary according to the volumes of asset managed and generally they also include the areas of personal financial advising, with *ad hoc* trained staff at the desk or by providing remote services by phone or through a call centre.

On the other hand, the delivery of financial services might not be economical if such activity creates insufficient operational volumes and margins, thus hindering the rationalisation of the branch network, while if banking institutions that are similar in terms of proximity and market target are already present in the same area they might be able to satisfy the demand from that particular market segment, thus reducing its potential. This is the case of Nordic countries which has already been described.

There are also intermediate solutions, consisting of differentiation policies in terms of branch types so that it is possible to make available a complete range of services, including financial services, only in areas that are economically profitable. The other existing services can be restructured, to include for example Post Offices in shops, points of contact in supermarkets, or travelling staff in case there are no fixed structures in the areas which provide for fewer operations and profits. The latter option is possible provided that there is no resistance on the side of trade unions aiming at safeguarding the employment level and organisation in the area and that there are no constraint in terms of the provision of universal banking services at the Post Office branches. This need is usually felt more strongly precisely in those types of low-density and low-profit areas[80].

As for the adjustment of prices made in order to increase the margins and profitability, it is necessary to bear in mind that, in most European countries, the greatest strength in the supply of financial services by the Post Office is the lower

---

[80] For more details see Chapter 5 in this volume.

pricing with respect to the banking system. This is also a consequence of the standardisation of service and of the limited added value given in terms of advisory and customisation activities.

If we analyse the current positioning and mission statement of postal operators in Europe, three strategic groups emerge:

- postal firms with a wide-ranging spectrum of financial activities (Germany, France, Italy, the Netherlands, Spain);
- postal firms focussing on a range of products and services that are basic, or even advanced, but in any case limited (UK, Austria, Belgium, Denmark and Norway);
- postal firms that are about to leave the financial sector (Sweden and Finland).

There are also countries that are still in a transition phase and might develop either in the direction of abandoning the sector – which according to the indications seems the most likely option in the majority of cases – or of a marked strengthening, presumably by creating strong partnerships. This is the case of Ireland, Portugal and Greece.

Among those operators who have adopted a global positioning strategy, in a more advanced position, we find DPWN which has already developed consolidated operations also in the trading on-line area. By acquiring specialised operators it has paved the way for activities in the area of loan granting. France and Italy are well established in the area of payments service and deposit collection - France also offers advanced managed saving instruments - therefore they should be able to develop successful global strategies. However they still need structural interventions in order to improve the organisation and to develop suitable specialised competencies aimed at achieving sustainable growth in a more sophisticated market. It should be mentioned that in France La Poste already has a consolidated image in the sector and the consolidated combination with similar public structures in the financial sector facilitates this development. In Italy Poste Italiane is still trying to build up on its image and massive marketing campaigns have been started for this purpose. In the latter case it is more difficult to find financial partners also due to the obstacles from the domestic banking system which opposes the entry into the sector of an operator still controlled by the Government. The losses and inefficiencies in the postal core business area are so substantial that a kind of subsidy is more or less unavoidable. As for the future prospects in both cases, the public base of the postal company and the absence of opening to private entities will probably cause the strategic management to be less flexible. This entails for example limitations in the choice of partners because the selection has to be made though a public tender procedure.

The picture thus drawn of strategic groupings does not show with sufficient clarity the other trend in positioning strategies, represented by choices related to the intervention methods. In this area the solutions adopted are often the key for the success or failure of the initiatives. The consequence in these cases can be either the sudden development or the declining trend followed by the decision to leave that particular business area.

3.4.1 Choosing Modalities of Intervention

In line with the trends in the financial sector – which are oriented, on one side, towards universal banking and integrated offer of products and services capable of meeting a wide range of needs and, on the other side, of specialisation within product area and phase of production process – the options available at the Post in the offer of financial services, are basically organised upon the following structure:

- **Internal production and distribution**
  - *traditional*
  - *direct*
- **Delegated production**
  - *captive*
  - *partnership*

  and distribution
  - *traditional*
  - *direct*
- **Distribution agreements**

In general terms, within those markets with a low level of evolution and specific regulation and special regimes to meet particular needs, the prevailing model is the one of internal production and distribution managed by the Post Office. The natural evolution of this structure is towards a clearer distinction of operational structures dedicated to the financial activities from an internal organisation point of view. As a matter of fact, in recent times, in order to avoid cross-subsidies with activities which are under legal monopoly conditions or under the reserved area and, at the same time, activities open to competition, the regulation has imposed an accounting separation of the different business areas. As far as internal production is concerned, however, the activities continue to be strongly integrated from the strategic point of view as well from the functional perspective with the postal group.

As above mentioned, originally the adoption of the above described model has been made easier because the Post Offices were already part of the public administration. Nowadays, the model can exist if the level of sophistication remains low, that is to say, if the market expresses a demand for elementary products, limited to standardised payments services and to very simple savings instruments. This flow of funds usually remains beyond the financial market. The offer of social banking services is usually organised upon this model: within this model itself, the financial activity is a kind of extension of public functions which were already given to the postal incumbent.

Maintaining such an organisation also in more advanced financial markets can help keeping special rules and regimes that might be more easily questioned by adopting new organisational models and different company structures. Therefore, from certain viewpoints, this could be considered as a transitory solution which is adopted to take time onto the market and to enhance some positions starting from generally advantageous conditions.

Besides the two above mentioned situations, the European experiences tend to develop towards forms of externationalisation of production which are delegated to specialised structures[81].

Moreover, in this field, a possible choice can be made between the exclusive externalisation of production to a specialised unit (captive), which is subject to a totalitarian control and integrated in the postal group or the setting up of partnerships with third partners which can bring technical know how, specialised management culture and proved experience image. Nevertheless, this second possibility has the traditional problem of a partnership: to keep and confirm in the time the different economical subjects' convergence and to elaborate successful strategies for the promoters.

If then we consider at the same time the wide range of activities (see the above mentioned Table 3.8), the partner that is being chosen for a determined activity area is not necessarily the best one for other areas and this fact can influence then the further development. Therefore, the choice is very delicate and in the European postal service, several experiences of difficulties in this respect are to be found, as the previous historical analysis shows. As the intermediation areas that are addressed and the product range that are offered become wider and wider, with growing levels of complexity, there seems to be no other choice than of specialised units, which is also what happens mostly in the banks.

In extreme terms, the fact of choosing the externalisation can be radical. In this case, the Post Office concentrates only on the distribution function, while the manufacturing process is carried out only by third parties with which they have long term relations and through commercial agreements. In this case, the relationship is developed on the basis of contracts which are more flexible and also the commissions are considered as a more often applicable tool in order to orient the different attitudes towards the expected results. As a matter of fact, the previous historical analysis shows that the fees due for the commercial activity

[81] For certain activities (setting up of insurance and social security policies, joint activity of saving collection and loans granting, management of mutual funds, direct intervention within the securities brokerage's activity, among others), the choice can be imposed by the regulation itself. For different reasons connected to the prevention of solvency and owing to the controls' effectiveness, the corporate purpose must be limited to specific areas of activity.

and, in particular, the splitting up of remuneration in a fix and a variable component following the real operativity have often been renegotiated by the post and financial partners. This is a confirmation of the lively dynamics to be found in the rapidly growing markets.

If the we consider jointly the two development vectors (business areas and intervention models) the following positionings emerge (Figure 3.1):

Figure 3.1

Post intervention areas and models while offering financial services

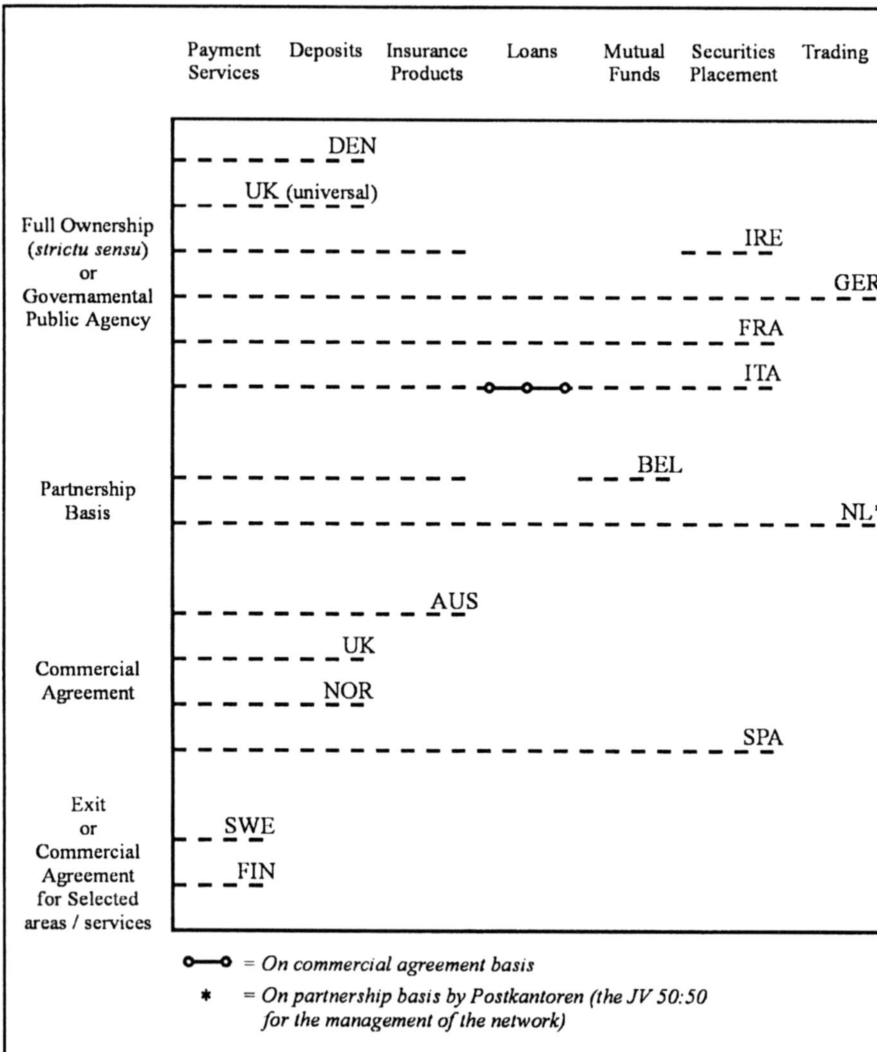

The above described administrative model typically chooses the first solution. On the other side, the "Postbank" look mostly at the delegated production solutions, in an ante litteram way, since the theory of this model has been set up after the Postbank's experiences.

While restructuring of postal systems and public administrations with separation of economical activities in private company structures, a certain rationalisation of partnership relationships has become necessary. As a matter of fact, the internalisation itself of all production and distribution processes called for accountant separation and setting up of explicit goals and intervention modalities in the financial area (within the management contract and statutes). This happened in many cases with the hostility of the bank system that, in new market conditions, invokes equal regulation treatment and prevention of cross subsidies with funds generated by reserved activities or subsidised in favour of financial services. These performances should be carried out following market rules. Moreover, there are conflicts also within the post groups themselves owing to competitive pressures, which have unusual strength - comparing to the past tradition - and a strong impact, within the postal activity as well as in the financial and banking sector.

In general, these strengths have strongly obliged to come to a high degree of efficiency and modernisation of procedures and a more rational use of human resources, while widening the offer spectrum, with a different layout as far branches are concerned, as well as for the management of relationship to the customers. Post services and financial services, under pressure, have taken up divergent and conflictual attitudes and the consequences on the offer of financial services have bee generally negative.

The Correos & Telegraphos and Caja Postal-Grupo Argentaria as well as the very first relationship between Deutsche Post and Deutsche Postbank are very clear examples of this.

Thanks to the externationalisation of activities in different structures which are separated from the juridical and organisational point of view, concentrating respectively onto a specific business area, the conflict can be reduced or, in any case, the strategies can be set up and the missions can be singled out in a more transparent way. Therefore, the strategies' final results will be more incisive.

As earlier described, the Netherlands have adopted an interesting solution: in this country, the historical evolution of postal and bank services have followed parallel paths. This has paved the way to the successful implementation of a strong partnership with a primary bank-insurance group with global operativity, from the viewpoint of geographical size as well as from the financial intermediation areas perspective. As far as the management of the branch network is concern, this partnership is possible through a joint venture. This solution has no doubt been facilitated by the fact that the Postbank had already become part of the bank group and contributed, in the retail segment, to the development of the future ING. In this experience, the privatisation of the postal area services and its financial sector take place, in fact, without any significant considerable time lag.

Nevertheless, the European TPG leadership position in the postal, transport and logistics sectors, may lead to emphasise excessively the pan-European vision of the market and, consequently, to reduce and nullify the importance of domestic operativity within the international context. The branch's operativity remains linked to the domestic market in this area and carries out its financial performances to the clients of the retail market.

The German DPWN had a more ill timed scheduled and more difficulties in the setting up a partnership with Deutsche Postbank. These difficulties have been solved by creating a strong partnership model where the post group has complete control over the bank group.

In general, the credit activity (i.e loans granting) remains excluded from the operativity area: in this sector the access is mostly limited to modest financing for the clients of the retail market, in order to face cash needs and limited personal loans or, more often, connected to the use of credit cards. On the side of the investment of funds raised by postal deposits, they generally choose bonds, Treasury bills or investments within the banking sector.

On the other hand, for what concerns their activity within the framework of offer of loans to private subjects, generally connected to the purchase of a house, or offer of support to business for their productive activities - that is to say for a type of activity which implies a deeper evaluation of the credit background itself and the subsequent monitoring of risks positions - the post groups prefer commercial agreements. To this purpose, they become then brokers without taking any risk on their own.

This seems to confirm the Posts' interest to come to the financial market mostly with that type of activities that generate commission and fees, without taking financial risks.

3.5 References

BELGIAN POST GROUP (2001): Contribution to the Conference "Postal Offices & Financial Services", February 12-13, EFMA, Paris.

BRAGA M.D. (1999): The Norwegian Experience: the Case of Den Norske Bank, in RUOZI R., ANDERLONI L. (1999), Banking Privatisation in Europe. The Process and the Consequences on Strategies and Organisational Structures, Springer-Verlag, Berlin-Heidelberg.

CHANNON D.F. (1977): British Banking Strategy and the International Challenge, The MacMillan Press, London.

CORIGLIANO R. (1977): La Cassa Depositi e Prestiti e le Casse di risparmio postali, Franco Angeli, Milano.

DEL BURGO S.S., TURNABELL CARRIÓ (1998): The Spanish Experience: Argentaria Privatisation, in RUOZI R., ANDERLONI L. (1999), Banking Privatisation in Europe. The Process and the Consequences on Strategies and Organisational Structures, Springer-Verlag, Berlin-Heidelberg.

DON CRUICKSHANK (2000): Competition in UK Banking. A Report to the Chancellor of the Exchequer, March, The Stationery Office, London.

EUROPEAN CENTRAL BANK (1999): The Effects of Technology on the EU Banking System, July.

HARKER P.T., ZENIOS S.A. (1998): What Drives the Performance of Financial Institutions? W.P. 98-21, The Wharton School.

HEIDENREICH L. (2001): Presentation of Postversicherung AG, Contribution to the Conference "Postal Offices & Financial Services", February 12-13, EFMA, Paris.

HURLEN J. (2001): The radical transformation of the Norwegian Post Office, Contribution to the Conference "Postal Offices & Financial Services", February 12-13, EFMA, Paris.

LA POSTE, Rapport annuel, (various years).

LLEWELLYN D.T. (1999): The New Economics of Banking, SUERF Studies, n°5.

LLEWELLYN D.T. (1997): Disintegrazione del processo bancario: l'esperienza delle banche inglesi, in European Banking Report.

LOPEZ-FALDE J.M. (2001): Partnership banking. Correos/Deutsche Bank agreement, Contribution to the Conference "Postal Offices & Financial Services", February 12-13, EFMA, Paris.

PILLEY O., ANDERLONI L. (1999): European Post Offices in Financial Services. Competitors or Strategic Partners?, Lafferty, Dublin.

PILLEY O. (1998): Cross-Sector Alliances in Financial Services, Dublin, Lafferty.

POSTBANK, Annual Report, various years.

SALVEMINI M.T. (1999): Il punto di vista della Cassa depositi e prestiti, in CESARINI F. - COSTI R. - TUTINO F., Bancoposta e mercati, Il Mulino, Bologna.

THE POST OFFICE, Annual Report, various years.

WATKINS J. (1998): Information Technology, Organisations and People. Transformation in the UK retail financial services sector, Routledge.

WORLD BANK (2001), World Development Indicators 2001, April.

4

The Posts: a Full Range of Payment Services

Lucia Leonelli

4.1 Introduction

The payment service market is changing according to many different patterns. Economic globalisation has led to an increase in transaction volume and frequency, with the result that the risks associated with settlement are emphasising the need for a reliable payment system.

Technological development has created new payment instruments as well as new ways of transferring money. Furthermore, it has significantly contributed to changing the context of market competition. On the one hand, new opportunities to enter the market and participate in the production process, in full or in part, have emerged for new operators; on the other, traditional operators have been forced to reorganise their range of services in order to retain their market shares.

The enforcement of new regulations has modified market boundaries. The advent of the European Monetary Union has increased the need for cross-border payments, whose costs and timing have to be consistent with those of domestic payments.

The restructuring process that has affected the supply framework is an important aspect of the changes that are still underway in the payments sector. This paper examines the role played by the postal system. In particular, it focuses on how the supply of postal payment services – which traditionally consisted of collection services on behalf of the State - has evolved over time. This study is based on a comparative approach between the main European countries and points out how different cultural and legislative conditions, together with the institutional models adopted in the various countries, can affect the postal system operation in relation to the supply of payment services.

This chapter is divided into four main sections. The first section highlights the major differences in the way payment systems are structured in the various countries and the role played by the postal system. The second section examines the payment services the Post Office can supply, focusing in particular on their range, technical features and spread. The third section analyses the degree of integration existing between the banking and the postal payment system, considering its profound significance and the way it can heavily affect the structure and effectiveness of the supply. The forth section examines a few aspects concerning the availability of postal services on the Internet, paying special attention to the activities related to e-commerce.

4.2 The Payment System Structure in the Main European Countries: the Role of the Post Office

The payment systems available in European countries differ in terms of user preferences for one service or the other, the structure of supply, its terms and conditions and the way control measures are implemented.

This section analyses the payment systems available in the main European countries, with particular reference to the aspects associated with user interest for payment services in general and special services in particular. The historical differences underlying the success of certain services are briefly analysed while emphasising the main current trends. Within this framework, the requirements of customers that traditionally prefer the postal system are studied, in order to evaluate the role this operator has played in history and its prospects.

4.2.1 The Use of Payment Services in the Main European Countries

The propensity to use payment services is heavily affected by the role cash continues to play, especially when small/medium amounts are paid personally.

The ratio of cash in circulation to GDP has considerably changed, partly as a consequence of the greater interest consumers have shown for alternative ways of payment. A high ratio may have different meanings and reflect, for example, the strong role of the informal economy or the value reserve function strong currencies usually have, with the result of weak currency countries feeling encouraged to increase their demand. While Germany shows a growing ratio, Belgium, France and the United Kingdom show a declining index. Despite its shrinkage, the Italian ratio is still higher than in the other countries, except for Germany and Spain.

Table 4.1

Cash in circulation/GDP ratio in the main European industrialised countries

	Belgium	France	Germany	Italy	The Netherlands	United Kingdom	Spain
1981	10.1	5.4	5.5	6.4	6.6	4.2	n. a.
1991	6.0	4.3	6.5	5.4	6.9	2.7	n. a.
1999	5.1	3.3	6.6	6.0	4.6	2.9	9.7*

* *This figure refers to 1998*

Source: Bank for International Settlement, Statistics on Payment System in the Group of Ten Countries, 1992 and 2001, European Central Bank, Payment Systems in the European Union, 2000.

As for the number of per capita transactions settled with instruments other than cash, Italy is far behind the average of the other countries. Yet, the trend towards the use of payment services is certainly on the rise if we consider that in 1993, in Italy, only 31.7 per capita transactions were settled with instruments other than cash.

Table 4.2
Per capita transactions settled with instruments other than cash

	Belgium	**France**	**Germany**	**Italy**	**The Netherlands**	**United Kingdom**	**Spain**
1998	122.5	181.1	166.5	42.5	154.5	150.8	46.2

Source: Banca d'Italia, Relazione annuale, 1998, table aH 2 (Bank of Italy, Annual Report, 1998, table aH 2).

Table 4.3
No. of accounts per inhabitant

	Belgium	**France**	**Germany**	**Italy**	**The Netherlands**	**United Kingdom**	**Spain**
1991	1.0	2.0	1.0	0.4	1.1	2.4	n. a.
1998	1.4	1.1	1.0	0.5	1.3	2.5	n. a.

Source: Bank for International Settlement, Statistics on Payment System in the Group of Ten Countries, 1992 and 2000, European Central Bank, Payment Systems in the European Union, 2000.

Italy confirms its high propensity to use cash, which partly derives from the lower number of current accounts than in the other countries. The greater use of current accounts in the other countries is due to different causes. To start with, current accounts are more widespread where the charging system provides for free payment services to account holders in return for receiving no interest on credit balances. Other reasons may be traced back to cultural attitudes and the way they have been influenced by the authorities' decisions in the various countries. Limits on cash payments have been enforced in France since the Second World War, whereas in Italy their adoption has come only recently following the enactment of money laundering legislation. Furthermore, the circularity of the networks responsible for payment card management can affect the number of current accounts held by individuals. Indeed, if payment cards can be used to withdraw money from any automated teller machine, regardless of the issuer, users will be able to complete their transactions at any ATM available with one card only (even if different costs will be charged). If said circularity does not exist, users will feel encouraged to open more current accounts with different operators so as to have more cards and be able to take advantage of more ATMs. This is one of the reasons behind the considerable number of current accounts in the United

Kingdom, where circularity between ATM management networks has become effective only since January 2001[1].

Table 4.4
Cash deposits by the public as a percentage of GDP

	Belgium	France	Germany	Italy	The Netherlands	The United Kingdom
1991	13.6	19.9	15.6	31	17	45.8
1999	20.1	21.7	21.2	33.3	30.4	59.8

Source: Bank for International Settlement, Statistics on Payment System in the Group of Ten Countries, 1992 and 2001, European Central Bank, Payment Systems in the European Union, 2000.

4.2.2 Cheque-based and Giro-based Countries

As far as the use of payment services is concerned, cheques are preferred in France, United Kingdom and Ireland (Figure 4.1), whereas giros are more widely used in Germany, The Netherlands and Belgium (Figure 4.2).

Figure 4.1
Use of cheques in transactions not settled in cash (%)

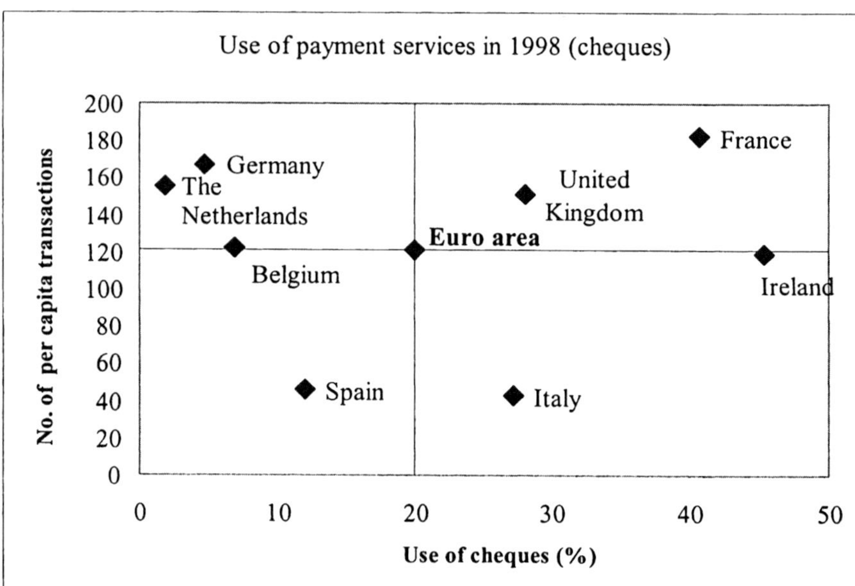

Source: BIS data.

[1] See www.apacs.org.uk

This diversity may be attributed to several factors. First of all, the supply structure should be considered. The need to make remote payments has resulted in the need to take advantage of a payment service provided by a financial institution that can transfer available funds in all parts of the country.

Figure 4.2
Use of giros for transactions not settled in cash (%)

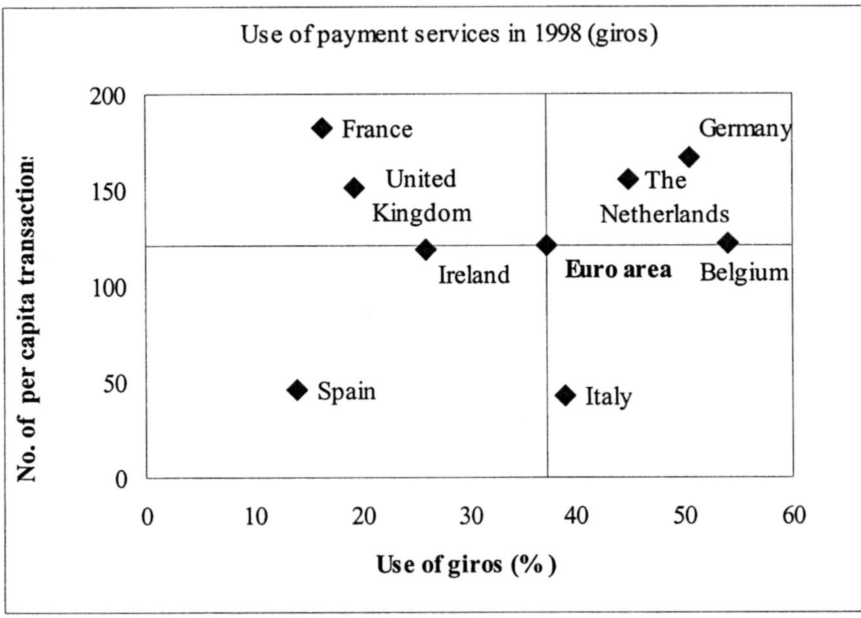

Source: BIS data.

In some European countries (for example in the Netherlands) the need for remote payment services has been fulfilled by such national institutions as the Post Office with its dense branch network. Since the payment service offered by this type of provider usually has the structure of a giro payment, this instrument has become more popular than the cheque in the users' culture. In other countries such as France and the United Kingdom, traditionally known as cheque-based countries, the relationship between correspondent banks has been backed by regional agreements that have guaranteed the development of an efficient cheque trading system, allowing cheques to become the most popular means of payment[2].

[2] See Committee on Payment and Settlement System (1999), p. 9.

Table 4.5
Breakdown of non-cash payments
As a % of the volume of transactions settled with instruments other than cash

	Belgium	France	Germany	Italy	The Netherlands	United Kingdom	Spain
Cheque	5.8	40.7	4.0	25.6	1.0	29.0	12.1
Card payment	28.9	18.2	5.2	17.6	28.6	34.6	22.1
Credit transfer	51.9	16.4	50.6	37.2	41.6	17.6	14.0
Direct debits	9.4	13.3	40.2	10.4	28.9	18.9	46.0

These data refer to 1999 except for France and Spain, whose data refer to 1998
Source: Bank for International Settlement, Statistics on Payment System in the Group of Ten Countries, 2001; European Central Bank, Payment Systems in the European Union, 2000 .

The payee's risks differ according to the method of payment chosen by the payer. Risk diversity has resulted in different forms of payment with varying degrees of acceptability. Some countries, such as France and, more recently, Italy, have enforced provisions that aim at providing more guarantees to cheque receivers, thereby making the instrument more acceptable.

In some countries, such as Germany, the spread of giros has been further favoured by a close integration between companies and banks, which has contributed to encouraging direct crediting of salaries into employees' accounts[3].

The current trends show a generalised increase in the use of payment cards and an overall rise in settlements performed through automated payment services, which can be easily completed without the need to fill in paper forms. Cash continues to play a prominent role, especially to settle transactions that payers do not want to be traceable. The use of cheques is generally considered to be on the decline. This is partly due to the need for a definite charging system in countries like France, where the issuance of cheques has always been free, and partly due to the fact that the Eurocheque card, which has traditionally guaranteed cheques for domestic and international settlements and cash withdrawals, will no longer fulfil this function as of January 2002[4].

With regard to the changes in payment culture that have occurred in individual European countries, a few significant elements are worth mentioning. In the United Kingdom, preferences in the use of payment services have considerably changed over the last decade. Card-paid transactions have strongly increased, whereas the use of cheques has diminished, even though cheques are still the most widespread means of payment. The large use of cheques is the direct consequence of efficient settlement systems and the use of guarantee cards, which have traditionally strengthened the acceptability of cheques. The strong development of payment services in the United Kingdom is further witnessed by the low ratio of

[3] Brizi R., Tresoldi C, Sasso F. (1999), p. 49.
[4] For further information, see www.europay.com/common_nav3_empty.html.

cash in circulation to GDP, which is among the lowest in Europe. Card settlements are reported to be increasing substantially in France, another country which usually falls in the cheque-based group. The country is very much oriented towards the development of electronic payment systems. Towards the end of the 80s, the country introduced chips in payment cards to enhance their safety and potential for use. Here, too, the ratio of cash in circulation to GDP is very low. In contrast, the ratio of cash in circulation to GDP is high in Germany and the Netherlands, where cheques do not play a prominent role and giros are preferred to settle large purchases. Likewise, these countries show a growing use of payment cards as a substitute for cash, whose role is increasingly waning.

4.2.3 The Evolution of the Role of the Bank-post

The role played by the Bank-post in the provision of payment services has changed over time. Since the second half of the 19th century, the postal system has supplied financial services in competition with the banking system to meet social needs that, with respect to the payment sector, were associated with facilitating the transfer of money to any part of the country and abroad, thereby establishing a channel for public revenue collection (taxes, rates,...) and making payments on behalf of the State.

Given the size of its branch network, the Bank-post has formed the backbone of the payment and collection system used by the State, public authorities and public utilities. As for payment services, the Bank-post has mainly focused on the provision of collection services.

Therefore, at the beginning, it played its role in the payment service sector within a segmented, hardly competitive market, where banks mainly served prominent clients making high-value transactions, whereas the Post Offices performed lower-value payment and collection transactions[5].

Starting in the '80s, a number of changes have occurred which have led the banks to compete with the postal system in areas the latter had always controlled. Banks have extended and strengthened their presence in economically more developed areas, have widened their service range and have enhanced the efficiency of their services, also thanks to several initiatives adopted at system level. In many cases, this evolution has resulted in a reduction of the postal system activity, even in relation to payment services. Within other contexts, marked by low income levels, the banking system has reduced its presence, leaving financial service requirements unmet.

An example of the way banks have started to supply services that had always been a prerogative of the postal system is provided by the payment of pensions and benefits. In European countries, this activity had traditionally been carried out by the postal system, mainly because of its capillary presence over the territory and the privileged relationship existing between the postal system and the State.

---

[5] See Tenaglia Ambrosini M. G. (1996), p. 485.

However, over the last ten years, banks have entered this market segment, offering direct crediting of pensions into bank current accounts. Over time, this has led to a lower incidence of the pensions paid by the Post Offices. In Great Britain, this service is currently provided by the Post Office and Girobank on behalf of the UK Government's Social Security (DSS) and direct crediting of benefits amounts to 30 billion pounds. From the year 2003, direct crediting of benefits will be entrusted to Nat West, a market leader in the automated payment service industry. Post Offices will only be responsible for order book or cash payments[6]. In Belgium, Post Offices are compelled to make door-to-door payments of retirement and minimum pensions[7]. In France, 95% of all payments on behalf of the *Caisse Nationale d'Allocations Familiale (CNAF)* are made through giros by the banking system (approx. 75%) and the postal system (approx. 25%)[8]. In Italy, pensions paid by the Post Offices on behalf of *INPS* total approximately 80 million; this figure is however gradually diminishing owing to the increasing role played by banks (*Corte dei Conti*, 2000 - Italian National Audit Office, 2000).

In spite of its strengths, resulting from its management of most of the payment and collection transactions on behalf of the State and its ability to establish close contacts with customers[9] as a consequence of its capillary presence on the territory, the postal system has been obliged to face keen competition for a restricted range of services that were qualitatively unable to meet the growing customers' needs in a satisfactory manner.

The social purpose of postal payment services has gradually lost its strength over time and, partly in consequence of the legal transformation of the various entities, an entrepreneurial management philosophy has progressively taken root. This new philosophy is aimed at finding suitable conditions to encourage the development of real competition in terms of range, efficiency and cost of the services provided[10].

The adoption of this different management philosophy has also been made possible by the removal of legislative constraints affecting the category of payment and collection services.

According to the regulations enforced in the various countries, payment and collection services can be classified as:

- "universal", non-exclusive services – a definition that applies to services that have to be supplied at conditions ensuring that no customers are excluded, i.e. with limits to charges and wide accessibility;
- "non-universal" services, supplied under competitive conditions.

---

[6] See Pilley O., Anderloni L. (1999).

[7] La Poste, Contrat de gestion entre l'Etat et la Poste, 1997-2001.

[8] Groupe de réflexion et de concertation sur l'évolution des relations entre les banques et leurs clients, Rapport exercice 1999-2000, p. 205.

[9] See Forestieri G. (1999), p. 75.

[10] See Bank of Italy (1998), p.287.

Table 4.6
Regulations governing payment and collection services

Country	Regulations	Universal services: services that must be supplied under conditions ensuring that no customers are excluded	Non-universal services, supplied under competitive conditions
Belgium	Contrat de gestion entre l'Etat e La poste	Issue and payment of postal money orders	Other payment services
France	Law implementing directive 97/67		Payment services
Germany	Postal Act of 22nd December 1997		Payment services
Italy	Legislative Decree no. 261 of 22nd July 1999 *		Payment services
The Netherlands	Postal act 1988		Payment services
United Kingdom	Post Services Act 2000		Payment services
Spain	Ley postal no. 24 of 13th July 1998	Giro services, whereby payments to natural or legal persons are ordered on behalf of other persons through the public postal network	

** The new "Contratto di Programma" published on G.U. n° 221, September 21st, 2000 based on the legislative decree mentioned above, partially changes the situation. In fact financial services are no more included in the universal services.*

Passing from the first to the second category means removing a number of constraints that hinder range enrichment, customisation and freedom in the definition of bank charging criteria. By adopting the directive 97/67 of 15 December 1997, European countries have preferred to assign a minimal relevance to this category, which necessarily includes postal services under non-competitive conditions. In implementing the directive, some countries like Italy and France, have preferred not to include payment and collection services in the category of universal services. Other countries, such as Spain and, to a certain extent, Belgium, continue to regard payment services as universal services, forcing them to meet precise profitability and accessibility requirements.

4.2.4 The Presence of the Post Office in the Payment System

Customers that traditionally take advantage of the payment services supplied by the Bank-post are private individuals, companies and the public authorities. Private individuals are usually the following:

- non-banked individuals, i.e. people that live in places where there are no banks;

- individuals without a bank current account, even though they live in places where there are banks;
- individuals that prefer the postal system even though they have a bank current account because its costs are lower and they are more familiar with postal procedures, they have a poor financial culture, there are no limitations (except in terms of amounts) in making and receiving payments, they can take advantage of more services at a single counter (e.g. collecting their pension and paying utility bills);
- individuals holding a postgiro account.

As for companies, in addition to the reasons mentioned for private individuals, special collection requirements should be highlighted. In this respect, a distinction may be drawn between:

- large service companies that benefit, in particular, from collection services to collect utilities bills;
- commercial businesses with customers living in different areas of the countries that rely on the postal system to provide payment facilities that can be easily accessed by everyone;
- companies that prefer to leave their customers free to decide whether to make their payments at the bank or the Post Office.

By tradition, the public authorities also take advantage of the postal system for collection and payment transactions. An example is provided by tax collection and the payment of pensions and benefits.

Data shown in table 4.8 belong to 1998. In year 2000 the subscription of postgiro accounts sharply increased in Italy. In September 2001 the situation is 1.462 thousands of postgiro accounts due to the more focused strategy of Poste Italiane supporting the new offer of postabank services.

Table 4.7

No. of Post office branches

	Belgium	**France**	**Germany**	**Italy**	**The Netherlands**	**United Kingdom**	**Spain**
1991	3,142	16,944	25,909	14,412	2,715	20,638	n. a.
1999	1,386	16,926	n. a.	13,976	2,247	18,775	10,386(*)

(*) no. of Post Offices that perform financial transactions

Source : Bank for International Settlement, Statistics on Payment System in the Group of Ten Countries, 1992 e 2001; European Central Bank, Payment Systems in the European Union, 2000, Universal Postal Union, Statistics, 1998.

Table 4.8
No. of postgiro accounts (thousands)

	Belgium	France	Germany	Italy	The Netherlands	United Kingdom	Spain
End 1991	1,200	30,800	5,100	500	5,950	15,800	-
End 1998	1,271	10,089	3,950	413.6	7,500	16.1	-

Source: Bank for International Settlement, Statistics on Payment System in the Group of Ten Countries, 1992 and 2000; European Central Bank, Payment Systems in the European Union, 2000, Universal Postal Union, Statistics, 1998.

Unlike what happens with banks, where service users are usually also bank account holders, the users of postal payment services often ask for services that do not oblige payers to be postgiro account holders. These are generally-available payment services, i.e. services that may be requested by anyone, even in case of no previous relations with the Bank-post[11]. Sometimes a limitation may be the need for the payee to be a postgiro account holder, as it is the case for the collection services offered to companies and the public authorities.

The payment services supplied by the Bank-post mostly fall within the category of money transfer procedures, which provide the payee with a certain amount of money paid by the remitter on service activation. By its very nature, this procedure does not generate any credit risk for the payee. This feature has increased service acceptability, fostering its spread.

4.3 Analysis of the Supply

The range of payment services offered by the postal system has considerably widened with time, meeting the customers' demand more exhaustively. However, there are still profound differences between the postal systems of the countries under examination in terms of range diversification, service efficiency and ways of establishing contacts with customers.

This section examines the range of payment services offered by the postal system, highlighting the features of the systems in the various countries and the capacity or the limits of such services in fulfilling payment requirements. For reasons of clarity, our analysis will start from the postgiro account, since it represents a base relationship necessary to access some types of payment and collection services; all the other payment services are then examined, starting from the services than can be activated without holding a postgiro account, to finish with the services that move the funds available on the accounts.

---

[11] See Leonelli L. (1999), p. 31.

Finally, contact channels with customers are examined, pointing out the main initiatives that have been or are still being implemented to improve the existing channels and to open new ones.

4.3.1 The Postgiro Account

In the countries under examination, the postgiro account is provided by all postal institutions with a banking nature (Belgium, Germany and The Netherlands) as well as by French and Italian Post Offices. The Post Offices in the United Kingdom and Spain have no products of their own; however, they allow the customers of the banks that have entered into business agreements with them to access their accounts through post counters.

The customers that make use of this type of account are households, companies and the public authorities. By depositing money on a postgiro account, depositors entrusts the custody of their money holdings and the execution of payments and collection transactions on their behalf to the Post Office, so as to ensure a more efficient and cost-effective management of their available funds. The postgiro account also meets information requirements with respect to performed transactions. It may be regarded, especially by households, as a base relationship allowing them to access a wider range of financial and insurance services.

In some countries, the function of this account has changed with time. In Italy, the postgiro account offered by *Bancoposta* has traditionally been an instrument mainly used by large invoicing agencies to collect utility bills, since the account did not permit easy and rapid transactions[12].In May 2000, a new postgiro account was launched, addressed in particular to household customers. The new account plays a more significant monetary function and provides access to a range of financial and insurance services, in addition to a series of channels to take advantage of the account. Moreover, *Bancoposta* is presently studying a new account to meet the special needs of companies'. In Belgium, the *Postcheque* account is addressed to household or private customers. It is a typically monetary account which provides a wide range of payment services, mostly free. In the United Kingdom, the banking activity of the post office has been historically carried out by Girobank, which was transferred to Alliance & Leicester towards the end of the 80s[13]. In contrast, the role played within the payment system by the Post Office in France is extremely prominent. There are more than 10 million active postgiro accounts and the *Poste* is the second largest financial institution in France[14]. The postgiro account enables account holders to have cheque-books issued at any Post Office or sent directly to their homes. Furthermore, the French Post Office and, more recently, the German *Postbank*, have increasingly oriented

---

[12] La Torre M. (1996), p. 22.

[13] For more details see Chaper 3, § 3.2.2 in this volume.

[14] See www.lapostefinance.fr.

their activities towards the corporate segment, supplying cash management services as well.

As far as charging is concerned, different approaches are being taken in the European countries. In France, no charging policy has been adopted for the use of postgiro accounts and only an annual account management fee of 1.67 € is due. In the Netherlands as well, no charges are debited for account management. In Belgium, no fees are due in relation with the postcheque account at the *Banque de la Poste* for account management, sending bank statements, withdrawals from Post Office counters and ATMs, national giros, standing orders, domiciliation as well as cheque or electronic purse payments. In Italy, the *Bancoposta* account fee is 1,000 lire (0.52 €) per transaction, up to a maximum annual ceiling of 60,000 lire. A stamp duty of 49,500 lire is payable every year and a 27% tax rate is applicable on interest receivable. No fees are charged for such account transactions as opening, managing and closing an account, requesting a monthly statement of account, customer correspondence, checking the account balance, requesting the issue of a cheque-book or debit card (which will be dealt with in the following pages) and utility bill domiciliation. In Germany, the *Postbank* applies a monthly fee of 4.35 € on postgiro accounts. However, if the holder is under 26 or payments exceed 1,000 € per month, no charges are debited. A Eurocheque card or a card to withdraw money from ATMs is given to account holders over the age of 18.

As for the funds collected through postgiro accounts, they are managed by the same institutions in Belgium, Germany and the Netherlands, owing to their banking nature. In France, until 1 January 1999, all collected funds were transferred to the Treasury. After that date, in compliance with art. 126 of the 1999 Financial Bill (no. 98-1266 of 30 December 1998) and the programme agreement 98-2001, the amount collected through account deposits over five years will be gradually transferred to a Post Office subsidiary involved with investment banking. In Italy, a convention due to expire at the end of 2001 provides for the transfer of all funds collected through postgiro accounts to the *Cassa Depositi e Prestiti*, even though the 1997 Financial Bill established that "since February 1997, in relation to postal giros, except for postal giros held by public authorities or agencies, the *Ente Poste Italiane* may use the increase in deposits compared to the fourth quarter of 1996 for direct commitments to the Treasury and the purchase of State Bonds". These funds can therefore be used for other types of investments.

4.3.2 The Supply of Payment and Collection Services

To examine the payment and collection services supplied by the Post Office, we will start from the services that can be requested by anyone, even without holding a current account, to finish with the services that generate movements on the accounts.

The money order

The money order is a payment instrument used to transfer legal currency within a country (domestic money order) or abroad (international money order); sometimes amount and place limits are established (e.g. the Post Office is designated by the payer).

The money order can be used by any customer, even customers who do not hold a postgiro account. The instrument is issued after the necessary amount has been paid in cash to the selected post office. Besides requesting the money transfer, the customer can ask for a number of additional services including sending a message to the recipient, asking for a receipt or payment notice, enquiring about the outcome of the money order, seeing the paid instrument as well as requesting the non-transferability clause and the certification of issue or payment.

The domestic money order can be transferred by endorsement. The limitations of this instrument are its maximum amount and, as a result, its scope, as well as the long time required to obtain ordinary money order payment.

Table 4.9
No. and amount of money orders issued

	Belgium	**France**	**Germany**	**Italy**	**The Netherlands**	**United Kingdom**	**Spain**
No.	238.749	13.354.000	618.218 (*)	13.992.000	n. a.	29.693.740	20.329.037
Amount (SDR[15])	126.792.161	1.745.471.147	n. a.	2.358.218.908	n. a.	356.453.608	1.059.521.773

(*) This figure refers to 1998

Source: UPU statistics – items 10.1 and 10.2 www.upu.int.

International money orders can also be issued and received. Although international money orders are payable at the office specified on the instrument, they can also be cashed at any other office. The money order value is denominated in the currency of the country of destination or in another currency agreed between the parties. The money order coming from abroad can be transferred by endorsement.

The crediting money order is an instrument that allows the beneficiary to be credited with a certain amount directly on the postgiro account rather than in cash.

[15] SDRs are special drawing rights, i.e. a particular type of currency created by the International Monetary Fund. Its value is based on the average value of the 5 major world currencies.

The instrument can never be endorsed, nor can it be cashed. In Italy, to prevent Post Offices from running any credit risks, the service can only be received but not provided. The international money order is used exclusively to refund the senders of correspondence or parcels sent or received from abroad with the corresponding cash being paid on delivery.

Furthermore, the Post Office has entered into agreements that provide for funds to be transferred abroad in a very short time, approx. ten minutes. The companies that provide this service are Western Union and Money Gramm. The Italian and the British Post Office have entered an agreement with Money Gram. The Spanish Post Office has entered an agreement with Western Union to transfer funds in 180 countries.

Table 4.10

No. and amount of international money orders issued

	Belgium	**France**	**Germany**	**Italy**	**The Netherlands**	**United Kingdom**	**Spain**
No.	546.373	3.359.726	851.134 (*)	1.189.291	200.000 (**)	1.581.150	354.521
Amount (SDR)	107,089,824	558,105,793	n. a.	401,283,683	n. a.	2,570,699	58,538,069

Data referred to 1999; (*) This figure refers to 1998; (**) Including inpayment money orders.

Source: UPU statistics, items 10.3 and 10.4 www.upu.int.

Table 4.11

No. and amount of international money orders received

	Belgium	**France**	**Germany**	**Italy**	**The Netherlands**	**United Kingdom**	**Spain**
No.	112,746	508,285	2,583,339 (*)	1,127,276	180,000 (**)	25,476	341,225
Amount (SDR)	30,084,197	116,582,308	1,780,807,687 (*)	333,992,604	n. a.	1,079,385	66,297,025

Data referred to 1999; (*) This figure refers to 1998; (**) Including inpayment money orders

Source: UPU statistics, items 10.5 and 10.6 www.upu.int.

The giro inpayment

This service allows customers to credit a certain amount of money to the postgiro account of a recipient. The payer is issued a payment receipt as evidence of payment completion. Compared to the equivalent bank service (bank transfer), this service is less expensive because transaction fees are considerably lower.

Table 4.12
No. and amount of domestic giro payments

	Belgium	France	Germany	Italy	The Netherlands	United Kingdom
No.	54,278,907	34,927,000	20,323,278(*)	670,169,000	60,000,000	102,415,000
Amount (SDR Thousands)	4,401,625	29,807,488	12,367,583(*)	118,280,743	n. a.	102,796,824

Data referred to 1999. Data for Spain are not available ; (*) This figure refers to 1998
Source: UPU statistics – items 10.9 and 10.10 www.upu.int.

Giro cheques

Giro cheques are used to move the funds deposited on a postgiro account. To draw a giro cheque the drawer must be a postgiro account holder, have enough available funds and have the necessary paper forms. Giro cheques are mostly used to transfer funds from postgiro to bank accounts or to pay periodical or perpetual annuities or pensions.

Post cheques are certified cheques issued by some postal administrations[16] to their postgiro account holders; these instruments can be collected at Post Offices in Europe, Japan or the United States. The Italian *Bancoposta* does not provide this service since the enforced regulations do not allow it to take insolvency risks. The instrument allows the customer to go to any Post Office and cash the cheque showing a guarantee card or identity papers. Once paid, the instrument is given back to the issuing Administration and a link account in the creditor country is debited. After receiving the instrument, the issuer debits the customer's account. Therefore, the account is debited after the cheque has been paid; during that time lapse, the issuer runs the risk of insufficient funding, as cheques may be totally or partially uncovered.

---

[16] This is the case for Belgium, Denmark, France, Luxembourg, Norway, the Netherlands and Switzerland.

The postal giro

The postal giro allows customers to transfer funds from their own postgiro account to another postgiro account holder. Funds can be transferred within a country (domestic postal giro) or abroad (international postal giro).

This instrument is used for retail payments, to settle utility bills and invoices, to pay taxes and contributions. Funds are usually transferred between households, households and companies and, in case of domestic postal giros, between households and large issuing bodies.

Table 4.13
No. and amount of domestic postal giros received (credit transfer)

	Belgium	France	Germany	Italy	The Netherlands	United Kingdom
No.	45,679,311(*)	1,299,697,024	986,072,357(*)	11,628,244	n. a.	4,506,946
Amount (SDR thousands)	510,039,406 (*)	432,278,573	614,356,944 (*)	68,316,737	280,000	n. a.

Data referred to 1999 – Data for Spain are not available. (*) This figure refers to 1998
Source: UPU statistics – items 10.11 and 10.12 www.upu.int.

Table 4.14
No. and amount of domestic postal giros ordered (outpayments)

	Belgium	France	Germany	Italy	The Netherlands	United Kingdom	Spain
No.	112,746	508,285	2,583,339 (*)	1,127,276	180,000 (**)	25,476	341,225
Amount (SDR thousands)	30,084	116,582	1,780,807 (*)	333,992	n. a.	1,079	66,297

Data referred to 1999; (*) This figure refers to 1998; (**) Including inpayment money orders
Source: UPU statistics – items 10.13 and 10.14 www.upu.int.

A further service the Post Offices provide to meet the needs of customers that have to transfer funds abroad is Eurogiro. The Eurogiro system allows customers to make cross-border transfers of limited amounts of money between two postgiro account holders living in countries that participate in the Eurogiro network. This procedure eliminates the need for paper forms since funds are transferred electronically. This system allows the Post Office to credit the sum due to the payee within four days of its sending; the number of days can be reduced to two in case an urgent transfer is requested (this last procedure has been activated only in a few countries).

The Eurogiro system was developed following a study carried out by a Group of European Postal General Managers. To implement the project and international organisation was set up in 1993 - EUROGIRO Network/AS, based in Taastrup, Denmark – whose mission is to manage the electronic procedure that allows to transfer funds across borders. The company shareholders include the following countries: Austria, Belgium, Denmark, Finland, France, Germany, Ireland, Iceland, Italy, Luxembourg, Norway, the Netherlands, Spain, Sweden, Switzerland, Portugal and the United Kingdom. The countries taking advantage of the network as users include: Japan, Morocco, Turkey and the United States. The procedure allows customers to make and receive payments to and from other countries for a limited amount, at a reduced cost and in very safe conditions. It also reduces manual processing, thereby streamlining accounting procedures.

Payment cards

Payment cards allow customers to make payments without using cash, to withdraw money from automated teller machines and to obtain information about their current accounts. They include debit cards, credit cards and pre-paid cards.

The use of payment cards has increased following the adoption of measures concerning service charging, network development, payment procedures and the interoperability of payment circuits. The new technologies make it possible to execute payments in a faster and safer way at a lower cost. Moreover, payment cards have largely developed following their use to settle e-commerce transactions.

The European countries where the use of payment cards is most widespread include: the United Kingdom, France, the Netherlands and Belgium. In France, credit cards are also used as debit cards. In virtually all countries, projects are underway to foster the use of microchips inside cards, to enhance their functionality and, most of all, their security features.

Figure 4.3

The use of payment cards in the European countries

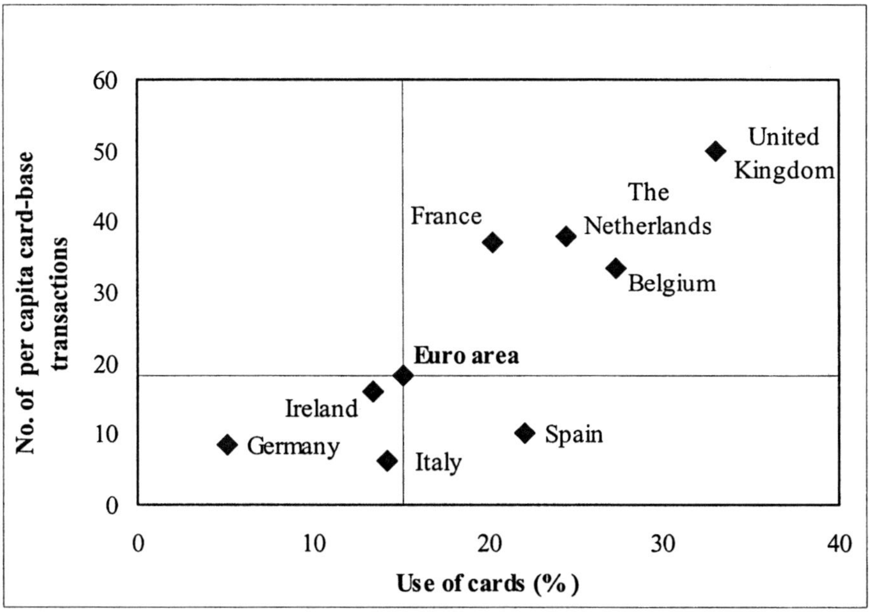

Source: AFB – la banque en chiffres 1999 – www.afb.fr

Table 4.15

Main postal payment cards available in the European countries under examination

Belgium
Postamat Plus
This is a multipurpose card that allows holders to access *Bancontact /Mister-cash* and *Proton* (in Belgium) and *Maestro* (abroad) cash dispensers. It allows holders to withdraw money 24 hours a day, 7 days a week, from 1,100 automated teller machines and to purchase goods at 66,000 POS terminals. As previously mentioned, it is an electronic purse. Abroad, money can be withdrawn from 450,000 *Maestro* ATMs and 4.5 million POS terminals. Domestic transactions are free of charge, whereas fees are payable for transactions abroad.
Eurocard-Mastercard
This is a revolving credit card with a monthly ceiling of 2,000 Euro. The amount of purchases can be paid in instalments equal to 10% of the total amount due, with a minimum payment of 24.79 Euro. The annual card fee is 17.35 Euro. This card is accepted by 65,000 retailers in Belgium and 13 million retailers abroad.

(continued)

(continued)

France

Carte premier Visa

It allows holders to make withdrawals 7 days a week. In France, the ceiling is 6,000 francs, whereas abroad it is 10,000 francs. Money can also be withdrawn from *VISA* ATMs. Payments can also be made abroad at 17,000 participating retailers in 200 countries. It offers free insurance services and medical assistance for holders and their families abroad.

Carte Réalys

This is a card that checks the current account balance every time it is used so as to prevent the user from spending a sum exceeding the available funds. It can be used every day. In France, it can be used to make payments at retailers' showing the label "CB", while abroad at shops showing the label *Visa Electron*. In France, cash withdrawals cannot exceed 3,000 FF from the ATMs of the Post Office and 2,000 FF from other cash dispensers. Abroad, users can withdraw up to 4,000 FF from ATMs that show the *Visa Electron* label.

Carte Blue Visa

It allows holders to make payments at 17,000 participating retailers in 200 countries. In France, cash withdrawals cannot exceed 3,000 FF from the ATMs of the Post Office and 2,000 FF from other cash dispensers. Abroad, users can withdraw up to 4,000 FF from ATMs that show the *Visa* label. It includes a free insurance policy for holders and their families in case of travel accident, provided travel tickets were purchased with the card. It also offers medical assistance to holders and their families in France and abroad.

Italy

Postamat Maestro

The *Postamat* debit card is an access key to the *BancoPosta* account. It fulfils the typical functions of a debit card. It relies on the magnetic strip technology and participates in the *Bancomat* circuit through the *Maestro/Cirrus* circuit; it can be used at bank ATMs showing its label (26,000 in Italy, 210,000 in Europe and 480,000 in the world).

The card's economic conditions include free withdrawals from the Post Office circuit and a fee comparable to that charged by banks for withdrawals from non-proprietory cash dispensers in case of withdrawals from bank ATMs. *Postamat* enables holders to access the company's and Cirrus circuit to withdraw cash from bank ATMs and the *Maestro* circuit to make purchases at retailers'. The *Postamat* card is on line with the customer's account. Usage is unrestricted if the card is used at POS terminals within the Post Offices (the only limit is funds availability on the postgiro account); in shops participating in the *Maestro* circuit, purchases can total up to one million lire, with a maximum of three million lira per month; conversely, in case of withdrawals from postal and bank ATMs, there is a daily ceiling of one million lira without monthly limitations other than that of funds availability.

(continued)

(continued)

Bancoposta MasterCard This is a revolving co-branded credit card; the amounts spent on purchases at s hops Participating in the *MasterCard* circuit (in Italy and the world) are refunded by the holder through monthly instalments, whose amount is arranged when the contract is signed. Card issue, in co-operation with Agos Itafinco Spa, is subject to the opening of a *BancoPosta* account. The card is issued only after the reliability of the perspective holder has been assessed (the assessment is made by the above-mentioned partner company). The customer is initially granted a credit line of three million lire, which can be increased upon request. The customer is also authorised to withdraw cash up to 500,000 lire every day from the ATMs showing the MasterCard label; since this transaction is regarded as a cash advance, a fee is charged. The amount withdrawn by the customer is refunded by monthly instalments. The card holder can also choose to have the entire loan credited on the current account by simply contacting the freephone number (which has to be contacted also to enable the card and to ask for card to be stopped in case of loss or theft). Following an agreement with *Deutsche Bank*, two new cards have been issued: *Bancoposta* "classic" and "gold". They allow holders to make their purchases at retailers participating in the *Mastercard* circuit and to obtain cash advances. The amounts spent are refunded in one amount, at the end of the month.
The Netherlands **Interpay(Euro/Master)** is a Travel & Entertainment card. **PIN Card** This is a debit card backed by the banking system. In the Netherlands, is it the most widely used card, as the figure of 20 million cards issued shows. Seven million cards have been issued by *Postbank*.

Through credit cards, the Post Offices, which do not have a banking nature, grant their customers the opportunity of taking advantage of a current account that is similar to a bank account. Their inability to grant a credit line is overcome through the credit line granted by their cards. However, we should bear in mind that these cards cannot be used to settle payments with all counterparts and that cash advances are usually rather expensive.

Pre-paid cards can be used to purchase goods and services directly from retailers that have the necessary technological facilities to debit the card of the amount of purchase[17].

The first cards to be launched on the market were disposable and could only be used to pay a single item or service. They are generally issued by the same entity that provides the service and mainly rely on magnetic strip card technology.

The electronic purse is an instrument designed to settle frequent, low-value transactions. It can directly compete with cash because of its convenience and

---

[17] See Working Group on Payment Systems in the European Union (1994), p. 1.

relative ease of use. With the forthcoming introduction of the Euro, the use of these cards may, in principle, facilitate the settlement of recurrent, low-value purchases due to the lack of familiarity users will have with the new coins and banknotes at the beginning.

The Post Offices presently offer this instrument in Belgium, where the multipurpose card *Postomatplus* can be used as an electronic purse to make payments at 45,000 terminals and at 10,000 public phones. In France, the *Poste* has developed *Modeus*[18] together with other companies involved with e-commerce (Rapt, Sncf, Group Casse d'Epargne, Societé Genérale). In The Netherlands, the *Postbank* has launched *Chipper*. The electronic purse has been developed thanks to a joint venture with KPN telecom and, since September 1998, by all the other banks belonging to the ING group. It is a multipurpose card. In 1998 there were 5 million *Chipper* cards issued, 45,000 terminals installed and 20,000 telephones available for card recharge.

Table 4.16
Electronic purse characteristics

Country	Name	Disposable/ Rechargeable	Use on the Internet	Multipurpose	Electronic purses per 1,000 inhabitants
Belgium	Proton	Rechargeable	No	Yes	n.a.
France	Modeus	-	-	-	-
Germany	GeldKarte	Rechargeable	No	Yes	536 cards issued
Italy	Minipay Visacash	Rechargeable	No	Yes	14 n.a.
The Netherlands	Chipknip Chipper	Rechargeable Rechargeable	No No	Yes Yes	764 318
United Kingdom	-	-	-	-	-
Spain	Visa cash Euro 6000 Monedero 4B	Rechargeable Rechargeable Rechargeable	No No No	Yes Yes Yes	87 n.a. n.a.

Source: Forschungszentrum Karlsruhe 1999, p. 176.

[18] Pucci E., La posta in rete con nuovi servizi, Il sole 24 ore 16-06-2000.

4.3.3 Getting in Touch with Customers

The need for payment service users to access the postal system varies according to the monetary instrument used to settle their transactions.

When cash is used, people have to go to the Post Office and ask for a money transfer, which is carried out once they have paid the corresponding amount.

If payers hold a postgiro account, their need to access the postal system obviously increases, as they will have to open their account, ask for information to check credit and debit transactions and account balance or give instructions about payment and collection transactions (e.g. paying through a postal giro after filling a form, cashing a cheque).

The advent of electronic money and electronic payment has partially changed the way users access the postal system. While direct contact between seller and purchaser is still necessary to start the postgiro account relationship or to request special services, such as automatic debiting of accounts or the issuance of credit or debit cards, users no longer need to go physically to the Post Office since such services can be requested by mail. The need for direct contact to make or receive payments has diminished, if not disappeared. Payments being the result of an electronic transmission of information, they can be arranged through channels that allow users to get in touch with the Post Office in different ways (POS, home banking via a PC, etc.). Likewise, information requests can be answered through these channels and no longer oblige users to go to the Post Office (telephone banking, home banking, etc.).

New and more numerous channels have been recently made available to Post Offices as well, allowing them to get in touch with customers and provide them with payment services. The traditional channels represented by multiproduct and multifunction counters have been coupled with automated and electronic channels.

The features of each channel are examined below. Emphasis is put, in particular, on the functions they fulfil in the retail payment service market, their advantages and drawbacks in meeting customers' demands, the difficulties their application still poses, their current relevance and some indications about the role these channels may play in the future.

The Post Office counter

In the last few years, several projects have been launched in the various European countries to computerise Post Offices in order to enhance service quality and range.

In some countries, such as the United Kingdom, the capillarity of the postal system over the territory has fostered the drawing up of commercial agreements with banks to allow bank account holders to make transactions on their bank account at the Post Office. The British Post Office has traditionally supplied bank services through their main bank partner, Alliance & Leicester (which incorporated Girobank). In 1999, other agreements on bank transaction processing were reached with Cooperative bank, Lloyds TSB and Barclays. Their aim is to allow customers holding a personal cheque account to deposit and withdraw money from 15,500 Post Offices in England and Wales. Cooperative bank's customers can deposit money and cash cheques in addition to transferring money. Lloyds' customers can deposit cash and withdraw it through cheques. Abbey National's customers can withdraw cash. In all cases, the Post Office is paid a fee for every completed transaction[19]. Likewise, the Spanish *Correos y Telegrafos* have entered into a distribution agreement concerning the services of *Deutsche bank* and *Banca Argentaria*[20]. Since May 1999, when the *Deutsche bank*'s products and service were made available at all Post Offices, there have been more than 18,000 customers. At the same time, more than 23,000 contracts for different services have been drawn up, for a total turnover exceeding 16,000 pesetas[21].

Table 4.17
Post Office branches

	France	Germany	Italy	The Netherlands	United Kingdom	Spain
No. of branches that accept financial transactions 3.10	17,080	n. a.	13,980	18,393	2,214	10,386
Average area covered by a permanent counter (Km^2) 3.5	32.58	25.49	19.98	13.31	17.30	126.39
Average no. of inhabitants served by a single counter 3.6	3,490.85	5,863.57	3,802.64	3,202.66	6,696.32	9,869.81

Data referred to 1999 – Data for Belgium are not available

Source: UPU statistics – items 3.10, 3.5, 3.6 www.upu.int.

[19] See Post Office, Annual Report 1999-2000.
[20] See Espinosa J.M. (1999), p. 182.
[21] Correos y Telegrafos, 1999 Financial accounts.

ATMs

The ATM (Automated Teller Machine) allows debit or credit card holders to receive information and give instructions. Sometimes it also provides a "circular" service, whereby a customer holding a card issued by an entity other than the owner of the automated teller machine can perform a limited number of transactions, usually against a fee. ATMs are increasingly widespread. Their number is bound to rise as a consequence of the higher number of card holders and the increasingly improved functions these customer interfaces are acquiring.

In the United Kingdom, all the major ATM owners have joined the Link network . Since 1 January 2001, this has enabled card holders to make use of all the available ATMs. When the service is provide against the payment of a fee, a message is displayed on screen before the transaction is performed[22].In Italy, 2,000 postal ATMs should be installed by the end of 2001. In Germany, *Postbank* owns 1,700 ATMs.

Table 4.18
Cash dispensers and ATMs

Country	**No. of existing networks**	**No. of counters per one million inhabitants**	**No. of transactions per inhabitant**	**Average value of transactions ($ USA)**
Belgium	12	608	17.4	104.8
France	1	549	20.5	70.7
Germany	4	562	18.4	156.0
Italy	1	523	8.6	150.9
The Netherlands	1	423	33.4	78.4
United Kingdom	1	476	33.1	88.8
Spain*		863	15.4	74 ECU

*Data referred to 1999; * Data referred to 1998*

Source: Bank for International Settlement, Statistics on Payment System in the Group of Ten Countries, 2001; European Central Bank, Payment Systems in the European Union, 2000.

POS

POS (*Point of Sale*) terminals are devices located at participating retailers' outlets that allow payment card holders to settle their purchases of goods and services with their card. POS terminals usually provide this service within the "circular"

[22] www.apacs.org.uk

interbank agreement framework. In Germany there are several EFTPOS networks; however, a high degree of uniformity and standardisation can be observed in the payment circuit. Any debit card may be used to withdraw money from any German ATM as well as with EFTPOS terminals. In the Netherlands, there is only one *PIN Card* processing centre (the bank-owned Interpay Nederland BV). The British credit card acquisition market is controlled by Nat West Streamline and Barclays Merchant, which hold a 60% market share[23]. The British Post Office has outsourced card payment management to Nat West since October 1998

Table 4.19
EFTPOS terminals

Country	No. of existing networks	No. of counters per one million inhabitants	No. of Transactions per inhabitant	Average value of transactions ($ USA)
Belgium	2	9,767	38.6	55.7
France	1	13,529	41.3	48.7
Germany	28	3,658	5.2	84.4
Italy	1	7,542	8.1	79.3
The Netherlands	1	9,186	44.2	48.6
United Kingdom	3	11,765	n. a.	n. a.
Spain*		16,691	8.8	48 (ECU)

*Data referred to 1999; *Data referred to 1998*
Source: Bank for International Settlement, Statistics on Payment System in the Group of Ten Countries, 2001; European Central Bank, Payment Systems in the European Union, 2000.

The electronic communication channels

The so-called electronic communication channels establish the connection between supply and demand through technology, whereby the data processing capabilities of information technology are integrated with the information transmission speed of telecommunications.

Home banking

Home banking systems allow customers to connect to the Post Office to make enquiries, give instructions about transactions or book services. Customers can connect through different channels. The main channels rely on:

---

[23] See Forschungszentrum Karlsruhe (1999), p. 37.

- electronic communications: Internet;
- other technologies: Videotel, telephone, interactive television;

Home banking - PC

This channel allows customers to connect to the Post Office from their home or place of work through a personal computer. Customers can send orders, receive information and manage transaction accounting. These services are addressed to high-end retail customers.

The Post Office provides customers with online banking services via the Internet. The main problem still associated with these services is security, i.e. the protection of information travelling over the Net. The advantages for customers are considerable, since they only need to go to the post office to request special services or make deposits. The more customers use electronic money to settle their collection and payment transactions, the less often they will need to go to the Post Office. However, the post office has been compelled to make rather considerable investments in information systems facilities and organisation, staff management and marketing.

Home banking -Telephone banking

Users can connect to the Post Office via the telephone only to receive information or also to give instructions about their transactions. Telephone banking can involve an automatic interaction system (IVR[24]) and/or the possibility of interacting with an operator (call center). In the first case, customers can be provided with a series of basic information (account balance, last transactions, etc.) while the Post Office can reduce the costs it usually incurs in providing such services, since information is given automatically and the service can be guaranteed 24 hours a day; it can also prove particularly useful to help customers get familiar with this type of channel.

Conversely, setting up a call center staffed with telephone operators is necessary when the post office wants to provide information and advice and allow customers to give instructions about their transactions. In this case, the call center may be organised so as to provide a first answer automatically and to involve the operator only when necessary; alternatively, the system can be organised so as to make the operator answer the call directly from the start.

---

[24] With the Ivr systems, the telephone becomes a real terminal in the customer's hands. The precondition for this service to develop is the spreading of multifrequency telephones. See Violano M., Van Collie S.M., (1995), p. 143.

Table 4.20
Home banking services provided by the Post Office

Belgium	The banque de la poste provides the postphone service, which allows users to make enquiries about their latest transactions and account balance, to order giros, to request documents (such as cheque books) and to obtain product information. The PC-based home banking service can also be accessed by connecting to the www.laposte.be site.
France	The Poste has offered its account holders the home banking service since December 1997 through Vidéoposte Micro; in November 1999 it launched Vidéoposte Net, an Internet-based service including home banking.
Germany	From the www.postbank.de site the postbank allows customers to manage remotely almost all the financial products and services available.
Italy	Poste Pay service – Since January 2001 all Visa or Mastercard holders can connect to the www.poste.it site to settle on line the transactions that would have normally required filling in a pay-in form at the Post Office even they do not hold a Bancoposta account. The service fee is 4,000 lire per form. This service, in addition to postgiro account information, is free for Bancoposta account holders.

4.4 Banking and Postal Systems Integration

In principle, the subject of banking and postal circuits integration may be set within the framework of co-operation and competition in the payment system.

The need to foster co-operation projects between different providers stems from the nature of the service generated by the payment system. From the economic viewpoint, the circulation of money should be regarded as a "collective property", whose production requires the co-operation of all the operators involved in order to share capital costs on an equal basis and define technical standards and common procedures[25].

Co-operation agreements are therefore necessary to overcome technical and economic barriers that would otherwise prevent single companies from operating and be successful on the market. Beyond certain limits, standardisation can generate diseconomies due to the higher vulnerability that strongly centralised systems have compared with more pluralistic solutions. An approach based on full co-operation deprives the payment system of the spur to achieve greater efficiency, which is typical of competitive contexts. In the relationship between co-operation and competition, neither of the two should attain primacy over the other, the best solution being a balance whose characteristics depend on environmental, institutional and technical factors that change according to places and time[26].

---

[25] See Marchetti P., Merusi F., Prosperetti L. (1996), p. 302.
[26] See Padoa Schioppa T. (1992), p. 37.

The patterns of development followed by the integration process can be analysed according to three different elements: demand, supply and regulations. As far as demand is concerned, bank and Post Office customers have the opportunity of being allowed to take advantage of any payment service in both circuits as this enhances service accessibility, friendliness and cost-effectiveness. As far as supply is concerned, integration is encouraged since it reduces the risk of developing payment systems customers do not appreciate, owing to their little usability. Regulations, through their monitoring function in particular, aim at promoting payment system efficiency and reliability.

Integration is an essential requirement to attain payment system efficiency. In some countries, like in Italy, integration was hindered by such factors as regulatory limits that prevented the enlargement of the scope of *Ente Poste* and insufficient automation in the postal system. Although these constraints have been recently removed, full integration between the two circuits has not been achieved yet.

The degree of integration reached between the two circuits can modify the competitive framework of supply, since customers' choices are especially influenced by the range of services supplied by the producer. All service conditions being equal, however, customers tend to value service efficiency in terms of both time and costs.

Keener competition is a true spur towards innovation and the search for greater efficiency to meet customers' requirements more exhaustively.

However, this should not jeopardise system stability following the inability of some operators to face competition pressure owing to different control policies enforcement. The functional standardisation of control regulations is therefore mandatory to avoid competition inequality in the payment sector.

The integration process should aim at a progressive standardisation of tools, circuits and regulations.

The current degree of integration between the banking and postal circuits can be assessed in respect of the participation of Post Offices in clearing and settlement circuits, in decision-making bodies responsible for the standardisation of payment circuits and procedures, in providing payment services that can be obtained from both circuits and, finally, in the "circular" use of the channels service providers exploit to get in touch with customers.

As far as the participation in decision-making bodies responsible for the standardisation of payment circuits and procedures is concerned, a different approach has been identified in the countries under examination. In the United Kingdom, the Post Office is a member of the Association for Payment Clearing Services (AIPA), which deals, among other things, with the definition of standards for the payment industry. Moreover, it belongs to the Cash Service Group, which deals with cash management. In France, the *Poste* belongs to the Committee for the Organisation and Standardisation of Banking Procedures. In Belgium, Germany and The Netherlands, the Post Administration it is an integral part of the system bodies since it provides financial services through a banking institution. In

Germany, in particular, a Credit Central Committee and an Information Group on Payment Systems have been set up. In The Netherlands there is a body in charge of co-ordinating development strategies for payment systems (Steering committee). In Italy, at present, the *Ente Poste* is not part of the bodies responsible for standardisation such as CIPA or SIA. However, art. 10 of *Bancoposta* Regulations, which were passed in March 2001, provides for the Bank of Italy to adopt all the necessary measures, in compliance with art. 146 of the Consolidation Act on Banks, to ensure the integration of the Post Office in the payment systems and the interoperability of the postal and banking payment circuits. Therefore, it is likely that, in the future, the Italian Post Administration will participate in the decision making process concerning standardisation.

As for the possibility of taking advantage of bank payment services in the postal circuit and vice versa, there are still significant limitations in Italy. The Italian Post Offices perform the same procedures: high value transfers, transfers to the retail sector, cheque truncation, electronic outcome of cheques. Customers, however, are strongly limited in their use of banking instruments in the postal circuit. A postgiro account holder cannot, for instance, pay a cheque drawn by a third party in his/her own account. The Italian Bank Association (*Associazione Bancaria Italiana - ABI*) ascribes these inefficiencies to the non-observance of the agreement reached in 1988 by and between the Italian Post Administration and ABI itself concerning the negotiation, exchange and settlement of banking and postal instruments. According to ABI, the Italian Post Office has not implemented yet a number of standardisation measures required to harmonise postal instrument procedures with the technical standards enforced in the banking sector, even though they should have been implemented by March 2000. Therefore, the enforcement of the new agreement, which would allow the Italian Post Office to negotiate endorsed bank account cheques, is subject to technical standards adjustment, as requested by ABI[27]. Within the retail transfer circuit, it is usually difficult for postal customers to transfer funds to bank customers. In these cases too, the implementation of art. 10 of the new regulations governing the *Bancoposta* will favour the removal of the existing limitations, fostering full integration between the two circuits.

As far as automated access channels are concerned, the banking and postal circuits are marked by broad interoperability. In the United Kingdom, an agreement is about to be signed by the cash dispenser network Link with the Post Office to connect its 18,000 branches to the circuit of banks and building societies. This initiative is a furthers step towards the creation of a "Universal Bank", strongly promoted by the British Government and supported by all the major British banks and the Post Office. Link provides the technology required to allow bank account holders to take advantage of the Post Office to make basic

---

[27] ABINEWS, Assegni: Poste inadempienti, non rispettano gli accordi, n°2 febbraio 2001.

transactions such as making enquiries about one's account balance and withdrawing cash[28].

4.5 The Post Office and the Internet

Post Offices offer services through the electronic communication channel, whose complexity and scope differ according to the operator involved. This section provides a first analysis of the services supplied by the Post Administration through the Internet. This is, however, a constantly developing area because of the technological solutions and the growing range of products available. Therefore, the aim of our discussion is to draw a global picture of the main activities carried out, and special emphasis in put on the objectives the different types of services pursue. More details on the services provided by the operators in the various countries under examination are given in Table 4.23 (at the end of the chapter).

Initially, the presence of the postal operator in the web was regarded as an opportunity to support and improve traditional postal services and to provide services at the same time as deliveries. Later on, the possibility of developing e-commerce related activities and other services, not necessarily related to the core business, was considered.

In particular, the possibility of gaining a competitive edge from the establishment of an integrated multiservice platform was evaluated, in order to enable a single operator to manage the different activities related to e-commerce. They include both the material activities associated with the delivery industry (express courier, transportation, logistics, etc.) and the activities that can be performed through the electronic channel (direct contact, transaction execution, payment, etc.).

All the major European postal operators take advantage of the electronic channel to provide information services. By visiting their web sites, users can obtain information on the services they provide, with differences concerning information wealth and complexity, the attention paid to economic aspects and the regulations that govern the postal administration and the completeness of the site English version. Users can access these services to obtain the information they need more easily, rapidly and at a lower cost. Besides minimising the costs related to this type of activity and promoting information wider accessibility, suppliers are given the opportunity of updating the information contained in their site in real time, according to their needs. To help customers get familiar with the electronic channel, many European postal operators provide Internet terminals inside the Post Offices.

---

[28] postinfo.upu.org

Figure 4.4
Activities and operators in the delivery industry

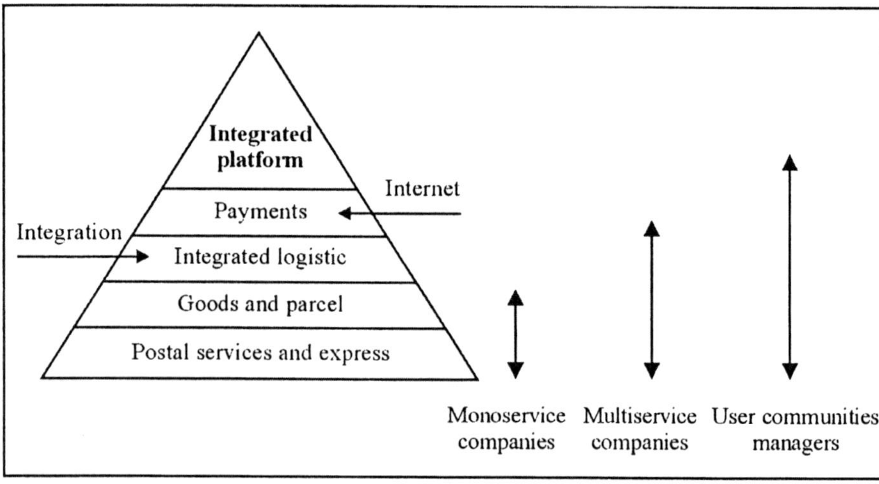

Source: Istituto di Economia dei Media (IEM), Letter no. 3 March 2000, p. 1.

Some postal operators have supplemented their information services with mail-related services. These are hybrid mail services that can integrate the traditional mail, for instance allowing business or retail customers to send the postal operator the text of a message via the electronic channel, delegating to the latter the task of printing and delivering it to the recipient. Services designed to substitute the traditional mail can also be provided, such as free e-mail addresses. Some operators offer the opportunity of managing address change procedures on line. The German Post Administration has entered into an agreement with the American company E-Stamp for the sale of digital stamps.

Some of the operators under examinations offer services within the framework of track & tracing activities. This type of activity is related to goods transportation, storage and delivery. Customers can access the web to obtain information about the route followed by their goods: from withdrawal to delivery. The Post Office can rely on the capillary presence of its branches and a network of operators that provide door-to-door delivery services daily. However, for this type of service, speed of delivery and the strengthening of information support services are essential. Considerable investments in information process quality and architecture have been necessary to meet such requirements[29].

Furthermore, Post Offices allow users to make payments electronically, via the Internet, especially to settle invoices and e-commerce transactions.

---

[29] Istituto di Economia dei Media – Fondazione Rosselli, 2000: Consegne e-mmediate, n° 4 aprile.

A primary role may be played by the Post Office in respect of the security requirements deriving from e-commerce and Internet-based transactions. In many of the European countries under examination, the Post Office certifies digital signatures. By digital signature we mean a special message validation or coding technique relying on a public-key cryptographic system. The technique is based on the use of two cryptographic keys every user is given. One is public and the other is private. Every document coded by using one of the two keys may only be decoded with the other key and the signature on the (private) key may only be checked with the public one. The certifying body is the public or private entity that carries out the certification, issues the public key certificate, publishes it together with the public key and updates the lists of suspended or withdrawn certificates as well as the lists of public keys. The essential task of the certifying body is to ensure the correct match between an entity and its public key through the certification it provides. Certifying means stating that a certain duly identified entity corresponds to a precise public key and specifying the key validity period. This information can be checked electronically. Many European postal operators act as certifiers and provide ciphered data and message transmission to ensure the highest level of confidentiality.

Some European postal operators have considered the possibility of developing Internet portals to supplement their service range. This shows that the Post Office is willing to play a key role in e-commerce, taking advantage of the opportunities resulting from the integrated supply of services and the control of effective delivery to the recipient thanks to its capillary presence on the territory.

According to a study published from Killen & Associates, the Post Office may become a future market leader if it enhances its competitiveness related to postal services and widens its service supply via the Internet, as e-document deliveries, e-commerce and e-messaging services show. While an annual 7% growth is expected for postal services, the other services should record an annual 19% rise.

Table 4.21

The Post Office and the Internet in Europe – ideas underway and projects

France La Poste	**e-Pap** (pret à Poster èlectronique): an hybrid postal service. **Cyberposte:** Internet-connected terminals located in 1,000 Post Offices. Access is time limited and subject to a fee. **@laposte.net**: free e-mail addresses. **L'@nnuaire** de La poste: a directory addressed to professionals that can be accessed via the Internet. It is a list of around 4 million French companies and organisations registered with the Registre national du commerce et des sociétés. **Track and Tracing**: a service provided by Chronopost and Tat Express, two subsidiaries.

(continued)

(continued)

	E-commerce: an agreement with France telecom to become the leading carrier of purchases made through the e-commerce portal known as Telecommerce, developed by France telecom together with IBM. Post@xess means data transmission and management for B2B e-commerce La Poste and CertiNomis have launched a project known as **PackSociéPoste**, designed to serve approximately 600 small-to-large size companies which regularly use the Internet. Users are granted 5 SociéPoste certificates. Further to the joint venture with Sagem, it has created an Authority for **Certipost** certification. The www.illiclic.com portal addressed to consumers is due to be launched soon.
Germany Deutsche Post World Net	**ECard**: a hybrid postal service addressed to business and retail customers alike. **EPost Target**: a hybrid postal service addressed to business customers of all sizes interested in direct marketing. **Ebusiness communication solutions**: safe transmission of data and documents. **E-Stamp Corporation**: an agreement reached to launch the electronic stamp. **World Wide Address Checker**: it checks the formal correctness of addresses worldwide. **Track and Tracing**: developed by the EuroExpress network and DHL. **Evita**: an horizontal portal . **New Business**: a comprehensive e-commerce solutions package designed for German small and medium sized companies . **Deutsche Post Signtrust**: a certification body complying with the provisions of the German Digital Signature Act. It produces smart cards for electronic signature and provides certificates for the Federal Chamber of Notaries.
Italy Poste Italiane	**Postel**: a hybrid postal organisation for business customers. **Postemail**: a freely-available e-mail box. **Interposta**: it allows users to deliver to non-connected people a message sent over the web, duly printed, put into an envelope and delivered by the postman. **Track and Tracing**: provided by SDA Express Courier, Postacelere and Posta Raccomandata. The Italian Post Administration has set up Postecom for the development of Internet-based services, in particular postal and Bank-post services, e-commerce services and digital signature certification. The **Eboost** portal has been developed to promote e-commerce. It allows companies that sell their products over the web to have a single interface throughout the process: from order management to storage, payment procedures, goods packaging, transportation and delivery. Postecom has registered with the Aipa association of digital signature certification. The **Postcert** service provided on the site will certify digital signatures, allowing users to send and receive digital legally valid documents

(continued)

(continued)

	Signature certification for the public administration network will be implemented and managed by Postecom. At the beginning, the service will be addressed to central public authorities whereas in the future it may be extended, for instance, to purchase and sell agreements between private individuals with the online signature of a notary.
United Kingdom Post Office	**RelayOne**: a hybrid postal service for business customers and consumers **Via Code**: a system to protect the exchange of messages via the Internet **Track and Tracing**: implemented by Parcelforce. **E-commerce**: a project being developed together with AT&T and Cap Gemini – designed to set up a virtual shopping centre.
Ireland An Post	**Billpay.ie**: it offers the opportunity of sending and paying bills on line. **Post Trust**: a digital signature certification service.
Spain Correos y telégrafos	Terminals are expected to be installed in 80% of post offices to help customers get familiar with the use of Internet and e-mail services.
Denmark Post Danmark	It provides comprehensive, integrated solutions to e-commerce companies with partners such as IBM, DFDS Dan Transport and Microsoft.
Sweden Posten AB	**PostNet**: for e-commerce, electronic infrastructure and electronic business communications. **Postgirot** payment services.
Switzerland	Postgiro account holders living in the German cantons of Switzerland can shop on line. M-Online-Shopping is the name of the joint venture launched by the Swiss Post Administration together with Migros, one of the leading distribution chains of the Swiss Confederation. Goods can be purchased on line by indicating postcard and postgiro account numbers. In towns, goods can be collected directly at Migros centres or home delivered via a forwarding service associated with the distribution chain.
The Netherlands TPG	*Iconnections*: it offers e-commerce solutions.

4.5 References

AN POST (2000): Annual Report 1999.

ASSOCIATION BANCAIRE BELGE (2001) www.abb-bvb.be

ASSOCIATION BANCAIRE FRANCAISE (2000): La banque en chiffres 99-Comparaisons internationales, www.afb.fr

BALDRY T. (2001): E-commerce: Integral part of our corporate strategy, EFMA Conference, 13 & 14 February, Paris.

BANQUE DE FRANCE (1998): Les moyens de paiement et les systèmes d'échange et de réglement.

BANQUE DE FRANCE (1999): Direction des Systèmes de Paiement.

BOHLE K., RADER M., RIEHM U. (1999): Electronic Payment Systems in European Countries. Country Synthesis Report, Forschungszentrum Karlsruhe GmbH, Karlsruhe, www.itas.fzk.de/deu/projekt/pez/emuis.htm
BRIZI R., SASSO F., TRESOLDI C. (1998): Le banche e il sistema dei pagamenti, Il Mulino, Bologna.
BROWN K. (2001): Future of Post Office after deregulation is enveloped in mystery, Financial Times, March 24th.
COMMITTEE ON PAYMENT AND SETTLEMENT SYSTEM (1992): Retail Payments in selected countries: a comparative Study, Basle.
COMMITTEE ON PAYMENT AND SETTLEMENT SYSTEM (2001): Retail Payments in selected countries: a comparative Study, Basle.
Contrat d'objectifs et de progrès portant contrat de plan entre l'Etat et La Poste 1998 – 2001.
Contrat de gestion entre l'Etat e La Poste 1997-2001.
Contrat de plan entre l'Etat et La Poste 1995 – 1997
CORREOS Y TELÉGRAFOS (1998): Estatutos de Correos y Telégrafos.
CORREOS Y TELÉGRAFOS (2000): Memoria 1999.
CORREOS Y TELÉGRAFOS: Ley postal.
CORTE DEI CONTI (2000): Relazione della corte dei conti al parlamento sulla gestione finanziaria delle Poste Italiane s.p.a. (esercizio 1999).
CRUIKSHANK D. (2000): Competition in UK Banking – A Report to the Chancellor of the Exchequer, Mars.
DAVID, J. (2000): La Poste, September 18th.
DEUTSCHE BUNDESBANK, (1999): Annual Report.
ESPINOSA J.M.(1999), Hay un futuro para los correos? Reflexiones sobre la innovacion como elemento para la supervivencia empresarial, Rivista de direccion organizacion y administration de empresa, n°1,www.cepade.es/revista/revista21/art16.pdf
EUROPEAN CENTRAL BANK (2000): Payment Systems in the European Union.
FORESTIERI G.(1999): Le condizioni organizzative per l'innovazione, in Bancoposta e mercati, CESARINI F., COSTI R. TUTINO F., Il Mulino, Bologna.
GROUPE DE REFLEXION ET DE CONCERTATION SUR L'EVOLUTION DES RELATIONS ENTRE LES BANQUES ET LEURS CLIENTS, Rapport exercice 1999-2000.
ISTITUTO DI ECONOMIA DEI MEDIA – FONDAZIONE ROSSELLI, (2000): Consegne e-mmediate, n° 4 aprile.
ISTITUTO DI ECONOMIA DEI MEDIA – FONDAZIONE ROSSELLI, (2000): Dallo sportello al portale, n° 2 febbraio.
KILLEN & ASSOCIATES,(2001): Reinventing the Posts: A Strategic and Tactical Blueprint for transforming Postal Authorities into Competitive Information Carriers and Processors, www.Killen.com
LA POSTE (2000), Rapport Annuel 1999.
LA POSTE (2001): Résultats groupe 2000, Paris 29 Mars.
LA POSTE, Contrat de gestion entre l'Etat et la Poste 1997-2001.
LA TORRE, M., (1996): Il Bancoposta in Italia, Giappichelli, Torino.
LEONELLI L.,(1999): I servizi di pagamento. Mercato, gestione,

regolamentazione, Utet, Torino.
LOHMEYER J., (2001): Postal Bridge from old to new economy, Paris 12 January
LUK, PC., (2001): Building for the future, World Mail & Express Asia 2001 Conference and Exhibition, Hong Kong 20-21 February.
MARCHETTI P., MERUSI F., PROSPERETTI, L. (1996): Funzione, estensione, strumenti della sorveglianza sui sistemi di pagamento, in Banca Borsa e titoli di credito, maggio-giugno.
PADOA SCHIOPPA T.(1992): La moneta e il sistema dei pagamenti, il Mulino, Bologna.
PADOA SCHIOPPA T.,(2001): Consolidation of the payment systems industry: the Eurosystem's perspective, International Payment Systems Week 2001, London, April 2nd.
PASSERA C., (2000): Freedom to act. Turnround of Poste Italiane, Geneva, October 5th
PILLEY O., ANDERLONI L. (1999): European Post Offices in Financial Services, Lafferty Publications Ltd, Dublin.
Postal Act (Postgesetz- PostG) of 22 December 1997.
Postal Services Act 2000.
SHEPPARD D. (1996): Payment Systems, Centre for Central Banking Studies Bank of England,.
TENAGLIA AMBROSINI M. G. (1996): La presenza pubblica nel settore del credito: il Bancoposta, in Diritto ed Economia, Mag-Dic, vol. 9, n. 2-3.
THE DEPARTMENT OF SOCIAL SECURITY (2001): Payment at a Post Office, www.dss.gov.uk
THE POST OFFICE, Annual Report 1997/1998; 1998/1999; 1999/2000.

Web sites

www.upu.int
http://postinfo.upu.org
www.apacs.org.uk
www.correos.es
www.post.be
www.uk-po.co.uk
www.postag.de
www.postbank.de
www.laposte.fr
www.posteitaliane.it

5

Financial Inclusion and the Role of Postal Systems

Jean-Paul Pollin – Angelo Riva*

5.1 Introduction

Today the struggle against exclusions is a very current issue in Europe. Although increased growth and efficiency have come about as a result of sudden changes in production structures, the increasingly competitive framework within which economic players have to operate, liberalisation and deregulation of the markets, a growing number of people have been excluded from these positive effects. Within this context, ensuing budget cutbacks have led to a subsequent reduction in social policy resources allocated to deal with growing problems. It has therefore become an urgent matter to act in a more effective manner.

Social exclusion is a multi-faceted phenomenon. The creation of new and better job opportunities is undoubtedly the main strategy to tackle it. Nevertheless, the means deployed to promote inclusion involve different sectors that need to be carefully co-ordinated. Financial exclusion is one face of this problem and access to financial services is increasingly becoming an important step in the path towards inclusion into the labour market and into social life in general. Furthermore, financial inclusion can contribute to substantial cost savings for the community. It also encourages consumers to take ethical values into account to a greater extent when making their choices. Finally, it can bring new activities and customers to the financial system.

Financial exclusion is a somewhat complex, if not vague, phenomenon. What appears to be lacking in the current phase of research is a basic reflection as to how it may be defined. From a purely practical standpoint, there are a few indicators that may be used to define the degree of exclusion: access to a current account, access to basic banking services and to the complete range of payment instruments, as well as access to other financial products (emergency credit, insurance and social security). It is therefore possible to consider the concept of financial exclusion as a "gradual process of having one's financial ties cut off"[1]. within the framework described below. The purpose of this study is to outline the trends in the struggle against financial exclusion with particular regard to access to

---

* Paragraph 5.3 is by J.P. Pollin, the rest by A. Riva.

[1] Caisse des Dépots et Consignations (2001), p. 2.

current accounts[2] and basic banking services for people in difficulty[3]. The issue can be divided into four main areas of focus: which beneficiaries, which range of services, which rates, which forms of distribution. These issues seem essential in light of their impact on social policies and the privileged, although not mandatory, access that they give to the other financial products and the features of modern day society. Last but not least, the issue of access to other financial products follows a different logic that requires different methodological approaches.

The difficulty in finding the best possible solution to banking exclusion has to do with the friction between conflicting, though equally crucial, social, economic and legal aspects: contractual freedom of banks versus the fundamental right of citizens to gain access to basic services, the need to safeguard competition in the banking sector versus the strong public property nature of the payment system; profitability of banks as a primary means of guaranteeing the deposits versus the benefits to society as a whole derived from having as many people as possible involved in the banking network, which also reduces the collective costs of promoting inclusion. In other words, the conflicting interests of efficacy and social cohesion.

Within this framework, it is important to note the role that the Post Office plays in terms of providing access to financial services to the poor as part of its dual remit of regional development and universal accessibility. The introduction of competition in the postal sector is also bringing about deep changes in the strategies adopted by operators. In this chapter, we shall attempt to provide an overview of actions taken to promote financial inclusion. We shall then go on to assess future prospects by analysing the two largest networks in Europe: La Poste and The Post Office.

5.2 Social Europe and the General Economic Interest Missions

5.2.1 The European Social Policy

The extent to which monetary poverty and social exclusion has increased, despite the growth experienced over the past few years, explains the level of priority

---

[2] Current bank accounts, Girobank accounts and the like. This meaning, which may seem to be a broad and somewhat vague one, is justified, in our opinion, by a twofold reason: *in primis*, the sophistication of financial services associates means of payment with products which are not current accounts, technically speaking; *in secundis*, this is the acceptance of the term currently used in studies at European level.

[3] Financial exclusion is not only determined by poverty, but other causes contribute to it. That is the case of overindebtedness, which affects various social classes, although to a different extent. Here, the issue is envisaged from the point of view of vulnerable categories of persons.

assigned to these problems. About 18% (some 65 million people) of the EU population lives on less than 60% of the median national income, the low-income threshold set to measure relative poverty. The situation does not seem to be improving at all: on the contrary, over the past ten years a trend towards growing gaps and weakening cohesion has been observed. Only through social transfers has it been possible to keep the poverty rates at these levels. Without them, poverty would have struck 26% of the European population[4]. This is a major problem for the governments. Indeed, the relevance of exclusions within social policies becomes clear when we consider the percentage of GDP that goes to social expenditure within the member states[5]. From this standpoint, the issue of regionalisation is particularly relevant with respect to rural areas, former industrial zones and the urban suburbs where the lack of infrastructure represents a structural hindrance to economic and social development. According to other studies, the risk of poverty is greater among the unemployed (on average one out of three) and other people who are not economically active (more than one out of two)[6]. Even though unemployment is the first cause, social exclusion goes much further and manifests itself in various type of outcomes and obstacles which make social exclusion a multi-faceted phenomenon, as illustrated by the situation of the working poors[7]. Being such a complex phenomenon, exclusion should be seen from a voluntary perspective; it requires a targeted, innovative and integrated approach which should be concretely based on access to high-quality public and private basic services. In the case of the latter, the main driving force is the social responsibility of companies[8]. Given the current features of the economic and financial system as regards access to the labour market, it seems that this insertion process cannot occur without first providing access to banking services to those excluded. Such access must be part of a policy to define a strategy aimed at meeting the needs of less fortunate social groups.

The promotion of inclusion is one of the objectives of the strategy agreed upon in Europe to modernise social protection and allow it to respond to the changes in the economic environment. The Lisbon Summit highlighted the connection between economic growth and social model. As a result of this, the European Social Agenda is based on the concept of social policy as a production factor requiring increased deployment efficacy. In order to reach this aim, the elaboration of a social policy needs to take place through improved forms of

---

[4] Eurostat, Statistics in Focus 13/1999, quoted in European Commission, COM (2000) 79 final, p. 5. In these figures, pensions are not considered as social transfers.

[5] For example 26% in Denmark and 27% in the United Kingdom. These figures include pensions. European Commission, COM (2000) 379 final, p. 6.

[6] Eurostat PCM 1994, EU – 13, quoted in European Commission, COM (2000) 79 final, pp. 18-19.

[7] 12% of people holding a job live in poverty (working poverty). European Commission, COM (2000) 79 final, p. 18.

[8] European Commission, COM (2000) 79 final.

governance which bring together the European Union, the Member States, local and regional authorities, NGOs and enterprises. From a European perspective, a remarkable innovation is the extension of the principle of open co-ordination (thus far limited to employment) to other social policies. Even though the Member States still have responsibility for taking initiative in such matters, the new approach makes sure that the objectives in question are more easily followed up, from a quantity and quality standpoint, within the framework of the Union.

5.2.2 The General Interest Missions

Within the framework of market liberalisation for the services related to network enterprises, the EU has allocated the means to ensure that a balance is struck between competition and consumer protection (namely protection of the most vulnerable): general economic interest missions. These missions were created by the Treaty of Rome as a means of justifying exceptions to competition. Later on, they became a development and social concept in their own right[9]. Aware of the value of such missions, the Lisbon summit asked the Commission to update the 1996 Communication which defined them[10]. The latest Communication[11] confirmed the main points mentioned earlier, once again highlighting the basic principles: universal access, high quality and affordable prices of the services in question, taking into account the specific needs of certain categories of the population (the disabled and people earning a low income) guaranteeing complete coverage of the territory.

As for the application of these norms to the banking sector, there are not many Community documents on the subject. The interpretative Communication of the Commission dated 26 June 1997 on the freedom of service provision and the general interest missions in the Second banking directive lays down the necessary criteria for a general interest measure to ensure that the set objectives will be reached. The Report by the European Commission to the Council of Ministers on the general interest services in the banking sector, adopted by the Commission on 17 June 1998 and presented to the Ecofin meeting on 23 November 1998, states that the banking sector is already characterised by a satisfactory level of competition and that only a "major community interest" could justify the placing of constraints. Art. 35 of COM (2000) 580 final, draws on the Report suggesting an open list of general interest missions which have been entrusted to credit institutions in Europe. None of the Member States has given the banking sector a mission to provide basic banking services. The Communication goes on to say that

---

[9] The Intergovernmental Conference of Amsterdam introduced in the Treaty, signed on 18 June 1997 and effective as from 1 May 1999, Art. 7 d (new Art. 16), which places these missions among the common values of the E.U.

[10] European Commission, Paper 96/C281/03.

[11] European Commission, COM (2000) 580 final.

two Member States (Germany and Austria) regard providing a comprehensive regional financial infrastructure to be a general interest mission. A further demonstration of the prudent attitude adopted by the Commission on the matter is the decision that this type of regime should be the object of an individual evaluation. It can be noted that European institutions are concerned about the fact that financing universal service requirements, as part of a general interest mission to provide basic banking services, might jeopardise competition in the European banking sector[12].

5.3 Financial Exclusion as Affected by the Transformations of the European Banking Market

The vague and unclear positions taken by the Commission show the existence of a certain contradiction between, on the one hand, the expressed intention to create a social Europe and preserve the general interest missions, and on the other hand, the liberal inspiration of European construction as defined by the Treaty of Rome. Indeed it is not easy to reconcile the principle of competition with providing universal services, a principle that escapes pure market logic.

Prior to the financial deregulation which occurred in the mid-80s, the issue of a universal banking services was not frequently mentioned. This was due to the fact that in a world where banks had monopoly advantages (or at least were not subject to the pressures of competition), the unprofitable missions were financed by cross subsidies. Financial institutions did not have much information on the proceeds derived from their various activities. Analytical accounting was often non-existent and the concept of profitability of customer segments was almost excluded from banking culture. Indeed there were substantial pricing inconsistencies between the main functions of the bank: in particular, management of the payment means took place through intermediation (i.e. the distribution of credit as a counterpart to the collecting of deposits). It was therefore increasingly frequent, during an inflation period, to see an automatically growing gap between the nominal profitability of credits and the remuneration (non-existent or very low) of deposits. It was actually on this interest margin that most of the net banking profits were earned, while commissions (namely the charges imposed on instruments and payment operations) accounted for only a small portion. Therefore, basic banking services were offered almost free of charge, without jeopardising the balance of the system.

This situation started to be seriously called into question when financial deregulation led to increased competition between banks and between banks and financial markets. The intermediation proceeds (interest margins) started to

---

[12] In view of the aim of this research, the issue of the financing of universal service obligations will not be considered. See concerning this: Rodriguez S. (2000), p. 561 et seq.

dwindle; this led to increased commissions and the subsequent invoicing of payment means in order to find other sources of income. This orientation led to the gradual elimination of cross subsidising which had guaranteed universal access to basic banking services.

The creation of a homogeneous European monetary area is expected to consolidate these trends because it will change the competitive structure of the sector. The banking systems which appeared to be strongly concentrated at the national level prove to be extremely fragmented at the European level: if we consider the whole of the European Union, the five largest institutions account for about 12% of the market, compared to 22% for the United States and 25% for Japan. The result could be restructuring (in particular by cross-border concentrations), which will exercise new pressures on the margins. This movement will be all the more strongly felt because in the European banking industry there are substantial excess capacities, capable of generating situations of destructive competition.

Mention should also be made here of the introduction of new technologies which is also bound to boost competition and allow for a better targeting of customers. For one thing, new technologies make it possible for rapid (and almost limitless) extension of the area of activity of all existing or future banks. Moreover, the distribution of certain services becomes less expensive. However, electronic banking makes it easier for banks to select customers since the branch office becomes an "all-embracing" point of sale. At the same time, long-distance marketing makes it possible to directly contact a targeted group of customers on the basis of previous information. It is still early days to predict the future of direct banking, in particular whether it will be a way of replacing or complementing traditional forms of distribution. There is no doubt, however, that this form of commercialisation will make it easier to select profitable market segments: electronic banking will be addressed to a profitable clientele, abandoning problem customers (i.e. the less fortunate and less educated customers that cannot be easily charged for banking services rendered). This is bound to create an intolerable imbalance, considering that maintaining non-profitable customers or operations is all the more unacceptable because the latter are not homogeneously divided among the networks or distributions channels.

The combination of all these developments leads to exclusion from banking services. To tell the truth, this is a traditional problem which appears in all instances of deregulation of activities related to public service provision. Starting from the moment when an operator loses a monopolistic position, it is no longer possible to finance free access to a universal service through pricing differences (or in a more general sense, at conditions outside the market). The same type of difficulty was experienced with the deregulation of telecommunications, postal services or the distribution of electricity... In all these cases, it was necessary to devise new ways to combine the advantages of competition with the possibility of offering all citizens a service regarded as necessary for reasons of equity and economic efficiency.

5.4 The Phenomenon of Banking Exclusion

5.4.1 Quantification of the Phenomenon

Over the last twenty years, the use of banking services has been increasing all over Europe[13], but according to Eurobarometer[14] – which as far as we know is the only source of data established using a common method at the European level – within the region there are still substantial differences.

Table 5.1
Availability of a personal current account, giro account or similar (%)

Country	YES	NO	NSP	Country	YES	NO	NSP
B	92.7	5.1	2.0	**I**	70.4	22.4	7.2
DK	99.1	0.7	0.2	**L**	94.1	3.9	1.7
WD	96.4	3.1	0.5	**NL**	98.9	0.5	0.6
D	96.5	2.9	0.6	**A**	81.4	13.5	5.1
OD	97.0	2.3	0.7	**P**	81.6	16.7	1.8
GR	78.9	17.9	3.2	**FIN**	96.7	1.5	1.7
E	91.6	6.9	1.5	**S**	98.0	1.6	0.4
F	96.3	2.8	1.0	**UK**	87.7	10.6	1.6
IRL	79.6	16.7	3.7	**EU 15**	89.1	8.6	2.2

Source: Eurobarometer 52, Financial services, Europeans and financial services; May 2000

According to these statistics, 89% of Europeans have a personal current account. However, this percentage ranges between 99% in Denmark and 70% in Italy. These differences are related to specific features of the national markets as well as to cultural factors[15]. They emphasize the need for a strong concerted

---

[13] For example, in Germany between 1980 and 1998, this rate rises from 76.5% to 82%; in the United Kingdom, from less than 50% to approximately 80 % (78% according to the National Statistics Office Family Resources Survey 1995/1996, 83% according to the APACS 1996 survey, 85.5% according to the National Statistics Office Omnibus 1998); in Ireland, current accounts increase from 1.6 M to 1.8 M (approximately 80% of adults) between 1990 and 1998. IFF (2000), p. 13; Kempson E. - Whyley C. (1998), p. 32; CSR Europe (2001), p. 8.

[14] Eurobarometer 52 (2000), p. 74. The method according to which this survey was carried out was the subject of criticism, but we are obliged to point out the difficulty of this kind of evaluation. These data should therefore be considered as indicative and not an accurate picture of reality.

[15] For example, in France, a policy of mass bankarisation (bank utilisation) was carried out as early as the sixties whereas, in the United Kingdom, the possibility of being paid

action, on a European level, aimed at making the economic and social structure of the region more homogeneous and modern. It is necessary to point out that these differences in banking practices are also related to the use of means of payment (see Ch. 4).

5.4.2 The Importance of Access

It appears that, apart from the intrinsic differences in national systems, the difficulties encountered by those who do not have a current account are similar all over Europe. These difficulties exacerbated by the increasing number of people using banking services and the development of a cashless society.

The first serious difficulty which those who do not have a current account have to face is related to employment. The problem is particularly serious because nowadays the financial relations between employers and employees are increasingly carried out through the current account, which is the easiest and cheapest way to manage the payment of monthly salaries. As already mentioned, the "insertion path" is a key concept in European social policy which involves the use of all necessary means to facilitate access to the labour market. Therefore, within the framework of a global and integrated approach, the banking connection seems to be taking on an increasingly important role.

Another essential element related to the promotion of banking inclusion is the adoption of the concept of social policy as a production factor. The new approach requires the maximum efficiency level in terms of the reduced cost for the distribution of transfers and maximum usefulness for the beneficiaries. These aims can be reached simultaneously by providing people with access to banking services considering the low cost of payments on current account with respect to payments in cash and the advantages derived from the management of cash flows through current account for the beneficiaries. A good example of this policy is the decision by the British government, combined with the pressure on the banking sector to offer basic banking services (see below), to increase the payment of allocations on bank accounts between 2003 and 2005. Today the Benefit Agency and the Social Security Agency (Northern Ireland) pay 2/3 of allocations (about 60 bn £ to 18 ml beneficiaries) through the Post Office by means of order manually processed books and girocheques. These operations are very expensive for social security agencies (79 pence per operation) and not very safe (frauds amount to 140 ml £ a year). The total cost of distribution amounts to more than 600 ml £ a year. On the other hand the payment of allocations on bank accounts costs a mere 1 penny per operation and, provided that the practice becomes sufficiently

---

social benefits in cash did not encourage the phenomenon. Caisse des Dépots et Consignations (2001), p. 4. In Italy, the high level of charges and the relative inefficiency which characterised the banking system until recently, combine with cultural factors such as the financial head of family and the extent of the black economy.

widespread (the government has not imposed any obligation in the matter), the total cost of distribution will amount to less than 10 ml £ per year[16]. As far as France is concerned, even though there are no aggregate data on a national level, it seems that the payment of allocations into the account is already regarded as a normal practice. According to a survey carried out by the Caisse Nationale d'Allocations Familiales in February 1999[17] "transfers are by far the most widespread form of payment, accounting for 95% to 100% of operations (Author's Note: depending on the agencies considered) in terms of both quantity and amounts". Among the non-automatic methods of payment, only the cheque-letters account for a relevant percentage, although their use is becoming less prevalent because social security institutions encourage beneficiaries of their services to open a *Livret A* so that the allocations can be paid by other means, considering the difference in cost: 16 FF for a cheque-letter against 0.4 FF for an optical cheque-letter not payable in cash. Payments by cheque and money order, which are extremely expensive for the issuer (30 FF)[18], are rare and payment in cash now only exists at certain counters[19].

Access to a current account appears particularly important in view of the difficulties and costs experienced by those who use alternative payment systems. Mention should also be made of the fact that, in some countries, the providers of gas, phone and electricity grant discounts to those who choose to pay their bills directly from their account. Another relevant factor is the cost of going to the place where you have to pay and the problems related to cheque cashing. In the United Kingdom, this problem is particularly acute[20], but it is also present in the other European countries[21].

---

[16] Performance and Innovation Unit (2000), p. 67.

[17] Comité Consultatif (1999 – 2000), p. 205 et seq.

[18] The issuer, typically a social body, sends the CRSF (Regional Centre of Financial Services) an order to debit its Girobank account (CCP) for the benefit of a payee. The CSFR sends a postal order to the recipient's post office and the recipient in question withdraws the sum over the counter at La Poste or is paid at home if the amount is less than 5,000 FF. Delessy H. – Gobin S. (2000), p. 4 and p. 8.

[19] Unfortunately there is no national consolidation of payment transactions per type of payment, therefore a sample of 8 funds was chosen for the study. Furthermore, it should be noted that the new software Cristal, currently being installed, does not break down benefits according to different types of payment. Comité Consultatif (1999 – 2000), p. 205 et seq.

[20] Kempson denounces that, for excluded persons, these payments are "one of the key difficulties" in the fact that they do not hold a current account. This category faces up to its obligations through several methods, the common factor of which is high cost. For example, the most widespread method is the payment in cash at the local office of the creditor or Post Office, especially when collecting benefits, but a transaction of this kind can cost £0.9, and there are not many creditors who bear the full cost (the practice of paying a contribution is more widespread). The new network of PayPoints does not apply customer charges, but payment in cash prevents its being accessible at the reduced rates offered to those who pay by direct debit. Another much used method is the "pay-as-you-

People excluded from banking services are subject to the risk of theft because they have to keep all their cash with them. This type of problem is particularly serious in the case of homeless people.

Furthermore the bank account is the favoured way of access to financial services which become increasingly important as a consequence of the modernisation of social systems, such as insurance – housing and long-term savings, as well as for credit.

Finally it is necessary to consider social costs. Indeed the banking connection is increasingly associated with the concept of citizenship because it has become part of social standards and, as a consequence, increases the sense of involvement of the individual in social life.

5.4.3 The Barriers to Social Inclusion on the Demand Side

As for the socio-economic characteristics of exclusion, the Eurobarometer survey shows that women are more frequently represented than men (9.7% against 7.4%). As far as age groups are concerned, the most numerous group is represented by people older than 55 (7.5%) as well as, of course, by those between 15 and 24 years of age (21.1%). In terms of level of education, it is easier to find people without a bank account on the lower levels of the scale. As for the professional aspect, it is obvious that the unemployed are markedly over-represented (20%) among those who do not have a current account, overtaken only, and logically, by students (26.6%), while the other professional categories are far down on the list[22].

The data from Eurobarometer make it possible to provide a more detailed analysis of the experiences of outcasts, dividing this category between those who have never had a current account and those who have decided to close one of their own free will.

---

go". Several options are available among which a direct deduction at source for social transfers and prepaid meters. These methods are often imposed by the creditor as a result of previous payment problems and involve additional charges, which can reach one pound sterling per week. All in all, Kempson and Whyley calculate that the fact that it is impossible to pay by direct debit can lead to an additional charge of £46 per year on an average gas bill and £80 per year in the case of prepaid meters. Kempson E. - Whyley C. (1998), pp. 23 – 25; Kempson E. – Whyley C. – Caskey J. – Collard S. (2000), p. 54 and p. 55.

[21] For example, for France, Gueneau C. (2000), p. 49 et seq.; for Sweden, Konsument verket – KO (2000), p. 3.

[22] Self-employed 3.7%, executives 1.4%, white-collar workers 3.7 %, blue-collar workers 4.6 %, housepersons 13.4% and pensioners 7.2%. Eurobarometer 52 (2000), p. 75. The over-representation of the unemployed is confirmed by many national surveys: for example, Kempson E. – Whyley C. (1998), p. 4; IFF (2000), p. 8; Konsument verket – KO (2000), p. 3.

Table 5.2
People who have never had a current account (%)

Country	YES	NO	NSP	Country	YES	NO	NSP
B	40.7	50.9	8.4	I	55.7	41.8	2.5
DK	13.0	52.0	35.0	L	40.0	48.3	11.7
WD	55.8	32.1	12.1	NL	17.1	82.9	0.0
D	55.4	33.3	11.3	A	32.6	58.8	8.6
OD	53.1	39.6	7.3	P	54.9	38.0	7.2
GR	46.9	49.6	3.5	FIN	63.1	6.7	30.3
E	48.4	45.4	6.2	S	22.9	68.7	8.4
F	59.8	25.8	14.4	UK	45.8	50.6	3.6
IRL	61.1	34.8	4.2	EU 15	51.6	43.3	5.0

Source: Eurobarometer 52, Financial services, Europeans and financial services; May 2000

The data show that 52% of those excluded from banking services have never had a bank account. But here again the situation is highly heterogeneous - the percentage ranges between 13% in Denmark and 63% in Finland. Among those who have never had an account, there are young people who have not yet accessed this system, the older age groups who still have place their trust in money (cash – only generation) and people on a low income who live in disadvantaged communities. As far as the latter category is concerned, their main problem is that the reference group makes scarce use of financial services. This element is bound to lead to important hindrances to access: lack of the necessary training and information to make financial decisions, psychological barriers and lack of confidence with respect to financial institutions. The latter are regarded as hostile to low-income categories; finally there are cultural and linguistic factors and the perception that if you have a low income you do not need an account. Changing these ideas will be a long and arduous process; there is also a real risk that the targeted groups will not respond to the marketing stimuli from banks because the basic banking services on offer do not appeal to them (see Table 5.3 in the following page).

On a European average 21% of excluded people closed their account voluntarily. Once again the situation is very heterogeneous in Europe, the percentage ranging between 50% in the Netherlands and 3% in France. The weight of this category dramatically underscores the mindset of the excluded population. The lack of commitment is probably caused by the fear of not being able to manage one's own financial situation through the current account, related to a sudden loss of income caused by major events in life (unemployment, divorce, long illness, etc…).

Table 5.3
People who voluntarily closed their account (%)

Country	YES	NO	NSP	Country	YES	NO	NSP
B	19.7	74.5	5.7	I	14.5	82.8	2.7
DK	15.3	20.8	63.9	L	22.6	57.0	20.4
WD	24.0	64.3	11.7	NL	50.0	50.0	0.0
D	24.1	64.0	12.0	A	15.5	77.5	7.0
OD	24.4	62.1	13.4	P	18.9	70.7	10.4
GR	24.8	68.1	7.1	FIN	7.3	70.5	22.3
E	21.2	68.6	10.2	S	13.7	68.5	17.8
F	2.8	85.6	11.6	UK	38.8	54.7	6.5
IRL	14.9	70.3	14.8	EU 15	20.8	72.7	6.5

Source: Eurobarometer 52, Financial services, Europeans and financial services; May 2000

In both cases, even though on different levels, the solutions to overcome these barriers are, on the one hand, the supply of adapted and simple products and, on the other, financial education provided in close co-operation between banks, NGOs and social services.

5.4.4 The Barriers to Inclusion on the Supply Side

On the supply side, i.e. the banking sector, there can be different factors leading to the exclusion of low income groups: the refusal to open an account, the extension of services in connection with the account, the pricing system, the offer of products that have not been adapted and geographical access.

As far as the banks refusing to open current accounts is concerned, this does not seem to be a major obstacle at the European level. According to Kempson, in the United Kingdom, only 1% of those who have never had a current account were turned down by the bank when they tried to open one[23]. At the same time, however, banks are far from eager to attract business from this group. Indeed the Cruickshank Report points out the shortcomings of the market in terms of offer of bank accounts, especially to vulnerable groups: banks do not seem to be interested in these customers. Since account-related sales are excluded, the only way to prevent the accounts of such holders from being overdrawn is to cross subsidise them. In France, the survey carried out by the association Consommation

[23] Kempson E. – Whyley C. (1998), p. 14.

Logement Cadre de Vie[24] (see below) shows that 7% of the bank account applications that were turned down related to low income applicants, although there does not seem to be a standard policy on the matter[25]. On the other hand, the IFF strongly criticised the practice of rejecting these applications by German banks. These banks pointed out the lack of profitability of these accounts since account-related sales are impossible. Furthermore the relatively low number of complaints on this issue is explained by the condition of psychological submission and confusion experienced by the poor[26]. Within this framework, the post office continues to play its traditional role of unconditional acceptance (see below).

As for the issue of payment services related to an account, the Swedish experience clearly shows that opening an account is not sufficient in itself if it is not accompanied by suitable methods of payment (see below).

On the subject of pricing, the European Commission has expressed its concern that certain banking services that were either entirely or almost free of charge in the past might be subject to price increases exceeding the inflation rate. It is very difficult to make a comparison on a European level because banking systems are different not only from one country to another, but also from one bank to another or even one branch office to another. What is more, the rates indicated are not applied uniformly to all customers. The survey carried out following the request from the Commission highlighted the fact that billed amounts to maintain an account vary substantially across Europe and that no country charges the cheapest rates for all types of consumers. It should be mentioned, however, that banks in the Member States tend to encourage customers to use account management tools relating to new technologies by applying higher rates for traditional services for which banks have to pay more[27]. This trend might lead to the exclusion of some low-income groups which, for cultural and psychological reasons prefer the latter methods of payment (see below).

As are as banks closing accounts is concerned, Eurobarometer data do not indicate this as being a major cause of exclusion at the European level. Indeed, out of the 9% of the European population without a current account, banks took the initiative to close the account in only 2.8% of the cases. It is important to note, however, that the percentage in some countries is very different from the overall average: namely in Sweden (14%), France (11%)[28], followed by Germany (9%) and the United Kingdom (6%).

---

[24] This survey is centred on mistery shopping: militants of the association presented themselves in banks to ask for the opening of an account while declaring income between 2,000 and 5,000 FF.

[25] Comité Consultatif (1999 – 2000), p. 195 et seq.

[26] IFF (2000), p. 14 and p. 46.

[27] Comité Consultatif (1999 – 2000), p. 73.

[28] It should be pointed out that the French experts are very cautious concerning this information.

Table 5.4

The bank closed by account (%)

Country	YES	NO	NSP	Country	YES	NO	NSP
B	4.1	87.9	8.0	**I**	0.0	96.8	3.2
DK	0.0	36.1	63.9	**L**	0.0	79.6	20.4
WD	8.9	77.4	13.6	**NL**	0.0	100.0	0.0
D	8.9	77.5	13.6	**A**	2.1	88.2	9.7
OD	9.1	77.5	13.4	**P**	2.1	87.2	10.8
GR	1.2	91.0	7.8	**FIN**	0.0	70.5	29.5
E	1.1	85.3	13.6	**S**	13.5	68.6	17.8
F	11.0	74.6	14.4	**UK**	6.0	85.1	8.9
IRL	0.5	83.4	16.1	**EU 15**	2.8	89.3	7.9

Source: Eurobarometer 52, Financial services, Europeans and financial services; May 2000

As far as the offer of appropriate products is concerned, its role has been particularly stressed in the English literature. Kempson argues that banks need to develop products which are suited to the needs of the poor in order to fight financial exclusion effectively. The characteristics of these bank accounts are indicated on the basis of the wide-ranging research that has been carried out to date: desk operations, impossibility of overdraft, ATM cards with systematic authorisation, buffer zone allowing for withdrawals from cash dispensers and automatic teller machines of all sums available without interest[29], possibility of transfer to debit and credit and budget facilitation. Kempson explicitly excludes cheques because their use might lead to an involuntary overdraft[30]. It should be noted that this type of product would allow banks to manage the risks related to the payment methods, thus safeguarding their profitability.

New technologies allow for the distribution of financial products at lower costs with respect to bank counters. These lower costs also mean lower prices for consumers. But the use of the Internet for financial transactions requires a degree of confidence, specific skills and equipment which are not available to the most vulnerable categories. Many research studies have demonstrated their preference for bank counter transactions as well as the potential exclusion ensuing from the spread of new technologies. The reduction of costs down the line has been one of the main aims for banks; this has led to encouraging these new distribution methods and to pursue rationalisation programmes for the physical network, especially in the least profitable areas (i.e. rural areas and poor urban neighbourhoods). As a consequence of these trends, the situation in Europe is far from homogeneous. For example, in the United Kingdom, the closing of branch

[29] This facility does not seem to be able to be connected with the issue of credit.

[30] PFRC (2000), p. 42.

offices has reached dangerous levels: between 1989 and 1999 the number of branches has fallen from 17,000 to 12,000 (-30% approximately)[31]. The same has occurred in Scandinavia. In Germany, a traditionally over-sized country, the situation has not yet reached alarming levels, but the IFF points out that the trend is worrying if we consider the closing of 8,000 bank and post office branch offices (-12%) between 1996 and 1999. The general interest mission that has been entrusted to Savings Banks seems to have reduced the danger (the number of Savings Bank and co-operative bank branches went down by 1,000 units between 1996 and 1999)[32], but the General Directorate for Competition is still working on the issue. In France, the impossibility of competition on the deposit market in terms of price has led banks to try and differentiate themselves from the standpoint of service quality, particularly in terms of proximity. As a consequence, the banking system is over-sized and for the moment there has not been a reduction in the number of branches (between 1996 and 1999 the number of branches has gone from 25,434 to 25,501[33]), even though a restructuring of the network is under way, to the advantage of urban centres and to the detriment of rural areas and especially sensitive urban areas[34]. Although the end of the French exception will probably be a turning point, France still has a wide postal network which has been entrusted with a general interest mission of regional development (see below). There might be a contraction of the network caused by competition, but no substantial reduction seems planned for the time being. Indeed, post offices have covered the country in a capillary way for a long time and, for the moment at least, they have been able to safeguard the size of their networks. Now, with the opening of the postal service market to competition there is a risk that the situation might radically change, as shown by the situation in Germany (see below).

5.5 Banking Promotion and Exclusion in Europe: Current Solutions

5.5.1 The Market: Spain, Greece, Ireland and Italy

In these countries the problem of financial exclusion is not addressed, at least in a direct way. For the moment, the banking systems in these countries offer no

---

[31] CSR Europe (2001), p. 16.

[32] IFF (2000), p. 24.

[33] http://www.afb.fr.

[34] The banking industry admits the need for an improvement in networking in sensitive urban areas. Caffet M. – C. (2000), p. 126.

product specifically designed for vulnerable groups[35]. The extremely low rates of use of banking services in these countries indicate that, under current conditions, these markets are not in a position to solve the problem. Indeed, with the exception of Spain, Greece, Italy and Ireland have the lowest values in Europe, considering the specific situation of Luxembourg within Europe (see tab. 1 Eurobarometer). For the future, the method of open co-ordination will force these countries to take a serious look at the issue.

5.5.2 The Voluntary Role of Banks: France, Germany and Belgium

The situation is different in other countries where the public opinion and the attention of the Government have encouraged professional Associations to become aware of the problem and to deal with it by preparing Charters. This solution has been adopted in Germany and, more recently, in Belgium. France has a charter which acts as a complement to legislation. This approach has also been adopted in Finland and in the Netherlands[36].

In Germany, the Charter was adopted in 1995 following a survey which reported serious obstacles to gaining access to bank accounts. Numerous legislative initiatives have been suggested, but none successfully, since the Government preferred to entrust the solution of the problem to the initiative of banks. In June 1995 the Central Credit Committee (ZKA) of the German professional association launched the charter accompanied by the slogan «Current account for all» ("Girokonto für Jedermann"). The banks agreed to offer current accounts to all, regardless of their resources. This fee-based account would allow account holders to carry out traditional bank counter transactions. However, application of the Charter has been challenged by consumer protection groups. In June 2000, the Federal Government presented a status report of the situation to Parliament. According to this report, the number of "current accounts for all" has increased by 350% in 4 years (+ 876,000 in absolute figures). These data have convinced the Government that it is not worth changing the system currently in place. Udo Reifner points to inaccuracies in the Government's analysis. First of all, the report itself admits that banks themselves have different attitudes with respect to the Charter. Furthermore the data supplied by the banks do not include a differentiation according to the type of customer. Reifner suggests the possibility that these new accounts have been opened by a much more appealing category of customers (young people) rather than those on a modest income. Finally the author explains that, although the optimism of the Government can be justified by

---

[35] Only Ireland is initiating reflections on the subject and is studying the offer of a basic product by the organisation running the payment system. CSR Europe (2001), p. 23. In Italy, the initiative by Banca Etica is worth noting.

[36] CSR Europe (2001), p. 23.

the small number of complaints concerning the refusal to open an account, the psychological attitude of those excluded plays an essential role in this respect[37].

In 1996, the Belgian Government launched the debate on financial exclusion following a survey by the Centre Coopératif de la Consommation which reported the growing difficulty of vulnerable groups to establish a relationship with the banking system. This debate encouraged the Belgian banking Association to draw up a charter and to invite a number of banks representing about 80% of the retail market to subscribe to it. This Charter, presented in July 1997, includes the right of each individual living in Belgium to open a savings account, regardless of the amount and regularity of his/her income. This savings account consists of three basic transactions: manual or electronic monetary payment (transactions resulting in an overdraft are blocked); deposits (cash, cheques...) and withdrawals (with the possibility of a bank card being issued); bank statements (which can also be delivered only by cash dispensers). For their part, the account holders agree to deposit their salary there if they ever receive one. The opening of such an account must not be connected with the sale of other financial products. The Charter describes a minimum service supply which the banks are free to improve. The minimum service is offered by participating banks for at least 10 Euro per year, but the customer has the possibility of obtaining other services (debit card, direct banking, ...) by purchasing a package at a fixed price between 12 and 20 Euro. It is worth mentioning that the Charter explicitly lays down the application to these services of normal pricing (art 2). The Ombudsman is responsible for monitoring application of the Charter and acting as mediator between banks and customers.

In France, a Charter concerning basic banking services complementing the legislation was drawn up in 1992 within the framework of the Comité Consultatif des Usagers. For people on a low income, it includes the possibility of an ATM card as well as free access to the DAB dispenser of their bank, the possibility of long-distance payment, the availability of *relevés d'identité bancaire* (RIB), or banking identity statements, and a system of cheques whose number can be limited with the customer's agreement. These basic banking services are not based on the principle of free service. The application of this charter has been challenged by consumer protection groups. In particular, the Association Consommation Logement et Cadre de Vie (CLCV) carried out a survey (see note 34), in April 1999, on the conditions which banks apply to low income customers for the opening of a deposit account. Although, according to the Association, "there does not seem to be a fixed line of behaviour for the different agencies of the same bank," the survey reveals that branch offices never refer to the Charter, even if the question is raised directly. The survey also criticises a number of practices against the wording or the spirit of the Charter, underlining in particular the 7% account opening requests that were turned down. The Association Française des Etablissements de Crédit et des Entreprises d'Investissements (AFECEI) presented

[37] IFF (2000), p. 14 and p. 15.

its comments on the subject of this survey[38]. First of all, it underlines the local character of these "malfunctions" declaring that it is at least available to improve the application of the Charter in view of the 7% of refusals. Subsequently, it underlines its non-binding character. Furthermore, the Association points out that application of the Charter cannot imply the obligation to deliver methods of payment with uncontrollable risks (cheques and inter-banking cards) in "dubious" cases or in the event of reduced price sales or at a loss because competition is increasing on the French market, gradually making inroads[39].

5.5.3 The Government as a Mediator: the United Kingdom and the Attempt in France

The social crisis which hit Great Britain turned the struggle against exclusions into a priority for the Government. After the publication of the Report by the Social Exclusion Unit[40], the Government set up 18 teams (Policy Action Teams), in charge of studying the different dimensions of social exclusion. PAT 14 dealt with financial exclusion. Its report and the one by Don Cruickshank are the framework of the governmental action in this sector. The Government has had to take into account the shortcomings of the payment system market[41] as well as the mismatch between the needs of consumers and the products on offer. Spurred by the need to reform social security (see above), the government has exerted strong pressure on the banking sector and made latent threats to impose a universal service obligation in order to convince the banking sector to set up banking services based on the indications given by PAT 14. The banks answered the government's call by the deadline (October 2000). The services offered by these accounts are shown in tab. 5. Certain High Street Banks charge for the transactions which can be carried out from these accounts and ask for minimum deposits; for its part, the Government is insisting that all banks offer free every day banking and make it possible to open an account without leaving a deposit. Furthermore, Government programmes to

---

[38] Comité Consultatif (1999 – 2000), p. 195 and p. 199.

[39] It should be pointed out that, sometimes, beyond the boards of Professional Associations, banks do take initiatives in this field. That is the case, in France, of the Crédit Mutuel du Nord which offers a basic product free of charge, “Easy Access”, which includes a current account, deposit facility, a withdrawal card, statement of accounts and easy bill payments.

[40] Composed of officials, academics, businessmen and consultants, the aim of this team, directly dependent on the Cabinet Office, was to focus on the outstanding features of exclusions and draw up a national strategy, centred especially on sensitive urban areas, to contrast them. SEU (1998).

[41] Cruikshank (2000). This finding brought about a remodelling of regulations. See HM Treasury (2000).

promote financial inclusion place special emphasis on the Credit Unions[42]. Another priority area is the financial education of vulnerable groups[43]. Finally, within the framework of the Financial Services and Markets Act 2000[44], the FSA has been entrusted with increasing public awareness of the financial system and ensuring a high degree of consumer protection[45]. Also banking associations, under pressure from the Government and exacerbated public opinion, have acted as a centralised source of information, encouraging their members make efforts to comply with government expectations. From this standpoint, they have started to revise their customer relations programmes. This effort has led to a new code of good practice as well as to the acceptance of a new monitoring method[46]. A new Code signed by the BBA, APACS and BSA went into effect on 1 January 2001. This code provides for a minimal level of service that banks agree to offer customers in terms of information, protection of personal data and credit granted in the event of financial difficulties. As for the methods of monitoring to be used, the HM Treasury has set up a new structure within its organisation called the Banking Services Consumer Code Review Group. This new structure has been entrusted with this task and asked to reflect on the possibilities of implementing the Code[47]. Furthermore, the BBA has undertaken to draw up a report every year where the results of its action to promote financial inclusion are described[48]. In the first of these reports the banks underline their efforts in terms of facilitating access to financial services through the dissemination of cash dispensers and automatic teller machines, direct banking (phone, Internet) and longer opening hours. Secondly, they announce the newly established co-operation with the Credit Unions aimed at allowing them to expand their market share. Finally, they underline their commitment to the setting up of a national network for financial

---

[42] These non-profit cooperative financial institutions, which are marginal at the present time, (approximately 1% of the market), are called on to play a leading role through the creation of a central structure and through favourable new legislation. HM Treasury Task Force (1999); PAT 14 (1999).

[43] FSA (Financial Services Authority), DfEE (Department for Education and Employment) and local authorities are assigned to this task through an overall approach based on already existing structures so as to reach the target layers (especially young people, for example through the distribution of educational material in schools, and vulnerable adults, for example by fixing information points in employment exchanges set up as part of the "New Deal", the major programme for job promotion of the Labour Government). Adult Financial Literacy Advisory Group (2000).

[44] This law has reformed the British financial system in the sense that it creates harmonised major competition with transparency and consumer protection.

[45] FSA (2001).

[46] As a result of the remarks of the Cruickshank Report emphasising the inadequacy of the Code and the lack of coercive power of the Banking Code Standards Board.

[47] This group is composed of Treasury officials, consumer associations and bankers. A first round of consultation and inquiry was completed on 28 February 2001.

[48] BBA (2000).

advice and the offer of financial training through the Financial Literacy Education Program. Their stated aim is to help all social groups to take advantage of the new distribution systems. But the British Government has also taken into account the issue of the physical distribution of these basic services. Considering such factors as bank counter rationalisation programmes, the difficulty faced by vulnerable groups in dealing with the new distribution methods as well as the feelings of mistrust that some people have towards banks, the government has decided to avail itself of the most widespread network in the United Kingdom, the Post Office (see below).

Table 5.5
The basic services of British banks

	Credit scoring	Payments in by ACT	Direct Debits & standing orders	ATM card	Number of free cash dispensers (k)	Buffer zone (a)	Debit card	Cheque book
Abbey National	No (b)	Yes	Yes	Yes	3.000	No	Yes	No
Alliance & Leicester	No	Yes	Yes	Yes	30.000	Yes	Yes	(d)
Bank of Scotland	No	Yes	Yes	Yes	30.000	£ 10	Yes	No
Barclays	No (l)	Yes	Direct debit	Yes	30.000	£ 10	No	No
Clydesdale	No (e)	Yes	Yes	Yes	30.000	No	No	No
Co-operative	No (i)	Yes	Yes	Yes	30.000	No	Yes	No
Halifax	No (c)	Yes	Yes	Yes	30.000	No	Yes	Optional
Lloyds TSB	No (g)	Yes	Yes	Yes	30.000	£ 10	No	No
HSBC	No (e)	Yes	Yes	Yes	7.000	£ 10	No	No
NatWest	No (g)	Yes	Yes	Yes	8.700 (m)	£ 10	Yes	No
RBS	No	Yes	Yes	Yes	30.000	No	No (h)	No
Woolwich	No (i)	Yes	Yes	Yes	634	£ 50 (j)	Yes	No
Yorkshire	No (e)	Yes	Yes	Yes	28.000	No (n)	No	No

a. Free temporary overdraft so funds can be withdrawn from a cash dispenser when there is less than £10 in the account.
b. No credit scoring test but if a credit reference agency check shows previous records of bad debts of more than £500, then the application may be denied.
c. No credit scoring test but applicants may be turned down where credit checks show a bankruptcy order or significant bad debts.
d. Provided in many, but not all cases.
e. No credit scoring test but applicants with pending county court judgements or bankruptcy orders may be turned down.
f. The debit card facility means that the whole balance of the account can be withdrawn via cashback at a retail outlet.
g. No credit scoring test but undischarged bankruptcy may be grounds for turning down an application.
h. Planned for later this year.

i. No credit scoring test but undischarged bankruptcy and people with a prior record of fraud will be turned down.
j. Credit buffer, which will be free of fees, is applied to all new accounts. This buffer cannot be used to withdraw cash from a branch or cash dispenser.
k. From 1 January 2000, it is likely that virtually all 30,000 cash dispensers will be charge free.
l. Those with a record of fraud are likely to be turned down.
m. 30,000 from 15 December 2000.
n. Customers can use Yorkshire Bank branches to withdraw amounts less than the minimum amount given out by cash dispensers.

Source: BBA; http://www.bba.org.

In France, the Government has played a real mediating role by gathering representatives of the consumer protection groups from the Conseil National de la Consommation and of the banking system around a single table. This meeting was held as part of the *Mission de réflexion et de concertation sur l'évolution de la relation entre banques et leurs clients* and was intended to review banking relations and to strike a new balance. The discussion field was voluntarily extremely broad and went beyond the issue of the solution for the French exception of «neither – nor»[49].

The only obligation was to consider banking exclusion and the protection of fragile groups in order to implement the contents of a decree that had been announced in the law of 1998 against exclusions. Such a decree would cover the issue of basic banking services and the right to open an account (see below). Indeed one of the three sub-groups in the Mission was entrusted with the task of analysing this specific problem. In spite of the long and detailed phase of information exchange, complemented by interventions from scholars and experts, it was not possible to overcome the obstacles which had become apparent in the guidelines expressed by the parties present from the very start. Practically speaking, if we consider only the specific issues that interest us most, the consumer associations pointed out the need to avoid any type of stigmatising which might derive from the adoption of solutions targeted towards certain groups of people by indicating a specific type of institution, network or product. This would involve proposing an "obligation of universal service" aimed at granting to all citizens the same level of service on the basis of the principle of gratuity[50]. On the other hand the credit institutions pointed out that trust is the core of any banking relation and therefore any undifferentiated solution would go against the essence of their profession.

---

[49] Neither tariffing of cheques nor remuneration of deposits. This exception is destined to disappear with the introduction of the euro.

[50] It seems that this interpretation refers more to the concept of public service than to the legal label used of universal service.

5.5.4 The Government as Legislator: France, Portugal and Sweden

In the absence of an agreement between consumers' associations and banks, the French government had to implement the decree announced in Law 98-657 of 29.07.1998 (the anti-exclusion Law[51]) without the aid of consensual reference points. Article 137 of this Law amends the right to an account instituted by Article 58 of Law 84-46 of 24 January 1984 concerning activities and inspection of credit establishments in these terms: "Any natural person residing in France without a deposit account shall have the right to open such an account in the credit establishment of his or her choice or via the financial services of La Poste and/or the Public Treasury." The article goes on to stipulate that the opening of such an account requires the submission of a declaration upon the person's honour attesting to the fact that the person has no account. "If the chosen establishment refuses to open an account, the person may appeal to the Bank of France to designate either a credit establishment or the financial services of La Poste or those of the Public Treasury." The Law prescribes that the chosen institutions "may not limit the services linked to the opening of a deposit account to basic banking services except under the conditions defined by decree. Moreover, a body designated by the Bank of France that limits the use of the deposit account to basic banking services shall perform its mission under the conditions regarding fees established by decree." In the absence of an agreement between banks and consumers, the government took a position on the issue with Decree n° 2001-45 of 17 January 2001. This decree provides, in Article 1, for the following content for basic banking services: the opening, maintenance and closure of an account; one change of address per year; provision, on request, of banking or postal sort codes; establishment of a place of payment for bank or post office transfer orders; dispatch on a monthly basis of a statement of transactions conducted on the account; performance of cash transactions; collection of cheques and bank or post office transfer orders; deposits and withdrawals of cash at the branch of the body where the account is established; payments by standing order, interbank payment order or bank or post office transfer order; means of remote consultation of the account balance; a card for systematically authorised payments, if the credit establishment is able to provide it, otherwise a withdrawal card allowing weekly withdrawals from the credit establishment's cash dispensers; two bank cheques per month or equivalent means of payment offering the same services. As concerns fees, Article 2 stipulates that these services must be rendered to the beneficiary of the right to an account without any contribution on his or her part. Beyond the controversy sparked by the government decree[52], it should be noted that recourse to the procedure of the right to an account is rather limited, although it is on the

[51] This law poses the issue of inclusion in terms of access to basic rights.

[52] The banks contested the exemption from payment whereas consumer associations contested the number of beneficiaries.

increase[53]. This situation may be explained by various reasons such as the relative complexity of the procedure and lack of publicity in the media, but it seems that the existence of a financial institution that has not so far imposed any selection criteria on its clientele, La Poste, could serve as an explanation (see below). As concerns Portugal, the government decreed the institution of basic banking services with decree n° 27-C/2000 of 10 March 2000. Banks' compliance with the decree is voluntary, but as of February 2001, 14 banks representing about 90% of the market were participating[54]. The decree provides for basic banking services to be available to everyone, regardless of income or whether they receive the minimum social benefit. All the customer need do is complete a declaration on his or her honour stating that he or she does not have an account and authorising the bank to conduct the necessary verification. Fees are not fixed in absolute terms, but are based on 1% of the minimum wage as an upper limit. Banks consequently have a certain amount of freedom. Basic services include the opening and management of a current account, a debit card allowing for withdrawals at cash dispensers and automatic teller machines and payments, cash transactions at branches and a biannual statement of account (!).

Turning to Sweden, the first paragraph of the second section of the Banking Business Act stipulates that banks are required to accept deposits from the public and therefore to open accounts. As this obligation was not upheld in practice, the Financial Supervisory Board, after an initial circular in 1996, disseminated another in early 2000, stressing the fact that individuals, and in particular those with payment problems, were still complaining about difficulties opening an account. This circular reminded the banking system that the obligation must be upheld. However, banks are obliged only to open an account, and not to provide means of payment. Consequently, banks have the right to refuse these services and in some cases even refuse to issue cash cards, despite the Financial Supervisory Board's condemnation of this practice[55].

5.6 The Role of Postal Systems in the Provision of Basic Banking Services: the French and British Examples

In Europe, the postal model is changing rapidly due to the opening of this market to competition. Postal services have always contributed to social cohesion and the reduction of inequalities and exclusions, on the one hand via regional development, that is, by their usually unprofitable presence in rural areas and sensitive urban areas, and on the other hand by way of provision of universal

---

[53] According to the Documentation Office of the Bank of France: 2,959 beneficiaries in 1995, 2,958 in 1996, 3,364 in 1997, 4,329 in 1998, 6,368 in 1999 and 8,525 in 2000, private individuals and companies together.

[54] CSR Europe (2001), p. 26.

[55] Konsument verket – KO (2000), p. 4.

service to a socially disadvantaged population. With a view to evaluating future prospects, an analysis of the role played in this area by the two largest European postal networks, those of the Post Office and La Poste, would surely be meaningful.

5.6.1 The Post Office

The Post Office has survived privatisations by Conservative governments thanks to the affection users have shown towards the institution as it was, but it has felt the effects of years of under-investment, which has prevented it from modernising its network. Indeed, the Post Office is now in a difficult situation due to the decrease in (for example, the reduction in commission on bill payments) or even the disappearance of income generated by traditional business, led by the distribution of social benefits. Within the framework of rapid changes in the economic and social fabric of the United Kingdom and the opening of the postal market to competition, New Labour, by modernising the network and promoting new types of business, has aimed to make the Post Office a major actor in the country's economic life and a powerful tool of its social policy thanks to its coverage of the national territory, its capital of trust, its clientele and its role in the circulation of money and the distribution of benefits. The government's reflections, which began with the White Paper published by the Department of Trade and Industry (DTI)[56], were continued within the framework of the Performance and Innovation Unit (PIU), a think tank attached directly to the Cabinet Office, which was supposed to take stock of the conditions of the network and its prospects and to propose workable solutions, which were then accepted in their entirety by the government, with a view to maximising its potential.

The Post Office's network is the most extensive in Europe with 18,400 branches[57], including 9,900 in rural areas and 8,500 in urban locations. It seems to provide easy access for the population[58] all over the country, in rural areas as well as sensitive urban areas. The Post Office has a strong presence in rural areas: 70% of villages with a population of between 500 and 1,000 and virtually all market towns (more than 3,000 residents) have a post office. This coverage is much more extensive than that provided by other services, such as schools and retail shops, for example. A 1997 survey by the Rural Development Commission demonstrates that in rural areas the rate of coverage provided by the Post Office was six times

---

[56] DTI (1999).

[57] It is worth recalling that only 3% of the network (600 offices located in the centre of major cities) are run by Post Office employees, whereas the remainder 97% is run in partnership by sub–postmasters/postmistresses. Performance and Innovation Unit (2000), p. 12.

[58] 99% of the population live within less than 3 miles of a counter whereas 94% live within less than a mile. Performance and Innovation Unit (2000), p. 15.

that of banks[59]. Nonetheless, over the past ten years, the number of branches in rural districts has dropped by about 10%[60], despite the Post Office's policy of maintaining branches and opportunities for aid within the framework of partnerships between the government and local communities. As concerns sensitive urban areas, the problems responsible for economic desertification also have an impact on activities associated with post offices[61], leading to high turnover among sub-postmasters and affecting the quality of shops that often survive thanks to relatively stable income from postal activities. The Post Office's policy has not been to abandon these areas, which often have a higher density of post offices than other urban areas.

Obviously, maintaining this type of network is costly, given that only 40% of rural post offices and a very small percentage of offices in sensitive urban areas are profitable. With a view to preserving the network, the Post Office applies a policy of cross-subsidies between urban post offices (90% of which are profitable) and other branches[62]. But this does not seem to be sufficient. The Performance and Innovation Unit, observing that the post offices that lose money often have a higher social value, and that in an increasingly competitive environment, the Post Office could be forced to close them, has asked the government to make a formal request to the Post Office to avoid closing post offices wherever possible until 2006[63] and to establish a fund for the modernisation of rural offices and those in sensitive urban areas. The government responded by budgeting £270 million over three years. Moreover, within the framework of the renewed fight against exclusion, a new fund worth £15 million has been earmarked to support post offices in sensitive urban areas[64], while additional aid in the amount of £2 million for rural post offices, announced within the same context, has been made available[65].

---

[59] And the ratio must have increased in view of the acceleration of the rationalisation of bank networks over the last few years. Performance and Innovation Unit (2000), p. 35.

[60] By comparison, the number of bank positions has fallen by 25% and the number of service stations by 30 %. Performance and Innovation Unit (2000), p. 25.

[61] The report by the SEU showed that post offices are often associated with one of the rare retail shops of the area and contribute to maintaining it, through the stability of income. SEU (1998).

[62] The remuneration of sub–postmasters provides for a variable part, according to over-the-counter transactions, and a fixed part: offices which receive a low flow of variable payments see the fixed part increased. In short, the urban network subsidises the rural network and the network in sensitive urban areas. Performance and Innovation Unit (2000), p. 29.

[63] The proposal was accepted by the Post Office. DTI (2000). The fixing of a term would imply a real commitment, to the mind of the Performance and Innovation Unit.

[64] SEU (2001).

[65] *http://www.postoffice-counters.co.uk*, Press Release Archive, 15 February 2001.

To maintain the density of post offices in sensitive urban areas, parallel to financial aid, a Code of Practise negotiated between the Post Office and the Consumer Council for Postal Service[66], provides for the establishment of a broader process of consultation to prevent closures or manage relocations of post offices. Moreover, the Social and Environmental Guide to the Post Office Commission[67] stipulates that the Postal Services Commission must take into account the impact of post regulations on the maintenance of the rural network and of post offices in disadvantaged urban areas.

This strong connotation of local service and the attitude of sub-postmasters make the Post Office the label that enjoys the greatest confidence of any in the United Kingdom. This confidence translates into a service to a broad range of customers that explains, along with the range of services offered, the postal operator's importance in the monetary circuit. In fact, about a quarter of virtual money is distributed by the Post Office and returns in the form of deposits of cash.

Among the services offered, cash payment of benefits and pensions is the leading one in terms of turnover. In fact, about 2/3 of the benefits and pensions paid in the United Kingdom, for an absolute figure of about £60 billion a year, are distributed by the Post Office, which depends on them for about 40% of its income, or £400 million, thanks to an average remuneration of 49 pence for each transaction on an order book and 79 pence per giro cheque. About 18 million beneficiaries receive their benefits at Post Office branches. It goes without saying that the government's decision to shift towards the payment of benefits to current accounts between 2003 and 2005 seriously threatens the balance of the postal operator.

All the elements described above explain that although 28 million people visit the Post Office every week, most of its customers are from the older and more modest segments of society[68].

The Performance and Innovation Unit has established a framework focusing on automation with a view to enabling the Post Office to maximise its network's potential. Project Horizon, scheduled to conclude in spring 2001, was intended to computerise the Post Office's hitherto completely manual operations via the deployment of 40,000 computers and training of 70,000 people. The new activities under consideration including e-commerce, provision of government services and information and access to and training in use of the Internet. Most importantly, however, the link between the Post Office's computer system and those of banks will lay the groundwork for the growth of a new financial

---

[66] This body was created by the Postal Service Act 2000 so as to increase the presence of consumers in the regulation process.

[67] Document laid down by the Postal Service Act 2000 [sec 43(4)], supposed to inform the Postal Services Commission of the major lines of the social and environmental policy of the Government.

[68] Performance and Innovation Unit (2000), p. 20 e seq; p. 67 and seq.

institution managed by the Post Office and expected to earn it new income while serving as a powerful tool for promoting financial inclusion -- the Universal Bank.

Proposed in the Cruickshank Report and announced in the DTI's White Paper, recommended by the Performance and Innovation Unit and sharply criticised by banks, this new entity is not yet operational[69], but on 20 December 200, after six months of difficult negotiations, an agreement in principle in favour of its constitution[70] was signed by the government, the Post Office and "high street" banks. The Universal Bank, of which the Post Office will manage only front office operations, as the back office will be entrusted to a bank by means of a call for tenders, will be active in two areas. First, it will constitute a point of easy access for customers of banks with which it has reached an agreement with government support[71], and second, it will offer an own-label product, the Post Office Card Account. As concerns the first type of service, the Post Office, with a view to providing physical points of contact for the distribution of basic banking services, will allow customers of high street banks to conduct cash transactions involving basic banking accounts administered by the banks themselves at all its branches. The restrictions to which customers of banks that already have a distribution agreement with the Post Office[72] are currently subject (such as an additional processing delay of three days) will be eliminated in the wake of the introduction of a computerised system linked to the bank network. Banks will pay a commission on each transaction conducted at the Post Office, but in return they will be able to pursue their programme of branch rationalisation. Moreover, the Universal Bank will offer the own-label Post Office Card Account. The decision to offer such a product was taken for two reasons. On the one hand, research has shown that many people without current accounts do not trust banks[73], while the Post Office enjoys broad trust. On the other, government experts emphasised the fact that the basic banking services offered by high street banks may be too complicated for the poorest people, who are not used to handling anything but cash. This product (calling it a current account would be stretching a point) comes with only a few basic functions allowing accountholders to receive and manage their benefit payments at no cost: cash withdrawals (but only at the Post Office), everyday transactions, access to account with on-line card.

In terms of strategic positioning, the Universal Bank does not aspire to compete with banks. Lacking specific powers, it will consider itself a distributor and not a producer, and therefore will not develop a range of financial products, as the French and German postal services have done. Moreover, even the Post Office Card Account is not intended to compete with banks' basic banking services. If a

---

[69] On 1March 2001.

[70] *http://www.postoffice-counters.co.uk*, Press Release Archive, 20 December 2000. On 1 March, the legal status of the Universal Bank had not yet been determined.

[71] Seven to 31 March 2001. Gilliland K. (2001).

[72] Alliance & Leicester Girobank, Co–op Bank, Lloyds TSB and Barclays.

[73] PFRC (2000), p. 32.

person who already has an account comes to the Post Office, he or she will be encouraged to use this account. If a person has no current account, the Post Office will provide a list of banks with which it has an agreement and encourage the person to open an account with one of them. The Post Office product will be offered only to those who do not want the complications of a complete account or refuse to use a bank. The Post Office Card Account will not be highly publicised to avoid the appearance of competition with the banking world.

Obviously, the purpose of this card is not to generate profit (certainty of losses on the product, lack of opportunity for sales of related products), but to provide financial education to the most disadvantaged individuals by helping them to develop a relationship to the financial world[74]. Obviously, therefore, management of the Universal Bank will result in losses to be financed by the state with a contribution from banks. Officially, the amount of the fund, its legal status and details of burden sharing between the state and banks have not yet been settled[75], but the burden will be a heavy one that the government will attempt to shed by encouraging holders of the Post Office Card to use the basic banking services offered by high street banks, not by obliging them but instead by educating them.

5.6.2 La Poste

La Poste is certainly already one of the "heavyweights in the French economy". The leading employer in the merchant sector and one of the top French companies in terms of turnover, La Poste has a major economic impact at both national and local level, where it has a vitalising effect on local markets[76]. Indeed, it seems to have adapted more quickly than the Post Office to changes in the economic and competitive environment[77], and understandably, the government and La Poste have ambitious objectives as set out in the Planning Contract concerning the company's positioning in the emerging single and deregulated European market[78].

A former state administration, La Poste became a public law corporation (public operator) in the wake of Law 90-586 of 2 July 1990 on postal and telecommunications services, which furthermore officialised its major role in

---

[74] Gilliland K. (2001).

[75] On 1 April 2001. According to press information, the amount of the fund should be approximately £400 M and the contribution by the banks should amount to 125 M, Cameron D. et Shrimsley R., "Banks agree deal on Post Offices services", 'Financial Times', 21 December 2000.

[76] Larcher G. (1997).

[77] For example, massive investments in computer systems which have made the network, composed of over 80,000 computers and 17 calculation centres, highly efficient. La Poste, Annual Report 1999.

[78] See Preamble and art 1 – 7 of the Contract of objectives and progress concerning the plan contract between the State and La Poste 1998 – 2001 (Plan Contract).

regional development by assigning it a mission of public interest[79]. The regional development mission was subsequently specified in the Specifications[80] and Planning Contracts[81]. The Planning Contract for 1998-2001 repeatedly establishes, as a limitation on the activities of La Poste in this area, the operator's "financial balance" and encourages the implementation of partnerships[82] with an eye to maintaining this balance via a reduction in the network while ensuring a satisfactory level of service, and of "renewed and reinforced" dialogue focusing on postal presence commissions. These commissions, composed of representatives of La Poste and local elected officials, were created for the purpose of "establishing a better distribution (note: of the network of contact points) throughout the country, while allowing La Poste to pursue financial equilibrium in its activities" as "the commission could not ask for an inappropriate location to be maintained unless partners associated with the request have agreed with La Poste on provisions for ensuring the financial equilibrium of the public operation."

La Poste has fulfilled its commitment with the most extensive network in France. In the wake of demographic movements linked to the rural exodus, but in an attenuated manner, the postal network was being reduced and undergoing changes: 13,905 offices in 1960 and 12,357 in 1992, but 3,800 points of contact other than post offices in 1970 and 4,800 in 1993. Concerned about the relative tendency concerning the presence of public services in rural areas[83], on 10 March 1993, the Prime Minister of the time, Edouard Balladur, decided to declare a moratorium on the closure of public services under state authority. This frequently renewed moratorium was ended in 1998 by the Jospin government. Today, the postal network has 17,071 contact points, including 14,086 post offices and supplemental branches and 1,959 postal agencies: 83% of the network is located in municipalities with fewer than 10,000 residents, while 17% of the network, established in municipalities with more than 10,000 residents, serves some 50% of the population of mainland France[84]. The postal network therefore offers better facilities in rural areas than in urban ones and incontestably provides the densest coverage of any French network enterprise. To make a comparison with the banking sector, in 1997, in municipalities with fewer than 2,000 residents, Crédit Agricole had only 1,365 branches and the Caisses d'Epargne had only 500, while La Poste boasted 10,526 contact points. The extent of the network is such that the

---

[79] See. Art 8, paragraph 8 and also art. 6 and art. 38 of the Plan Contract 1998 -2001

[80] Decree no. 90 – 1214 of 29 December 1990 concerning the specifications of La Poste and the posts and telecommunications code: articles 3, 21, 24, 25, and 35.

[81] Plan Contract 1995 – 1997, Art. 4; Plan Contract 1998 – 2001, Art. 4.

[82] Plan Contract 1998 – 2001, Art. 4 – 1: "Partnerships may take different forms: public service companies, public points, postal branches, agreements with other public or private actors".

[83] The number of postal contact points was being reduced by approximately 1% every 5 years.

[84] La Poste, Annual Report 1999.

average distance to a postal contact point in a rural municipality without a post office is about 6.4 kilometres[85].

Because the post network is so widespread, *La Poste* necessarily plays a major role also in the sensitive urban areas where it is the most widely present public institution. Even though a lot of work still has to be done in this field for its admission, *La Poste* is already present with 531 offices in these areas and the plan contract lays down that 10% of the new offices set up as part of the modernisation of the network will be installed there. In actual fact, if the necessary breathing space for the network involves contractions and adaptations, it also means extensions, to meet current challenges and provide appropriate access to its services. The strategic plan of *La Poste* actually budgets 3 M FF of investments for the creation of 600 new offices, 80 of which were already set up in 1999. Present at both ends of the territorial problems, the network of *La Poste* proves to be a key factor in solving them.

Although the network is the traditional mainstay of postal activity and financial activity, such a scale is not justified by commercial reasons since the first 1,380 positions (8% of the network) yield 50% of turnover and the first 7,300 yield approximately 90% of it[86]. Furthermore, in the financial sphere, when the overall progress of the market share of *La Poste* is compared to that of the banks, which undertook to rationalise positions in rural areas, there is no noticeable corresponding increase of the importance of *La Poste* faced with the decrease of banking positions in these areas[87]. Consequently, the justification of the extent of the network in rural and sub-urban environments is mainly a social one. If, in the countryside, the importance is mainly a matter of the presence of a point of contact, in disadvantaged urban areas, it goes well beyond that: postmen are often called on to play a social role, which far exceeds the mission of providing a service[88]. Obviously, this development planning mission has a very high cost for *La Poste*: according to the estimates by Senator Larcher, it amounts to 3.2 M FF[89] for 1995, considering the allowances against direct local taxes granted in return, i.e. approximately 4% of its turnover.

Apart from its local dimension, the action of *La Poste* in encouraging financial inclusion is also carried out through a lack of customer selection. It goes without

---

[85] In 1997. Larcher G. (1997).

[86] La Poste, Annual Report 1999.

[87] For example, the Crédit Agricole with a number of positions equal to approximately 1/8 of postal branch offices in municipalities with less than 2,000 inhabitants plays a role almost equal to La Poste as far as rural customers are concerned. Larcher G. (1997).

[88] See Guatrat – Gounouf (1995).

[89] According to La Poste, this cost amounted to 3.52 M FF in 1995 including 329,000 for sensitive urban areas (ZUS); according to the European Union, this is "at least" 1.32 M. FF for 1993; for the General Inspectorate of Finance about 4.4 M (Such an amount represents, for the rural part of the network, almost two and a half times the development planning budget for the Nation voted for 1997). Larcher G. (1997).

saying that *La Poste* is the banker as a last resort for the vulnerable population. According to a study by the French banking association (*Association française de Banques - AFB*) out of 508 persons over 18 years old in 25 disadvantaged council housing districts, *La Poste* is the bank of 19% of them. Although some occasional episodes of caution were detected, consumer associations fully and unanimously acknowledge that the postal operator has the role of "irreplaceable bank position for the most deprived social groups"[90]. A role that it plays without any legal or financial recognition by the State[91]. In actual fact, if the right to an account seems underused, the causes, of course, are to be found in the relative complexity of the mechanism and the small amount of media coverage that it receives[92], but also in the universal access that *La Poste* reserves for the most vulnerable layers of society through its products which offer the most competitive tariffs on the market[93].

If the use of Giro accounts (CCP) by customers of *La Poste* does not seem to be very different from the way in which bank customers use their current accounts[94], the "social" product above all else offered by *La Poste* is the Savings Account (Livret A). It was created as a product aimed at encouraging popular saving in the 19th century and today it has become a managed savings account[95]. The product is distributed by a legal duopoly composed of the National Savings Bank (*Caisses d'épargne*) and *La Poste*, although it seems that the latter is the only one to offer widespread distribution among the weakened population[96]. Consequently, it is not a current account, but its characteristics and the use that is made of it make the Savings-Bank Book (*Livret A*) the privileged means by which the fragile sectors of the French population relate to the financial system[97]. Evidence of this is provided

---

[90] Larcher G. (1997).

[91] Although it is likely that this attitude of La Poste will be part of the negotiations concerning the Plan Contract.

[92] It is worth recalling that the CLCV survey showed that the banks seldom communicate the existence of such a procedure to the private individuals to whom they refuse an account. Comité Consultatif (1999 – 2000), p. 197.

[93] Many studies have been conducted on the comparison of bank charges. For example, UFC – Which to choose, no. 376, November 2000, p. 42 et seq.

[94] Delessy H. – Badaoui K. (1999a).

[95] The rate of remuneration of the funds paid is determined by the State.

[96] It should be noted that although Art 1 of law no. 99 – 532 of 25 June 1999 concerning savings and financial security shoulders the networks of the Caisses d'Epargne (Savings Banks) with responsibility for "the implementation of the principles of solidarity and the fight against exclusions" and more specifically sets it the task of fighting "against bank and financial exclusion of all the actors of economic, social and environmental life, in particular through the funds collected on the savings account 'Livret' A, the specificity of which is maintained", this task is directed by the Caisses d'Epargne towards support for SMEs and not towards access to financial services for private individuals.

[97] Homeless persons (SDF) can open a 'Livret A' at La Poste if they are domiciled at an association.

by the share of the sums originating from social transfers paid to these savings-bank books: 36% of family allowances, 20% of retirement pensions and 12% of unemployment benefit[98]. It is likely that the design of this product has diverted it away from its institutional aim, for many fragile persons: savings-bank books, in actual fact, are not subject to a minimum balance, people are free to withdraw money at the counters as much and as many times as they want[99], no commission is charged for transactions, the account can be kept on a physical book, which means that it is possible to know the actual amount of the balance at any time. These facilities, wholly or partly lacking in standard current accounts, make it a real purse used for very modest amounts on an everyday basis. Consequently, some categories of savings-bank books (*Livret A*) are extensively overused. Although there is no analysis of these savings books (*Livret A*) according to the income group of its holders, it is possible to envisage an analysis on the basis of the average monthly assets and the annual credit flows, an analysis which makes it possible to highlight its social "role". The "small" [100] "credit" savings-books (Livret A)[101] represent 45% of all the credit savings-books. If they represent 1% of total credits, they carry out 55 % of the transactions made on these savings-books. A part of these small savings-books (*Livret A*) are subject to heavy overuse: 50% of small credit savings-books (8% of the whole, i.e. 1.6 M savings-books) carry out an average of 39 transactions per year versus an average of 16 for all the credit savings-books. They are therefore concerned by half the transactions of savings-bank books (*Livret A)* while they represent only 0.3% of outstanding credits (0.9 M FF). If we take a closer look at the "small" savings-books[102], they are involved in many more transactions, and even more so for debit transactions than for credit transactions: the modest *Livret A* carries out an average of 43 transactions per year, 28 of which are debit transactions. According to the type of transactions, these books are characterised by a high proportion of transfers corresponding to payments of social benefits or wages[103]. It is further worth noticing that savings-books with outstanding credit of less than 1,000 FF are present above all in rural areas, where they total 50% of outstanding credits and in sensitive urban areas

[98] Larcher G. (1997).

[99] Several are examples of withdrawals of a few francs (see post office of Trappes) whereas transactions cost approximately 30 FF. Larcher G. (1997).

[100] Having monthly resources less than or equal to 3,000 FF.

[101] Accounting for at least one transaction per year (debit or credit, excluding capitalisation of interest). In view of the widespread distribution of the 'Livret A' in France, the distinction is an important one because many 'Livret A' seem to have been "forgotten" by the holders; consequently, although they have small outstanding credits and modest yearly credit flows, they should not concern a fragile category of population, but rather a multi-bankarised population, keeping the savings book out of inertia.

[102] Among the small 'Livrets A', the savings accounts are considered modest if held by customers over 18 years of age, who make more than 8 transactions per year (2 per quarter) and if the yearly credit flow is less than 40,000 FF.

[103] Delessy H. – Badaoui K. (1999b).

(ZUS) where they represent 2/3 of outstanding credits. The management of the savings-book *(Livret A)* for *La Poste* shows a loss: for example, in 1995 the margin achieved on savings-book with a deposit of less than 5,000 FF was a negative one by 3.24 M FF whereas the profits on savings-books with a balance greater than 5,000 was 1.92 M FF. The result is a loss of 1.31 M FF according to the General Inspectorate for Finance. The loss of image for *La Poste* should obviously be added to this direct cost: "When someone has 100,000 FF to invest, he chooses a financial counter rather than a welfare counter", a financial adviser confesses[104].

This is not the only means, however, offered by the *La Poste* to deprived customers, allowing them to be integrated into the payment system without having a current account. In actual fact, even if it does not have a legal monopoly, *La Poste* is the only financial institution to offer a money order service, even though it shows a loss and overall traffic is suffering a setback. As a matter of fact, the money order is not merely a means of cash transfer, but also a means of payment and a means of receiving payments, even regular ones (integration minimum income-RMI, unemployment benefit, etc.). If simplicity is an asset which can explain its widespread use, its use is often a necessity: "I do not have a current account", "I have a current account but no related means of payment", „I don't know what I could use instead of it" and "my creditor does not leave me any choice because he wants to be sure of payment", are the most common answers given by the users of money orders in a study carried out by *La Poste*[105]. As far as the use of the different types of money orders by the disadvantaged population is concerned, this same survey points out that the account money order[106], with a slight increase in traffic, is used for the payment of bills or taxes (collection, EDF [electricity bills], HLM [council rents], Télécom [telephone bills], etc.). The cash money order[107], where traffic is declining as people switch to alternative methods, is used, on the debit side, for the payment of invoices (school canteens, etc.) or claims and instalments (bailiff, Cetelem, etc) whereas, on the credit side, it is used for receiving alimony and for various payments. The so-called social card money order is particularly interesting[108]. This type of money order is used especially for

---

[104] Larcher G. (1997).

[105] Delessy H. – Gobin S. (2000).

[106] The issuer, a private individual or artificial person, deposits cash at the post office for transfers to the CCP (Girobank account) of a third party.

[107] The issuer, private individual or artificial person, deposits cash at the post office and hands/sends a remittance to the beneficiary. The latter can withdraw the sum from a post office, or transfer it to his or her CCP (Girobank account) via his or her CRSF (Regional Centre of Financial Services).

[108] The issuer, typically a social body, issues a money order to be debited from its Girobank account (CCP) and that order is sent to the post office where the beneficiary is domiciled. The latter receives it directly at his or her home address if the money order is less than 5,000 FF. Otherwise he or she is notified by his or her post office.

the collection in cash of various social benefits, but the traffic is sharply declining for the benefit of alternative methods of payment (including the optical cheque letter and giro transfer) because it is expensive for *La Poste* and the issuer (30 FF). It is worth noticing that, in sensitive urban areas, the money order is used twice more than elsewhere. As regards the cost that *La Poste* has to bear to provide this service, the loss, according to the General Inspectorate for Finance, is approximately 400,000 FF in 1995 (income for 550,000 and expenditure for 950,000) and is determined by an overuse of money orders for small amounts[109]. Alongside the money orders, it is worth noting the use of the cheque-letter although it is not only offered by *La Poste*. The issuer, typically a social body, sends large numbers of the cheques to the beneficiaries and the cheques are either payable in cash (if the amount is less than 4,000 FF), or may be credited to a Girobank account (CCP) or a savings-book (*Livret A*) or to a bank account. At *La Poste,* traffic of letters payable in cash is sharply declining for the benefit of automated means because social bodies encourage beneficiaries to open a savings account (*Livret A*) to reduce the volume of them. The cost of the latter is 16 FF, whereas, for example, the optical cheque letter only costs them 0.4 FF[110].

La Poste also ensures, free of charge, the issue of bank cheques drawn on the savings account (*Livret A*). They were created to be used in transactions involving significant amounts and they have become a very popular method of payment because there is no risk that the beneficiary should not be paid. Consequently, they are frequently used to settle current expenses (water, electricity, rent, canteen, etc.) by those who do not have any other means of payment or by payers considered as being "questionable". This service costs *La Poste* approximately 1.5 M FF per year[111].

Besides these "traditional" means, *La Poste* is developing innovation by making available products to the general public which use the most recent technology so as to meet the needs of marginalised customers. Tested in 1999, *La Poste* generalised, in 2000, the systematic authorisation card, which avoids involuntary overdrafts[112].

Seen under another light, the activity of *La Poste* in the social field is carried out in the daily work of the post office employees as emphasised in a survey by the Last – Clerse laboratory[113]. This research clearly shows that the frequency of

---

[109] Larcher G. (1997).

[110] Delessy H. – Gobin S. (2000).

[111] Considering its very high cost and the fact that La Poste is the only institution to offer this service free of charge, in July 2000, La Poste announced that a rate of charges would be applied to this service, but the reaction by several trade unions, consumer associations and politicians led to the scrapping of this project.

[112] La Poste, Annual Report 1999. Although this product is offered also by other banks, it seems that it receives little media coverage and is not widely used for reasons of business opportunity.

[113] Gadrey J – Ghillebaert E. – Gallouj F. - Devetter X. – Duplaa D. (1997).

social benefits at post office counters is approximately 10% and the cost borne by *La Poste* is in the region of 9% of counter operating costs. Furthermore, as far as telephone calls to the CRSF (Financial Department Regional Centres) are concerned, social calls represent between 20 – 25% of the whole and they take up 1/3 of the working time while "social cases", in heavily urbanised areas, would seem to represent 20 – 30% of the cases handled for the same proportion of dedicated time. Lastly, as far as delivery is concerned, postmen in urban areas devote approximately 20% of their time to services linked to social cohesion. Consequently, for all the functions of *La Poste* (sorting not included), 10 – 15% of activity is made up of social cohesion services which do not concern development planning. If this percentage is related to personnel costs alone, a social contribution cost between 6 and 9 M FF is obtained for 1995.

La Poste, today, makes a substantial contribution to the scale of French financial citizenship by bearing significant costs, without any official recognition from the State.

5.7 Conclusions

Although the promotion of financial inclusion is now recognised as a European issue and the participation of the E.U. will become increasingly active through the method of open coordination, at the present time, a European discipline concerning basic banking services does not seem conceivable. The fight against exclusions, and therefore against financial exclusion comes within the initiative of Member States, with the principle of subsidiarity prevailing. Furthermore, the pronounced heterogeneity of the financial service markets in Europe seems to advise against such a solution. Even more so, European institutions seem extremely cautious regarding the regulation of a "sensitive" sector such as the banking sector, where, moreover, the European Union considers that competition is playing its role[114]. Lastly, the political problems connected with such a decision are great, particularly concerning the attitude of the banking sector. Today, the European Union gives priority to the way of consensus by relying on the social responsibility of banking companies. That is how the support of the Commission is to be interpreted for the initiative of CSR Europe, a network of socially responsible companies, which is reflecting on the drawing up of a European voluntary membership Charter. The advantages of such an approach are the active participation of the banks and the necessary flexibility so as to take into account

---

[114] Report by the European Commission to the Council of Ministers on general interest services in the banking sector adopted by the Commission on 17 June 1998 and presented to Ecofin on 23 November 1998.

technological progress and the heterogeneity of the European market of financial services[115].

The principles of European social policy should incorporate these reflections to be developed as part of new forms of governance associating regulators, the banking sector and consumer associations. The coordination of strategies in the fight against exclusion should map out a pathway of coherent integration, leading to full citizenship defined in terms of access to basic services. As far as the financial sphere is concerned, it is worth emphasising the paramount importance of financial education and the improvement of communication between the banking system and vulnerable people. As far as basic banking services are concerned, they must be quality services, adapted to vulnerable people insofar as they allow them to fully participate in the financial and economic system. Obviously, they should provide for the opening, holding and closing of an account. It seems to us that an essential feature of the services associated with this account is the absence of any risk connected with the means of payment: on the one hand, it meets the needs of vulnerable categories of persons, on the other hand, it preserves the profitability of the banks. More precisely, basic services should allow cash transactions at counters (it is worth recalling the preference of vulnerable people for this type of transactions) such as the deposit and withdrawal of cash, the cashing of cheques, etc., but provide instruments for receiving and making remote payments: transfers, debits and remittances between banks. A debit and withdrawal card with systematic authorisation is necessary. As already indicated, these accounts should not make it possible to allow an overdraft unless it should be decided to set up a buffer zone, necessary to withdraw all liquid assets through cash dispensers. It is important to ensure that statements of account are frequently available, which might go as far as offering budget facilities. Concerning the beneficiaries, the social policy of the Union, as far as the fight against exclusions are concerned, provides for targeted actions for the benefit of disadvantaged layers. If the prevailing solution in Europe gives whoever does not have an account the possibility of access to basic banking services[116], the beneficiaries could be determined on the basis of those receiving social minimum income according to limits specific to each Member State. This approach would also allow the charges for services to be modulated, which should generally be reasonable, according to the seriousness of the conditions of exclusion[117] even

[115] In this context, the question as to whether the supply of basic banking services is a matter of responsibility for certain institutions or all of them seems to be settled in the sense of associating the whole banking sector in the fight against exclusion. Of course, today and even in the near future (in some cases, longer) the role played in this field by some, typically postal, institutions will be all the more important.

[116] This solution implies, in view of the design of these services, that only those who require them will ask for them.

[117] It should be pointed out that in France, within the scope of the Jolivet Commission, an agreement on the basis of these principles had been reached between the banks and a part of

going so far as to offer services free of charge for the most serious forms of exclusion. In actual fact, the adoption of means of payment with controlled risk would allow the banks to align charges with actual costs and, as far as services free of charge or charges lower than the actual cost are concerned, a form of supportive financing could be envisaged[118]. As regards the distribution of these services, innovative solutions should be found so as to ensure the physical distribution of services throughout the territory in view of the rationalisation of banking networks: mobile counters, weekly opening counters, distributions of basic cash services through retail stores, bank-postal network partnerships are so many examples of solutions to be implemented according to the requirements of the different States. A specific effort is necessary for sensitive urban areas where the cooperation and the coordination of the various parties involved as part of town policies is the pathway to be followed.

These principles should be adapted to the different national realities according to the real impact of barriers concerning supply and demand and the initial conditions, which are very heterogeneous at the present time. At national level, however, regulators are called on to play a major role, not as legislators, but as instigators to stimulate discussion and controllers of the effectiveness of the implemented measures. As a matter of fact, if banking ethics seem to be the best solution to the problem both at operational and political level, they should be applied. For that purpose, it seems advisable to set up mediators, coordinated at European level and according to joint procedures and criteria, who would be expected to constantly evaluate the situation and monitor the progress by associating the parties involved. Widespread media coverage should be given to the reports of these bodies so that public opinion can evaluate the attitude of each bank in relation to its social responsibilities[119].

Up to now, postal systems have played a major role in providing bank access to vulnerable categories of persons. The upheavals caused by the competitive opening of the European market, by the adoption of a business logic by postal operators and by the re-definition of their strategies have dealt the cards differently in several cases. In prospect, the role of postal systems in social banking seems to be determined by the position targeted by operators in the liberalised market of Europe, by the role entrusted to financial departments to achieve the objective and by the attitude of governments. For example, The Post Office is not in a position to compete with the banks on the market for financial

---

consumer associations. The demand for free basic banking services for all citizens by other associations prevented it from being implemented.

[118] For example, a fund supplied by each bank in inverse proportion to the basic accounts opened out of the total.

[119] For example, in response to the rising ethical criticism regarding the choice of investments for private individuals, as from January 2002, Euronext will launch an index of socially responsible companies and the marking agencies chosen to assess those companies shall include their "social" performance in the assigned rating.

services and the role of the Universal Bank in the field of basic banking services, with the support of the Government and the banking sector, will enable it to face up to the drop in income caused by the changeover to the payments of benefits to bank accounts while waiting for the reform that will allow it to become a competitive actor on the postal market. As far as *La Poste* is concerned, this operator is perfectly able to compete with the banks on the market for financial services, as already proved by its activity, and it wishes to become a fully-fledged financial actor. Furthermore, in agreement with the French Government, the operator proposes to reach a position of leadership on the European and world postal market. Financial services are an essential asset which shall be able to release all its potentiality to overcome competition, in particular from the German operator which is already undergoing thorough restructuring (see Ch. 2). It therefore seems that operators aiming for a position of leadership are destined to reduce, according to the same logic of the banking sector, their action in the field of social banking as and when the authorities of administrative supervision gradually grant them increasing levels of autonomy[120].

5.8 References

ADULT FINANCIAL LITERACY ADVISORY GROUP (2000): Report to the Secretary of State for Education and Employment, Décembre.

BBA, British Bankers' Association (2000): Promoting Financial Inclusion, April 2000.

CAFFET M. C. (2000): L'application de la charte des services bancaires de base, en «Revue d'économie financière», n° 58, pp. 121 – 134.

CAISSE DES DEPOTS ET DES CONSIGNATIONS (2001): Etude pour l'élaboration d'une charte européenne volontaire sur les services bancaires de base, working paper, Janvier.

COMITE CONSULTATIF (1999 – 2000): Rapport au Conseil National du Crédit et du Titre, Banque de France.

COMMISSION EUROPEENNE, Communication 96/C281/03, «Les services d'intérêt général en Europe».

COMMISSION EUROPEENNE, COM(2000) 79 final, «Construire une Europe de l'inclusion».

COMMISSION EUROPEENNE, COM(2000) 379 final, «Agenda pour la politique sociale européenne».

COMMISSION EUROPEENNE, COM(2000) 580 final, «Les services d'intérêt général en Europe».

---

[120] That is the case, it seems, of La Poste destined to share the weight that it now carries with the banks. That will require time, nonetheless, and, to safeguard the financial citizenship of vulnerable categories of persons, a simplification of current French legislation.

CONTRAT D'OBJECTIFS ET DE PROGRES PORTANT CONTRAT DE PLAN ENTRE L'ETAT ET LA POSTE 1998 – 2001.

CONTRAT DE PLAN ENTRE L'ETAT ET LA POSTE 1995 – 1997.

CRUIKSHANK D. (2000): Competition in UK Banking – A Report to the Chancellor of the Exchequer, Mars.

CSR Europe (2001): Toward Financial Inclusions for All. A European Voluntary Charter on Banking Services: First Step of a Eropean Initiative. Working Document, Février.

DELESSY H. –BADAOUI K. (1999a): L'usage des moyens de paiement selon le montant des flux créditeurs sur les CCP, working paper, La Poste.

DELESSY H.– BADAOUI K.(1999b), Eléments sur l'usage à La Poste du Livret A, working paper, La Poste.

DELESSY H. – GOBIN S. (2000): Quelques informations sur les mandats, working paper, La Poste.

DTI, Departement of Trade and Industry (1999a): Modern Markets, Confident Consumers. The Gouvernemnt White Paper.

DTI Departement of Trade and Industry (1999b): Post Office Reform: A World Class Service for the 21st Century. The Government White Paper, Juillet.

DTI Departement of Trade and Industry (2000): First Annual Report to Parliament on the Progress of Reforms Set out in the White Paper, Décembre.

EUROBAROMETRE 52 (2000), Services Financiers, Les Européens et les services financiers, Mai. Rapport rédigé par INRA (Europe) pour la Direction Générale Santé et Protection des consommateurs, Direction A, Politique des consommateurs, «Services financiers» et géré et organisé par la Direction Générale de l'Education et de a Culture, «Centre pour le citoyen».

FSA, Financial Services Authority (2001): Policy Statement 45, Conduct of Business Sourcebook, Février.

GADREY J. – GHILLEBAERT E. – GALLOUJ F.- DEVETTER X. – DUPLAA D. (1997): Valeur ajoutée et coût des prestations sociales de La Poste, working paper, Laboratoire LAST – CLERSE (Université de Lille I et IFRESI).

GILLILAND K. (2001): Post Offices and Access to Financial Services, Congrès EFMA, Paris, 12 – 13 Février 2001.

GUATRAT – GOUNOUF (1995): Le rôle des bureau de poste dans l'insertion des populations marginalisé, Mission de recherche de La Poste.

GUENEAU C. (2000): Les besoins des personnes fragiles en matière de services bancaires, en «Revue d'économie financière», n° 58, pp. 47 – 56.

HM Treasury (2000): Competition in Payment System, Consultation Paper, Décembre.

HM Treasury Task Force (1999): Credit Union for the future, Novembre.

IFF, Institut Fur Finanzdienstleistungen (2000): Access to Financial Services: Strategies towards Equitable Provision – German National. Report, Hamburg, August. Preliminary Paper présenté à la Conférence international de Göteborg «Access to Financial Services: Strategies towards Equitable Provision», le 22 et 23 Septembre 2000.

KEMPSON E. - WHYLEY C. (1998): Access to Current Account. A Report to British Bankers' Association, BBA.

KEMPSON E. – WHYLEY C. – CASKEY J. – COLLARD S (2000): In or out ? Financial exclusion: a literature and research rewiew, FSA, Consumer Research 3.

KONSUMET VERKET – KO (2000): Tendencies in Access to Financial Services in Sweden. Paper présenté à la Conférence international de Göteborg «Access to Financial Services: Strategies towards Equitable Provision», le 22 et 23 Septembre 2000.

LARCHER G., SENATEUR (1997): La Poste, opérateur public de service public face à l'évolution technique et à la transformation du paysage postal européen, Rapport d'information au Sénat n° 42, Commission des affaires économiques et sociale, édition web.

LARCHER G., SENATEUR (1998): Sauver La Poste: est-il encore temps pour décider ? Rapport d'information au Sénat n° 463, Commission des affaires économiques, édition web.

LA POSTE, Rapport Annuel 1999.

OFT, Office of Fair Trading (2001): The OFT's New Approach to Consumer Codes of Practise. A Consultation Paper, Février.

PAT 14, Policy Action Team 14 (1999): Access to financial Services, HM Treasury, November.

PERFORMANCE AND INNOVATION UNIT (2000): Counter Revolution. Modernising the Post Office Network, Cabinet Office, Juin.

PFRC, Personal Finance Research Centre (2000): Access to Financial Services in the UK, Paper présenté à la Conférence international de Göteborg «Access to Financial Services: Strategies towards Equitable Provision», le 22 et 23 Septembre 2000.

PILLEY O. – ANDERLONI L. (1999): European Post Offices in Financial Services. Competitors or Strategic Partners ? Lafferty Publications, Dublin.

RODRIGUEZ S. (2000): La nouvelle régulation des services publica en Europe. Paris, Ed. Tec & Doc.

SEU, Social Exclusion Unit (1998), Brining Britain Togheter, a National Strategy for Neighbourhood Renewal, Cabinet Office, Juin.

SEU Social Exclusion Unit (2001): A New Commitment to Neighbourhood Renewal. National Action Plan, Janvier.

UFC – Que choisir, n° 376, Novembre 2000., pp. 42 - 45.

UNITED NATIONS, (2001): Postal Saving for development project, Departement of economic and social affairs, Janvier.

6

Postal Banks in the Digital Age: Creating a New Role

Greg Schmid

6.1 Introduction

The Posts have had a long and important role in financial services. They have used their close contact with households to build an efficient component of the payment system through the postal giro and a direct and accessible way to build patterns of small savings.

But over the last decade major shifts in banking and transactions have challenged this role of the Posts. Commercial bank accounts are now available to most citizens, payment cards and credit cards make the costs of transactions cheaper, and new competitors are offering services traditionally handled by the postal banks. These trends lower the value of transactions and financial services, while increasing the competition postal banks face.

Still, the digital revolution provides opportunities for postal banks to compete, by offering financial services in new and different ways. Postal banks can use information derived from transactions to build an interactive information exchange with those consumers who find value for themselves in such exchanges. By working with the Posts, the postal banks can provide a new service to individual consumers that provides timely and targeted information of great value. In fact, we see the digital age presenting a unique opportunity for postal banks to leverage some of their most basic attributes and carve a new role for themselves that would add value to their revenue stream - plus provide a valuable service to consumers.

6.2 Do Posts Belong in Financial Services?

European Posts have a long history in providing financial services. By reaching every household and every business every day, they were in an excellent position to offer their services for transmitting payments. It was a relatively simple step to offer a means into the remote payments system for those who did not have bank accounts by establishing simple current accounts that could be drawn on for payments. The postal payment system could easily be extended to holding savings for a dispersed population. Finally, as the postal role in financial payments grew, the development of a giro system that offered an efficient payments and settlement mechanism for society as a whole emerged.

Because of the efficiencies in servicing everyone in a country, whether banked or unbanked, the size and scale of the postal operation and the effectiveness of utilizing a well-established infrastructure enabled the Posts to compete with banks through an efficient payments system and simple savings plans.

But the digital age is challenging the basic premises of the system. Transaction costs in a digital world will fall, in some cases quite dramatically - probably to half the cost of a paper-based system. With national and international settlements systems all highly automated, the advantage of the giro system in reaching scale and being truly comprehensive disappears. In the digital age, most financial service players participate in efficient transactions and settlements networks; and much of the information about financial transactions is moving into digital form as well. The Posts' comparative advantage in the giro network and the ability to deliver physical account information and confirmations will shrink in this world.

In a digital age, the Posts must offer services associated with their unique role in financial services that provide value-added benefits to both their customers and themselves. This value-added component must be solidly based upon the foundation of services and relationships that can provide their own sustainable comparative advantage.

This paper explores the nature of the Posts' core assets in the digital age and how they may apply to financial services. Posts can find a comparative advantage for certain aspects of what they can uniquely provide in financial services - but only by rethinking what their role will be. They need to build that role on their traditional strengths of communication, regular consumer contacts, and a trusted brand. This new role can be successful and will ultimately place the Posts at the heart of the world of information and communication in the digital age.

To understand this new role for the Posts, it is necessary to appreciate the shift in the payments system over the last few years and how the banks are aggressively carving out a new role for themselves.

6.3 Banks Finding a New Role

The Posts are not alone in needing to redefine their role in the digital age. Every other industry that communicates or shares information with consumers on a regular basis, including those involved with the payments system, has needed to do (OR has done) the same thing over the last ten years.

A good case in point is the banks. Traditionally, the banks' basic role was as an information mediator between borrowers and savers. Banks had more information about investment possibilities and risks than did individual savers. Further, the banks could aggregate savings from many small accounts into large pools of investable funds. Using detailed information on local business and real estate markets, banks were able to locate acceptable risks in virtually every community.

They could sustain a good margin between the return that many small savers or deposit account holders were willing to accept and the rate borrowers were willing to pay for flexible credit.

The fall in the price of information undermined to some extent the banks' position as a key intermediary between borrowers and lenders. Many savers - both companies and individuals - discovered they could find a wider variety of investment opportunities outside of traditional deposit and savings accounts through direct access to markets. This direct access has been facilitated by the ease of obtaining market information through information brokers and electronic markets, and growing confidence in third party agents. Individuals have found they could better control their cash balances and minimize their account balances by using credit and payments cards.

This has made it easier for companies and individuals to place their money into investments that give higher rates of return than deposit accounts. In the United States, for example, deposit accounts as a share of total financial assets have fallen markedly over the last decade (see Figure 6.1). Banks have found it necessary to generate an increasing portion of their earnings from items other than deposit accounts.

Figure 6.1
Deposit accounts are much less important
(Share of all financial assets held in deposit accounts)

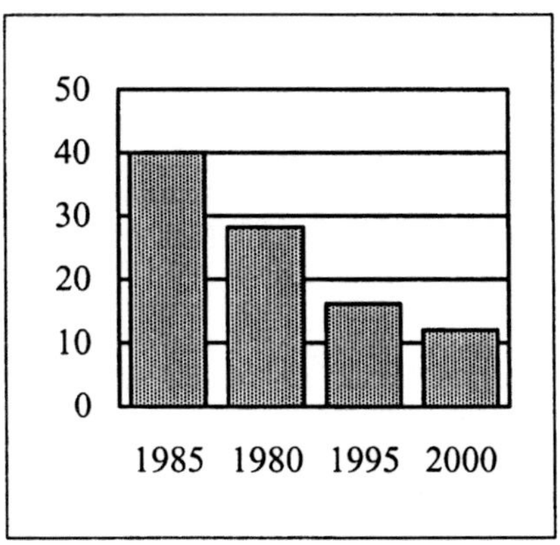

Source: Federal Reserve Board, Flow of Funds Accounts.

At the same time, many borrowers have gone directly to the markets—issuing more shares, commercial paper, bonds, or securitizing their debt in some form. As deposits have become less significant, banks have found funds in others places, often going to the market to borrow and build their investable assets. In fact, bank borrowing has increased markedly in recent years, in relation to deposits (see Figure 6.2).

Figure 6.2
Banks have gone to the market for funds
(Ratio of banks' market debt to deposit liabilities)

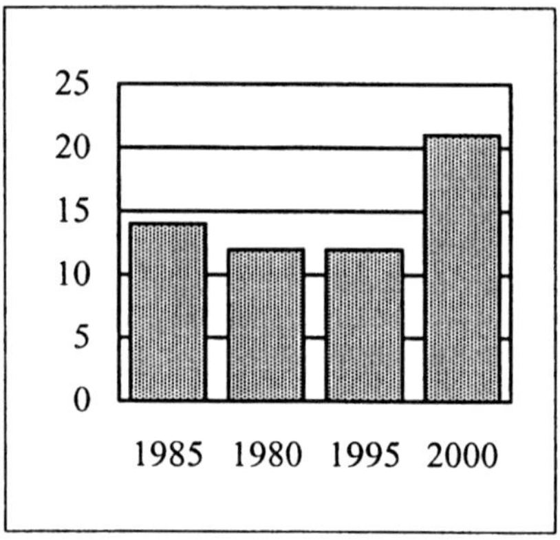

Source: Federal Reserve Board, Flow of Funds Accounts.

The faster and wider flow of digital information has changed the role of banks, both in building deposit accounts and in providing credit. But it also has affected routine activities such as transactions and payments. The ability to digitalize payments and send them instantaneously through settlement systems to a final payee account speeds up the process and reduces the number of parties needed to process the information. This makes it easier for alternate settlement systems to arise.

Thus, the digital challenge for banks is that their unique role in aggregating savings, in finding lenders, and in making a margin on transactions is undermined. Each of these losses threatens a key source of the banks' traditional revenue stream. Bank margins on these sources are likely to continue declining in the future. Banks have faced the fact that their traditional basic business - transactions and routine secured loans to households and businesses - will earn smaller and smaller margins as plentiful information becomes more available to everyone.

Banks have created revenue sources by appending value-added components onto basic services. Transactions have long been a key source of banking revenue. A recent study of large banks in the United States found that noninterest income accounts for about 40% of their total revenue. But of the noninterest income stream, only 15% came from transactions fees. The bulk of the noninterest revenues was accounted for by service charges on activities such as new loans, credit card accounts, handling of securities and documents, and aggressive market based activities such as foreign exchange trading and equity investments (see Figure 6.3). The range of skills needed to provide a greater choice of related services, to build fee income from financial market activity, and to generate returns from equity investment is critical to the profitability of the new bank of the digital age.

Figure 6.3
Varied sources of non interest income
(Share of total non interest income for 25 largest U.S. banks)

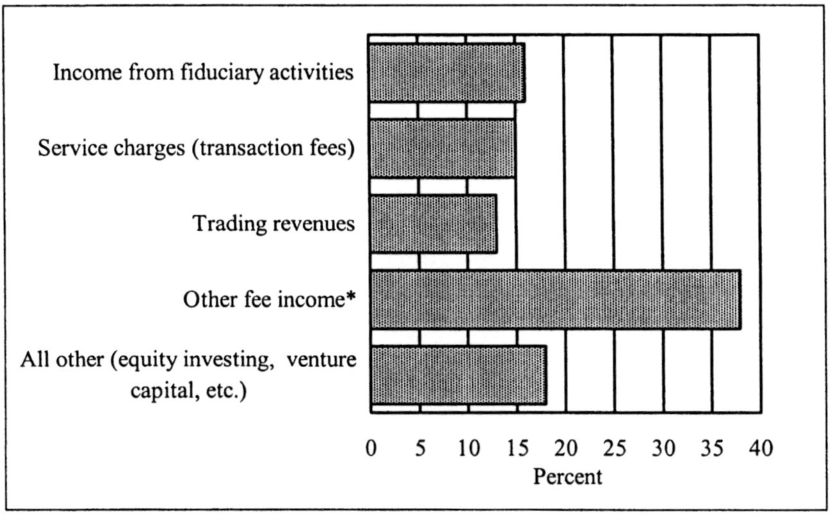

* *Loan fees, credit card fees and securutization, annuity commission, etc.*

Source: Derived from Radecki, L. Federal Reserve Bank of New York, Economic Policy Review, July 1999.

Banks have shifted their profit base from traditional services such as gathering deposits and settling transactions to using their expertise in areas such as handling important documents, assessing and running personal lines of credit, and making relative high returns on investments with risk attached. Banks are willing to accept lower earnings on transactions because they are using the transaction accounts as a means of building relationships through which they can develop higher valued services or grow a pool of investable funds where risk-taking can be rewarded.

6.4 Alternative Entries into Transactions Accounts

Banks have discovered in recent years that revenue earned from transactions is not as important as expanding the range of services that are provided to investors and participants in the payments system. Banks realize the importance of attracting people into their part of the payments system by offering prospective customers a larger menu of services. At the same time, there are other players emerging within the payments system with interests of their own, who challenge traditional postal accounts with new forms of competition. Let's mention five of these:

- *Larger banks.* Bank consolidations are creating a larger set of banks with sophisticated backroom technology. This makes it much easier for these banks to aggressively expand their marketing to smaller account holders and to operate a large number of small accounts more efficiently. Customers who found that only postal banks welcomed their modest accounts in the past, may now find much larger banks searching them out;
- *Internet and telephone banking.* New banks have appeared that offer banking services over the Internet. Without the legacy systems of branch offices, many of these banks have the potential to offer higher rates of return on deposit accounts. One such example is Scandia Bank, a telephone and Internet bank started by a Swedish insurance company. It has no branch offices, yet has 400,000 depositors and can afford to offer rates of interest much higher than other commercial banks in Scandinavia;
- *ATM networks.* Large banks are building ATM networks in populated areas. ATMs are appearing in stores, business complexes, airports and on street corners—wherever there are crowds of people. More ubiquitous than post office branches and without the lines of people, ATM networks allow easy and convenient access to deposit accounts;
- *Grocery stores.* Many large grocery chains are offering deposit accounts. Because they handle more cash transactions than most other businesses and have customers coming to their stores on average twice a week, grocery stores are well suited to offering their services as banks. The British grocery chain Tesco currently offers deposit accounts that shoppers can draw against to pay for groceries. These accounts supply basic deposit account services - and have higher interest rates than any bank in England. Tesco utilizes an existing infrastructure and a loyal set of customers, and provides the convenience of key banking services - cash withdrawals, instant credit transactions, deposits - at the same time customers are getting their grocery shopping needs satisfied. After only three years, the grocery chain has about 1.5 million accounts. Since regular grocery shoppers spend on average over € 50 per visit, store managers would be perfectly happy to offer checking accounts as loss leaders if they helped bring customers to the stores on a regular basis. But Tesco is profiting from its banking service and offering interest rates about twice as high as other leading deposit accounts in the United Kingdom. Thus, grocery stores may well follow Tesco's example and discover that being a bank is a natural and profitable part of their service offerings;
- *Credit card use.* Banks are aggressively managing major credit card programs and deriving an increasing portion of their payments-based income from these programs. But credit cards allow individuals to minimize deposit accounts or, at least, to exert more control over how much money needs to be in such accounts. Therefore, it seems that increased credit card usage will change the intensity of deposit accounts use.

Thus, we see many creative approaches to banking that new competitors are offering as viable alternatives to deposit accounts with traditional banks. To protect their payments income built on services, banks need to run efficient payments systems, minimize charges for transactions, and maximize the return on deposit accounts.

Banks have been forced to alter dramatically the way they earn money. Postal banks that want to continue in banking need to similarly adapt to this new competitive situation, because Posts - like traditional banks - are facing tough new competitors.

6.5 Posts Finding a New Role

6.5.1 An Imperative for Change

Like the banks, the Posts and postal banks need to find a new role in the payments system if they want to stay in the transactions business. Postal banks are especially vulnerable to some of the trends in the payments system, such as the move to networked settlement systems. They provide easy and cheap accessibility that reduces the postal giro system's advantage of a wider network of users, and undermines the giro system's ability to maintain a sizeable profit from a two- or three-day float.

As the European society's average income and education levels rise, there are fewer households that will not be welcome customers of the larger banks or even online banks; further, an even broader group of people will discover the grocery store may be the best place to open and establish their first transactions accounts. A much larger share of people will find that having and using a credit card will change their patterns of using transaction accounts.

Postal banks need to find a role that will allow them to offer an expanded range of services to more sophisticated consumers, services that will allow the postal banks to realize value-added returns, as do traditional banks.

Given the long-time strength of the Posts and postal banks, the comparative advantage of the Posts against the growing sophistication of the banks is not in the quick assessing of local credit risk, managing the intricacies of credit card balances, setting up venture capital funds, or operating actively in credit markets. It has to be something closer to the core attributes of the post - something that reflects the deep loyalty and trust that Posts have built with households, and their enduring popular brand image. The key for the Posts is to understand and build upon their strengths: having bonds of personal trust with households and providing access to needed and timely information.

6.5.2 The New Role of Information

Banks and other information purveyors have built new roles by responding to institutional changes brought by the information age. They are not responding only to new technologies that allow transactions to be done more efficiently or that make more information available. They also have adapted to the growing sophistication of their customers, who desire more complex, information-rich products. The key to the new digital age is understanding how the astounding changes in the cost and availability of information are allowing people to use it in new and different ways.

Consumers are learning how to use information in a way that empowers them to exert more control over commercial decisions. Consumers are using more channels of information and are using the information they get more selectively. This is forcing businesses to change the way they communicate with consumers and build successful relationships with them. Banks are learning that traditional activities such as transactions are not an end in themselves, but are tools for building relationships that lead to higher value-added activities that promise sustainable higher rates of return.

Posts must learn the same lesson; that success in the new digital age requires identifying and understanding the opportunities to add value to the way consumers conduct transactions. The future for Posts in financial services - as in other parts of the postal stream - will depend upon the Posts learning about the new consumer's expectations regarding information and carving out a key role as a trusted information agent for the new consumer.

6.6 The Consumer in the New Age of Information

The number of consumers who are learning how to use commercial information in new and different ways to help them with purchasing is growing rapidly. People with more education, knowledge-oriented jobs, and regular access to new forms of information technology are getting used to utilizing information for their own good. Many of these consumers - like many companies - have discovered that information leads to power and control. Let's spend a minute looking at some of the characteristics of this new consumer.

6.6.1 Demographic Shifts

Long-term demographic trends point to a profound shift - income and education are rising dramatically. Over the last few decades in the countries of the North Atlantic, educational attainment of the adult population is up dramatically[1]. If we look just at those who have pursued some college studies, the share of the adult

[1] North Atlantic countries include Canada, the United States, Belgium, Denmark, Finland, France, Germany, Ireland, Netherlands, Norway, Sweden, and the United Kingdom.

population that has attended college has risen four to five times faster than the overall growth of the adult population (see Figure 6.4).

Figure 6. 4
Educational attainment is up sharply
(Average annual rate of growth for Northern Europe, 1990–99)

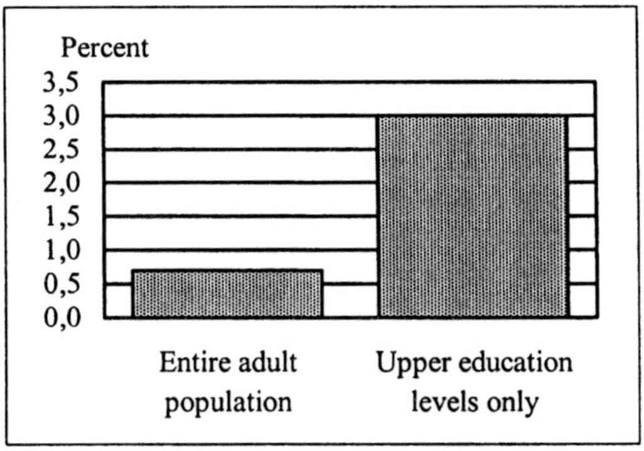

Source: OECD (Organisation for Economic Co-Operation and Development), Educational Statistics; Euromonitor.

The same trend is true for income, although the rate of change is somewhat slower, especially in Northern Europe (see Figure 6.5).

Figure 6.5
Higher income groups also rising fast
(Shift in share of households by income level, Germany 1990s)

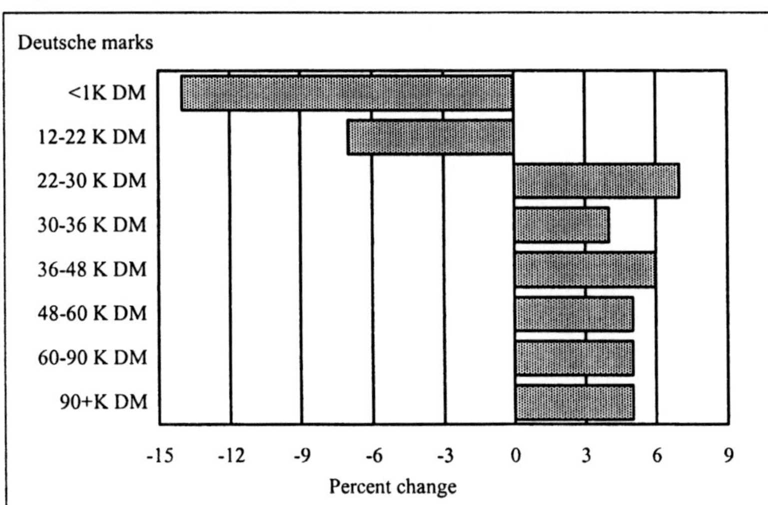

Source: Deutsche Statistisches Bundesamt, Statistisches Jarbuch..

The number of information-intensive jobs and the share of the population that has direct access to online information sources are growing even faster. If we put these trends together, we will find that about half the Northern Europe population lives in households with fairly high levels of discretionary income, or has completed the highest level of secondary education, or has regular access to the online world.

The trend for this part of the population to continue growing is demographically based. Since today's young people are going to colleges and universities at a much higher rate than did people who are now in their 70s, and since younger knowledge workers will have higher earnings than the majority of seventysomething blue collar workers, this trend toward an increasing share of the population with more income and more education should continue...

6.6.2 How Consumers Use Information

Our surveys show that these sophisticated new consumers gather and use information in different ways. This is especially true concerning the methods they use to obtain information about commercial decisions, that is, decisions regarding products and services they buy and use.

There is any number of examples of these differences. Consumers with higher levels of education use more channels to gather information. They not only utilize new digital formats to collect data, but they also turn to traditional sources such as newspapers, books, and mail more frequently than less-educated consumers (see Figure 6.6).

Figure 6.6
Sophisticated consumers like information in a variety of formats
(Share of adults who are frequent online users, by level of education)

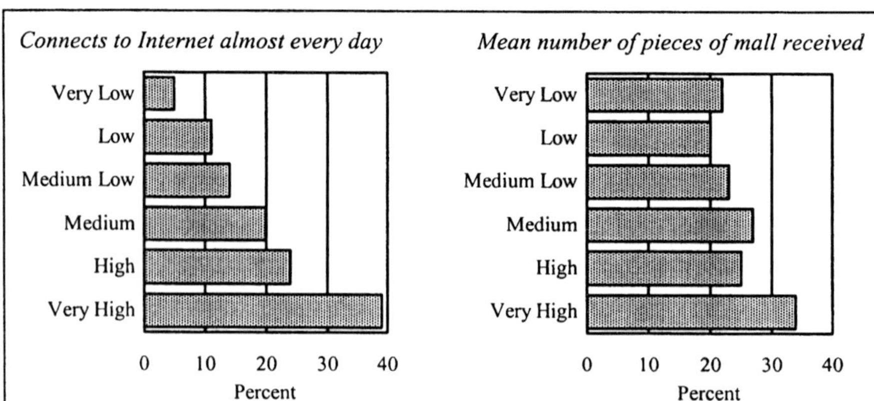

Source: Institute for the Future, Global Mail Household Survey, 2000.

Not only do these more sophisticated consumers use more channels but they get more information or have more commercial contacts with businesses through those channels. Our surveys have tracked perceived contacts with businesses across a broad range of different channels. In sum, the number of contacts rises with the level of education (see Figure 6.7).

Figure 6.7
Sophisticated consumers in Europe have more contacts with businesses
(Northern European consumers' perceptions of number of discrete commercial communications received each month, by level of education)

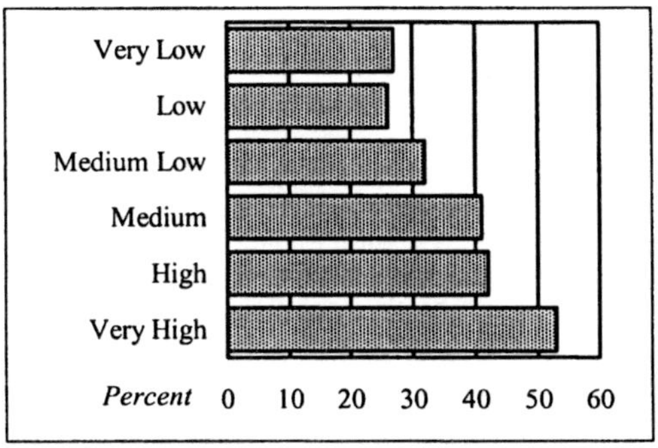

Source: Institute for the Future, Global Mail Household Survey, 2000.

Sophisticated consumers who utilize more information from more channels also have a strong preference for information that they sought on their own. The highly educated consumers believe that information they requested was much more likely to have been useful in making their last purchasing decision (see Figure 6.8).

Figure 6.8
Many Northern European consumers value requested information
(Percent of Northern European consumers who say information they searched for on the Internet or requested directly from companies was the most useful in making their last major purchasing decision, by level of education)

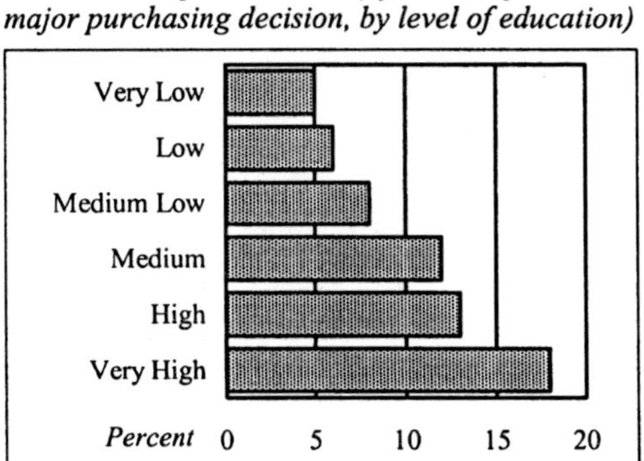

Source: Institute for the Future, Global Mail Household Survey, 2000.

Of particular importance to the Posts, these sophisticated consumers are not only open to the idea of getting targeted information but have actively done this in the recent past. While only about one-third of all adults in Northern Europe have given a company permission to send them targeted information, over 40% of well-educated consumers have done so (see Figure 6.9).

Figure 6.9
Sophisticated consumers are the most likely to leave permission for targeted information
(Percent of consumers in Northern Europe who say they have given businesses permission to send regular product or service information updates, by level of education)

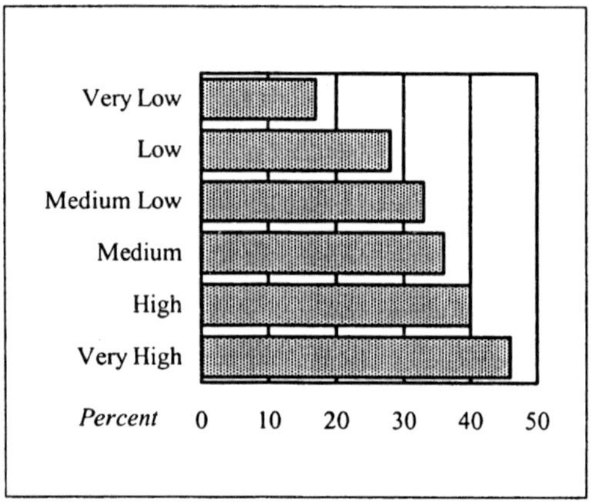

Source: Institute for the Future, Global Mail Household Survey, 2000.

New and sophisticated consumers, then, use more information in making their buying decisions, they use information drawn from a variety of channels, and they are more interested in information that is targeted to their particular needs. And a good portion of them is willing to share personal information with businesses in exchange for product or service updates they might want.

6.7 Trust and Privacy

The key to communicating with this new consumer is about building a relationship of trust. Any business that does this has to deal with the critical issue of public concern: privacy.

6.7.1 Concern about Privacy Is High

Privacy is a major concern of consumers of all kinds across the North Atlantic region. Today more than half of people express concern about their privacy (see Figure 6.10).

Figure 6.10
Privacy is important
(Share of consumers concerned about threats to their personal privacy)

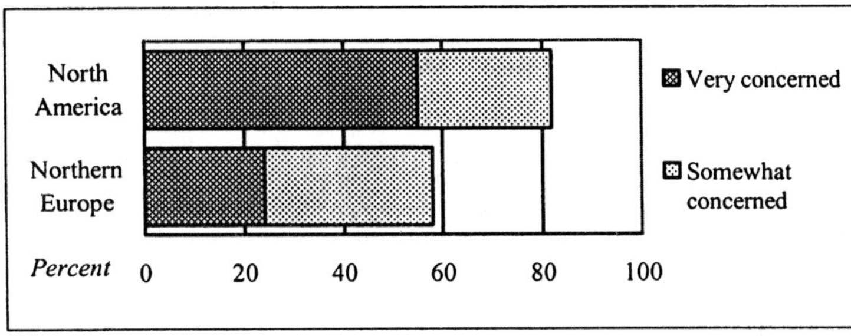

Source: Institute for the Future, Global Mail Household Survey, 2000.

While still high, the lower rates of public concern in Northern Europe probably indicate a tighter regulatory stance in the European Community toward privacy, and the resulting care taken by companies in dealing with personal information.

6.7.2 The European Directive

The European Data Protection Directive on privacy was approved in 1995 and came into force in 1998. It was developed to harmonize privacy regulation among community members and to establish basic minimum rules for privacy while giving states some leeway in customizing national rules. The Directive seeks to protect every individual's basic right to privacy in the midst of the high levels of concern about the increased ability of businesses to capture and process personal information.

The Directive is based on four specific principles that are meant to protect individuals from unwanted collection and utilization of personal information:

- any personal data collected from an individual should be for a specifically defined purpose;
- data collected should be used in a timely manner;
- individuals should have the right to access personal data about them;
- individuals should have the right to be informed about the uses of their data and the right to withhold permission for use.

The basic underlying thread behind these principle is that personal data should be used for the original purpose indicated and only with the informed consent of the individual. Use of data for marketing purposes is allowed but only if the individual has been notified and has the right to opt out. New systems of data gathering and use are emerging that reflect all of these concerns.

6.7.3 Permission-Based Systems

Businesses are experimenting with information gathering systems that ask individuals directly to share personal information in exchange for targeted information of value to them or for a reward of some kind. This is done only with the explicit consent of the user and it allows the consumer easy access to the system so they can voluntarily opt out. The most common form of this information trading is a loyalty card which tracks a person's purchases over time in return for benefits such as discounts.

But an interesting new version that is better at targeting is discount sites on the Internet. Swapping one's personal preferences for discounts or product information is much more interactive in nature. These Internet-based companies offer discounts to people who identify an interest that they would like to receive information about. A series of companies - Coolsavings.com, Iwon.com, and Grab.com, for example - are developing this new mode of information sharing on interactive Web sites. The real time interactivity of these sites brings them close to being permission-based marketing systems.

As a starting point, each company asks visitors to the site to register with their name and address. In exchange for this very basic information, visitors are offered discount coupons to use in a few popular stores or e-commerce sites. They are told they will receive more of these coupons in the future.

Visitors then are asked if they want to share information that is more personal in nature - there might be specific questions about family income, number of children, type of car, number of pets, and so on. The sites also ask for what areas of shopping interest the visitor might want discount coupons - clothing, music, home furnishing, or garden goods, for instance. At this stage, the consumer receives discount coupons regularly, for goods they have shown a positive interest in. Participants have the opportunity to revise their list of interests at any time.

If visitors respond positively to the first two stages, they receive a third level of questions that ask permission to send weekly or daily messages on substantive topics of interest, including such items as stock quotes, recipes, and sports news. Along with this regular flow of information come advertisements and coupons targeted to their special interest.

Each of these levels of inquiry sets up the potential for a dialogue between the site and visitors. The dialogue continually asks the visitors what they are interested in and, in exchange, the Web site provides information and discounts on products of interest to the consumers.

These models are rapidly gaining popularity on the Internet. Three of the 50 most-visited sites on the Internet - Coolsavings.com, Iwon.com, and MyPoint.com - are these permission-based systems. Recent tracking data indicate that in a typical month, each of these sites tallied between 7 and 9 million unique visitors. It is probably reasonable to estimate that in a typical month about 15 million different people are utilizing such sites.

Such information gathering will continue to evolve. As people gain confidence in the values they get for giving personal information, more detailed and individualized searches will emerge. If households identify particular items they are in the market for at the current time, information and discount coupons for that item can be sent to them in a timely manner. Or, in the approach favored by the new Respond.com, an agent can actually search for a series of specific product offerings around specified requests.

This form of interaction will surely evolve over the next few years; the service will be run by an information agent to which shoppers can express their interest in a given item and receive a flow of information and offers concerning that specific product. When that interest has passed or a particular product or service need is satisfied, the flow of information stops as well. Such continual interactivity regarding flows of timely information could well be a major attribute of a future post.

6.8 The Unique Value of Transaction Information

This flow of timely and targeted information will be extremely valuable to both interested shoppers and consumer-oriented companies. As we have seen, a large number of people in both North America and Northern Europe are experimenting with these types of information systems right now. But all these systems depend upon an active engagement on behalf of consumers.

There is another form of information, which provides the best up to the minute data on consumer behavior across a broad spectrum of activities, that does not depend upon the consumer actively updating files. That is transactions-based data. This data is gathered at the point of sale and combines two key streams of information: individual product information gathered by scanner at the point of sale, and the identity of the purchaser who has used a loyalty, payment, or credit card for the transaction.

An effective targeting would be at a fairly detailed level. A person who has recently purchased some recordings by Bach and Schutz, for example, may find it helpful to have an information agent ask if they would like to receive a tailored catalog once a month on recent Bach and Schutz recordings, along with reviews and descriptions of activity in the area. The offer is more likely to be accepted if it is tailored and focused and comes from a trusted third party. That trusted agent would find and deliver relevant material, send only what is requested, and continually provide consumers the option of dropping off that particular circulation list or switching to a slightly different one, with help from the agent.

While there are some current legal barriers to using transaction information for marketing purposes, the notion of "informed consent" opens up a means of utilizing such information in the consumer's interest. If a system is set up for a trusted third party to use detailed transaction information to provide valuable and useful information to the consumer, this would be consistent with the intent of the current European directive and would be seen as valuable by the sophisticated and active consumer.

The postal banks building on their brand image and the trust they carry with the public are in a great position to exploit such opportunities to become trusted information agents.

6.9 Let's Be real!

The postal banks are a long way from being able to do this. In fact, all current models of information exchange are far from offering valuable interactive response to consumers needs. The postal banks, for example, do not have the capacity to track records, do not have permission of the consumers, there are not permission-based systems in place, and the ability to respond quickly and flexibly to opportunities is not easy for the Posts, with their work rules and official procedures.

But Posts do have some unique advantages to build upon: they have a trusted brand, they interact with every household every day, they are associated with information delivery, and they possess a unique asset in having limited access to financial transaction information. How can these assets be used?

6.9.1 Five Concrete Steps

There are concrete steps that postal banks can take to prepare themselves for an expanding role as a leader in permission-based marketing. Let's look at these steps as a starting point.

- Become a key player in appropriate use of personal information. Become masters of the Data Protection Directive. Establish an information privacy office to set strong standards within the post.
- Understand and work to adapt the permission-based system. Work with your best clients to include letter mail as a key part of the rapid response to inquiries and information processing.
- Look for consumer value in transactions records. Consumers don't realize the potential value of information about their behavior patterns. Begin to work with retailers and catalog companies to determine which types of transaction data would provide insight into very specific purchasing behavior that could be influenced and aided by specific and timely information.

- Offer the consumer a range of good information. Often, the value of transactions information is not in the product that has just been purchased, but on supplemental or complementary items. Sometimes, it is offering alternatives. But in any case, the important point is that the Posts must be able to offer a flow of information from a variety of players so that the consumer can choose.
- Consumers must have the option of informed consent regarding tracking their data. Not only the initial set-up, but the flow of information over time has to be checked and rechecked. Each week, it's critical for consumers to identify what will help them now. The frequent contacts that Posts have with households are an advantage in these circumstances.

- Begin to work with your clients to develop targeted information products that are narrowly focused, can be produced in small quantities on demand, and that can be flexible in content. The promise of getting these into the hands of the very interested should produce some high quality responses.

As postal banks start to move in this direction, they will develop a diverse set of skills. They will be mastering the intricacies of privacy and permission-based marketing. They will be developing the tools to make transactions information valuable to consumers. They will be growing a flexible system of tailored catalogues that will be extremely useful for consumers and retailer oriented companies. They will be developing their reputation as a trusted information agent for the consumer.

6.10 A Future Vision

The future of the Posts is in information gathering, processing, and delivery. As an integral part of the Posts, postal banks should find a future role in utilizing the transactions information in ways that can benefit their customers. The future of the postal banks is not in maintaining a strong position in transactions, or even in entering the electronic marketplace, but lies in identifying their unique advantage in the transaction system in the digital age (just as every other large and successful bank is doing).

Postal banks will not make a living purely on transaction fees. Increasingly, other organizations such as grocery stores and telephone banks can offer the same banking services to today's unbanked. And the margins earned on transactions are likely to fall in the future. If postal banks want to compete with traditional banks for the sophisticated consumer, they will have to compete by adopting either the higher risk profile of banks or the sophisticated services that generate fees.

But the critical comparative advantage of the Posts is their high level of consumer trust and their being a key communicator of valuable and useful information. The Posts need to build on their ability to deliver relevant information on a daily basis and the implicit trust that they would use consumer information appropriately to connect financial transactions records with flows of relevant product or service information. It is this advantage in information flows and public trust that can thrust the Posts into a central role at the heart of the new economy.

Editors and Contributing Authors

Roberto Ruozi	*Professor of Banking Economics and Director of the Institute of Financial Intermediaries at Bocconi University in Milan*
Luisa Anderloni	*Professor of Financial Intermediaries and Markets at Genoa University*
Francesca Arnaboldi	*Ph.D. Student in Financial Intermediaries and Markets at Genoa University*
Ekkerard Bauer	*Lecturer and researcher at Hohenheim University, Chair of Banking and Foundation of Banking Studies*
Lucia Leonelli	*Researcher of Financial Intermediaries and Markets at Rome-Tor Vergata University*
Odile Pilley	*Case handler - Competition Directorate European Commission*
Jean-Paul Pollin	*Director of the Laboratory of Economics of Orléans University of Orléans*
Angelo Riva	*Allocataire de Recherche at the Laboratory of Economics of Orléans in joint supervision with DITEA – Faculty of Economics of Genoa University*
Greg Schmid	*Director - Strategic Planning Services Institute for the Future – Manlio Park, California*

Printed in the United States
102322LV00003B/38/A

9 783540 427773